THE CONCISE DICTIONARY OF CHRISTIAN THEOLOGY

THE CONCISE DICTIONARY OF CHRISTIAN THEOLOGY

REVISED EDITION

MILLARD J. ERICKSON

CROSSWAY BOOKS

A PUBLISHING MINISTRY OF
GOOD NEWS PUBLISHERS
WHEATON, ILLINOIS

The Concise Dictionary of Christian Theology

Original edition copyright © 1986, 1994 by Millard J. Erickson. Published by Baker Books, Grand Rapids, Michigan

Revised edition copyright © 2001 by Millard J. Erickson

Published by Crossway Books
        A publishing ministry of Good News Publishers
        1300 Crescent Street
        Wheaton, Illinois 60187

First Crossway edition, 2001

Cover design: Liita Forsyth

First printing 2001

Printed in the United States of America

Library of Congress Cataloging-in-Publication Data
Erickson, Millard J.
    The concise dictionary of Christian theology / Millard J. Erickson. —
Rev. ed.
      p.   cm.
    ISBN 13: 978-1-58134-281-9
    ISBN 10: 1-58134-281-0 (trade pbk. : alk. paper)
    1. Theology—Dictionaries.   I. Title.
BR95 .E75   2001
230'.03—dc21   2001002826

VP		16	15	14	13	12	11	10	09	08	07	06
17	16	15	14	13	12	11	10	9	8	7	6	5	4	3

To Wayne and Beverly Thompson
good friends
true Christians
and lay theologians

PREFACE

Every teacher of theology has had students raise their hands during a lecture to ask for an explanation of a theological term. Sometimes, however, a student sits silently, puzzling over the meaning of such a word or the identity of a scholar mentioned in the lecture.

This book is intended to be a companion to the study of theology. It is planned as a resource to be kept close at hand during class sessions and independent reading, readily available for reference. It was first conceived of during the writing of *Christian Theology*, when it became apparent that inclusion of complete explanations would make the manuscript unduly cumbersome. At least in part, it is designed to be a supplement to that work.

Since the first edition of this book was published, much has happened in the world of theology and of intellectual endeavor in general. This edition seeks to bring the original dictionary up to date by supplementing it with pertinent ideas and persons from the past fifteen years. At the same time, since I have found that most students have greater familiarity with recent thought than with earlier historical figures and movements, I have retained the emphasis upon the first nineteen centuries of the Christian era.

A number of persons have contributed to the production of this volume. I must especially acknowledge the countless students whose spoken or unspoken question, "What does that mean?" has furnished impetus for the writing of this book. My research assistant, Bonnie Goding, did much of the work of compiling the original word list. Pat Krohn typed the entire manuscript. Ray Wiersma edited the original edition and Ted Griffin the revised edition. I am appreciative to Crossway Books and its Vice President of Editorial, Mr. Marvin Padgett, for publishing this revised edition and once again making it available to students of theology.

Asking questions about theological matters is a very good thing. Getting correct answers to those questions is even better. May this book contribute to both of those ends.

Aa

Abba An Aramaic word for father that, like the English *daddy* or *papa*, connotes familiarity and intimacy. It is used by Jesus in Mark 14:36. Paul says that by the Holy Spirit the Christian uses the term in addressing the Father (Rom. 8:15-16; Gal. 4:6).

Abelard, Peter (1079-1142) A scholastic philosopher and theologian who is best known for his view of the atonement, often referred to as the moral-influence theory, according to which the death of Christ is a demonstration of divine love that moves humans to turn to God.

Abolitionism A pre-Civil War movement opposing the practice of slavery.

Abomination of desolation An expression used by Jesus in Matthew 24:15 and Mark 13:14 recalling Daniel 11:31 and 12:11. Some see it as a reference to the Antichrist, others to the practice of idolatry.

Abortion An intentional act of terminating a pregnancy with the aim of bringing about the death of the fetus.

Abortion, partial-birth A late-term procedure in which the fetus is partially delivered, the base of the baby's skull punctured, and the brain removed.

Abraham's bosom The place to which Lazarus was taken at his death (Luke 16:22-23).

Absolute In the thought of Georg Hegel (1770-1831) and some later idealist philosophers and theologians, a term for the ultimate reality. This is an all-encompassing reality, mental in nature, of which all finite entities are parts.

Absolute attributes *See* ATTRIBUTES OF GOD, ABSOLUTE.

Absolute inerrancy *See* INERRANCY, ABSOLUTE.

Absoluteness of God *See* GOD, ABSO-LUTENESS OF.

Absolution The forgiveness of sins. Derived from a Latin word meaning "to set free," the term refers in particular to the remission of sins by the Roman Catholic Church.

Absolutism A view that holds that certain conceptions are unconditional or nonrelative; in ethics, the idea that certain rules or judgments are unqualified or universally applicable.

Abstinence The withholding of oneself from certain practices, including sexuality. The term often refers to refraining from food or drink.

Accommodation of message The adaptation of a message to the context of the recipient, as in anthropomorphism.

Accommodation of revelation The adaptation of a statement or practice to certain situations. The term may mean simply that God expressed his truth in a form understandable by human beings, or it may mean that the truth has been distorted to be made suitable for fallible or erroneous human understanding.

Accountability, Age of The age at which a person becomes aware of issues of right and wrong and thus responsible for his or her actions.

Acts of God *See* GOD, ACTS OF.

Adam The first human being, a creation of God. Because the word *adam* in Hebrew also means "human being," some believe that Adam was not an actual individual person but simply a representative or symbolic character.

Adam, In *See* IN ADAM.

Adam, Last or second A reference in 1 Corinthians 15 and Romans 5 to Jesus Christ, contrasting him with Adam (the first Adam).

Adam's sin *See* ORIGINAL SIN.

Adiaphora Matters regarded as nonessential to faith; especially in Lutheran theology, matters regarded as neither commanded nor forbidden.

Adiaphorists A group of Protestants who were willing to tolerate certain Roman Catholic practices for the sake of church unity.

Adonai A Hebrew name for God, meaning basically "Lord."

Adoption That part of salvation in which God receives the estranged sinner back into the relationship and benefits of being his child. The term connotes positive favor, as contrasted with mere forgiveness and remission of sins.

Adoptionism A type of Christology according to which Jesus, a human being, was chosen by God to be elevated to divine sonship.

Adult baptism *See* BAPTISM, BELIEVERS'.

Advent The coming of Christ. The first advent refers to his initial coming in the incarnation. The second advent is the future Second Coming.

Adventism Belief in the second coming of Christ. The term is also used to refer to a denomination, the Seventh-day Adventists.

Aesthetic stage One of Søren Kierkegaard's stages or ways of life. The aesthete lives for immediate satisfaction or pleasure.

Affusion The pouring of water upon the head as a method of baptism.

Afterlife A state or condition of existence following the cessation of physical or bodily life.

Agape A form of love that is essentially giving (rather than possessive), unselfish, and independent of the merit of the one loved.

Age-day theory The theory that the days of creation in Genesis 1 are long periods rather than twenty-four-hour days.

Age, This The present earthly structure of reality as ruled by Satan (2 Cor. 4:4; Eph. 6:12).

Age to Come A future order under Christ's reign. This future divine rule is already partially present.

Agnostic Literally, "one who does not know"; in general, a person who professes uncertainty about whether God exists.

Agnosticism A view that professes inability to determine whether God exists.

Albertus Magnus (1193-1280) A Dominican scholar who attempted to integrate the thought of Aristotle with Christianity. He was a major influence upon Thomas Aquinas.

Alexandrian theology A school of theologians that flourished during the third through fifth centuries and attempted to utilize Platonic philosophy in the construction of Christian theology.

Allegorical interpretation A method of biblical interpretation that attempts to find a deeper meaning than the literal.

Allegory A literary device used to express a truth in a pictorial form.

Alms, almsgiving Acts of charitable giving to the poor.

Alpha and Omega The first and last letters of the Greek alphabet. Referring to the eternality of God, the phrase may be rendered "the first and the last" (Rev. 1:8; 21:6; 22:13; cf. Isa. 44:6).

Ambrose (340-397) A theologian and church leader who was trained in both Greek and Latin. He had a special influence upon Augustine, whom he taught and baptized.

American Council of Christian Churches A fellowship of churches and denominations that was founded in 1941. Carl McIntire was a major force in the movement. Much of its activity related to opposing the National (originally Federal) and World Council of Churches.

Amillennialism The view that there will be no period of earthly reign of Christ either before or after his second coming. The thousand years of Rev. 20:1-7 are regarded as symbolic, either of the completeness of Christ's reign or of believers' bliss in heaven.

Amoral Pertaining to that which is neither moral nor immoral. The term refers either to matters that are not relevant to moral judgment or to persons who are insensitive to moral considerations.

Anabaptists Members of a radical wing of the Reformation who denounced infant baptism, insisting upon a believers' church. They generally emphasized the authority of the Bible and the separation of church and state. From the Anabaptists have descended the Mennonites and various Brethren groups.

Analogia fidei *See* ANALOGY OF FAITH.

Analogy A method of reasoning in which one object, while not identical to another with respect to a given quality, is believed to possess a measure of that quality; also a method of inferring from the nature of the creation something of the nature of God.

Analogy of being The idea that there is a parallel or analogy between God and his creation, especially the human, so that inferences may be drawn regarding the former from a study of the latter.

Analogy of faith The idea that clearer passages of Scripture lend illumination to less clear portions.

Analogy of Scripture The belief that, Scripture being a unity, the meaning of one passage is illuminated by a study of other portions.

Analytical philosophy *See* PHILOSOPHY, ANALYTICAL.

Analytic statement A statement in which the predicate is logically contained within the subject.

Anathema An expression meaning "accursed." It is also used of excommunication.

Angel A created spiritual being. The name literally means "messenger."

Angel of the Lord, the A self-manifestation of the Lord in a perceptible form.

Angelology The study or doctrine of angels.

Angelophanies The assuming of visible form by angels for special occasions.

Angels, Fallen Angels who disobeyed God, fell from their place of service to God, and now serve Satan, the chief of such fallen angels.

Angels, Holy Those angels who have not fallen from their position of obedience.

Anglo-Catholicism High-Church Anglicanism, which feels a strong affinity for Roman Catholic beliefs and practices. John Henry Newman, an early leader of the movement, converted to Roman Catholicism in 1845.

Anhypostasia The belief that the Second Person of the Trinity, in becoming incarnate, did not assume the humanity of a specific individual but took on a generic or impersonal human nature.

Animal-nature theory of sin *See* SIN, ANIMAL-NATURE THEORY OF.

Animism The worship of physical objects in the belief that spiritual forces are present within them.

Annihilationism The belief that at least some humans will permanently cease to exist at death or some point thereafter.

Annihilationism proper The idea that those who do not believe, and thus are not saved, are to be obliterated by a direct act of God or as a result of sin.

Anointing An act dedicating a person through the applying of oil to his or her head.

Anonymous Christians The idea, found especially in the thought of Karl Rahner, that there may be persons who, without identifying themselves as Christians, may nonetheless be recipients of divine salvation.

Anselm of Canterbury (1033-1109) A medieval monk and theologian who had a strong influence upon Christian thought. He followed Augustine in using Platonic philosophy to construct theology. His major contributions included his view of faith and reason, his ontological argument for the existence of God, and his interpretation of the atonement.

Anthropic revelation Revelation given in human form or in forms familiar to humans.

Anthropocentrism The view that humans and human values rather than God and his values are the central fact of the universe.

Anthropological argument An argument that reasons from some characteristic(s) of human nature—such as the moral impulse—to the existence of God.

Anthropology The study of human nature and culture. Theological anthropology is a theological interpretation of humanity.

Anthropomorphism Conceiving of God as having human characteristics or existing in human form.

Anthropopathism Conceiving of God as having human emotions.

Anthroposophy A system of religious and philosophical ideas that combines conceptions from several different sources. It teaches that one can and should escape from the material world by discovering truths within humans.

Antiauthoritarianism Rejection of, and opposition to, any external authority.

Antichrist An opponent and impersonator of Christ. From 1 John 2:18, 22 and 4:3, Antichrist appears to be a spirit present throughout the age of the church. Some have sought to identify specific persons or offices as the Antichrist. The Reformers and others identified him with the papacy. It appears that there is a spirit or principle of rebellion at work in the world that will come to completion in personal form in the last days.

Anticlericalism Opposition to the authority of the clergy.

Antidenominationalism Opposition to the linking of churches into unions that are based upon common adherence to certain distinguishing beliefs.

Antilegomena A term referring to books about which there was dispute concerning whether they should be included in the New Testament.

Antimetaphysical Pertaining to opposition to raising metaphysical questions or attempting to give metaphysical explanations. *See* METAPHYSICS.

Antinatural Contrary to nature. The term is used by proponents of the view that miracles violate or break the laws of the physical universe.

Antinomianism An opposition to law; specifically, a rejection of the idea that the Christian's life need be governed by laws or rules.

Antinomy A contradiction or tension between two or more laws, rules, or principles, each of which is held to be true.

Anti-Semitism Hostility toward, and often persecution of, Jews.

Antisubstantialism An aversion to belief in and use of categories denoting substance. It often involves emphasis on function rather than substance.

Antisupernaturalism Aversion to belief in the miraculous activity of God in the earthly and human realm.

Antithesis Opposition or contrast; in Hegelian thought, an event, idea, or movement that arises in contradiction to a preceding thesis.

Antitrinitarianism A belief system that rejects the doctrine of the Trinity.

Antitype New Testament realities of which certain Old Testament persons, objects, or practices are types or figures.

Anxiety of finiteness *See* SIN, ANXIETY-OF-FINITENESS THEORY OF.

Apocalypse The book of Revelation.

Apocalyptic literature A genre of literature presenting revelations regarding the end of the world.

Apocrypha, New Testament Books dating from the second century and later that, being judged by the church to be spurious, were not accepted into the canon of the New Testament.

Apocrypha, Old Testament Books dating from the intertestamental period that, being judged by the church to be spurious, were not accepted into the canon of the Old Testament.

Apokatastasis A Greek word meaning "restoration." It refers to a restoration of all things in Christ (Acts 1:6; Rom. 8:18-25; 1 Cor. 15:24-28; 2 Peter 3:13). Origen and others taught that this restoration will involve the ultimate salvation of all humans.

Apollinarianism A fourth-century interpretation of the person of Christ: The divine Christ did not take on a complete human nature, but only its flesh; his human soul (rationality or *nous*) was replaced by the Logos or Word.

Apollinarius (ca. 310-ca. 390) Bishop of Laodicea who taught that in the Incarnation the divine Logos took the place of the human psyche, so that Jesus' humanity was in effect restricted to his physical body. Apollinarius and his views were condemned by the Council of Constantinople in 381.

Apologetics That branch of Christian theology that has as its aim the reasoned advocacy of the Christian faith. It includes both positive arguments for the truth of Christianity and rebuttals of criticisms leveled at it.

Apologia A defense of a particular view.

Apologist One who engages in arguing for the truth of a view, especially of the Christian message; in particular, one of the second- and third-century theologians who vigorously defended Christianity.

Apophatic theology A way of relating to God according to the belief that God cannot be conceptualized in human categories.

Apostasy A "falling away," usually a deliberate and total abandonment of the faith previously held.

Apostate One who departs from the faith.

"A posteriori" statements Statements that are logically posterior to, or dependent upon, sense experience.

Apostles' Creed A brief early summary of the Christian faith, formerly believed to have been constructed by the twelve apostles. In its present form, the creed probably dates from about A.D. 700. Its predecessor, the Roman Creed, probably originated in the second half of the second century.

Apostolic fathers A group of early Christian writers following the apostles and preceding the apologists (approximately the first half of the second century).

Apostolicity Possession of apostolic sanction and authority.

Apostolic succession The teaching that authority in the church has been transmitted by ordination or laying on of hands from the apostles to present-day clergy.

Apothegm stories According to form-critical interpretation of the Bible, stories that provide a historical setting for sayings or pronouncements, particularly those of Jesus in the Gospels.

"A priori" statements Statements that are logically prior to, or independent of, sense perception.

Aquinas, Thomas *See* THOMAS AQUINAS.

Aramaic A Semitic language. A cognate of Hebrew, Aramaic was probably the language usually spoken by Jesus. Parts of Ezra and Daniel are written in Aramaic.

Archaeology The study of ancient culture through the investigation of ancient artifacts. Biblical archaeology has as its aim the illumination of the biblical text.

Archaizing The making of modern things ancient. The term is used to refer to attempts to get modern persons to think in the thought forms of earlier cultures.

Archangels Chief angels. The only one named in Scripture is Michael (Jude 9). The only other reference to "archangel" (1 Thess. 4:16) does not give a name. The other angel named in Scripture, Gabriel (Dan. 8:16; 9:21; Luke 1:19, 26), is not identified as an archangel.

Archbishop In episcopal forms of church government, an official possessing higher authority than does a bishop. An archbishop presides over an archdiocese, which comprises a number of dioceses.

Arianism A view of the person of Christ according to which he is the highest of the created beings and is thus appropriately referred to as god, but not *the* God.

Aristotelianism An empirical philosophy that makes the form-matter distinction the key to metaphysics and holds that all knowledge is gained through sense perception.

Aristotle (384-322 B.C.) Greek philosopher who, though a student of Plato, developed an empirical system of philosophy quite contrary to Plato's ideas.

Arius A fourth-century theologian whose views of the person of Christ

were condemned at the Council of Nicea (325).

Armageddon A place referred to in Revelation 16:16. It is most frequently identified with the mountain of Megiddo. The final battle between the forces of God and those of Satan will be at Armageddon.

Arminianism A view that contradicts the Calvinist understanding of predestination. Arminianism holds that God's decision to give salvation to certain persons and not to others is based on his foreknowledge of who will believe. It also includes the idea that genuinely regenerate people can lose their salvation, and that some actually do. Arminianism often has a less serious view of human depravity than does Calvinism.

Arminius, James (1560-1609) A Dutch Reformed minister and theologian whose teachings gave birth to the theological system known as Arminianism.

Armstrongism *See* WORLDWIDE CHURCH OF GOD.

Article of faith A particular doctrinal tenet. The specific doctrines in a creed or confession are often referred to as articles.

Articles of Religion The standards of doctrine of the United Methodist Church.

Asbury, Francis (1745-1816) Methodist minister who was largely responsible for the introduction of Methodism in the United States.

Ascension Day The day of Jesus' return to heaven, the fortieth day after his resurrection (Acts 1:3, 9).

Ascension of Christ Jesus' bodily departure from the earth and return to heaven on the fortieth day after his resurrection (Luke 24:51; Acts 1:9).

Ascetical theology Theology dealing with the attempt to attain Christian perfection through various ascetic practices.

Asceticism The practice of self-discipline, especially the renunciation of certain bodily pleasures.

Aseity of God *See* GOD, ASEITY OF.

Ash Wednesday The day marking the beginning of Lent.

Asian theology Theology developed by Asians in attempts to conceptualize the Christian message in such a way as to be relevant to the Asian culture. Such attempts often stem from the perception that Western theology has corrupted the essence of the Christian message.

Assensus A Latin word referring to the aspect of faith that involves intellectual assent to certain propositions.

Assumption of Mary *See* MARY, ASSUMPTION OF.

Assumption of Moses An apocalyptic book purporting to be Moses' farewell exhortation to Joshua.

Assurance (of salvation) The divinely given confidence of the believer that he or she is truly saved.

Atemporality God is outside of time, rather than being of infinite duration within it.

Athanasius (293-373) Bishop of Alexandria who was a champion of the orthodox view of Christ and, in particular, effectively opposed Arianism.

Atheism The belief that there is no God.

Atheism, Christian *See* DEATH OF GOD THEOLOGY.

Atman In Hinduism, individual parts of the whole of reality, which is called Brahma.

Atonement The aspect of the work of Christ, and particularly his death, that makes possible the restoration of fellowship between individual believers and God.

Atonement, Day of The day on which the Old Testament priest made atonement for all the sins of the people (Lev. 16).

Atonement, Example Theory of The view that the effect of the atonement was through the example Jesus gave us of dedication to the Father, which we then should emulate.

Atonement, Governmental theory of the The teaching that the major effect of the death of Christ was to demonstrate the holiness of God's law and the seriousness of transgressing it.

Atonement, Limited The interpretation of the atonement that says Christ died only for the elect.

Atonement, Moral-influence theory of the The view that the effect of Christ's death was to demonstrate to us the love of God and thus to induce us to respond to God's offer of salvation.

Atonement, Particular *See* ATONE-MENT, LIMITED.

Atonement, Penal-substitution theory of the The idea that Christ's death is a sacrifice offered in payment of the penalty for our sins. It is accepted by God the Father as satisfaction in place of the penalty due to us.

Atonement, Ransom theory of the The idea that the blood of Christ was a ransom paid to Satan to deliver humans from his control.

Atonement, Satisfaction theory of the The view that Christ's death was a sacrifice to God in payment of the penalty for the wrong we have done against him.

Atonement, Universal *See* ATONE-MENT, UNLIMITED.

Atonement, Unlimited The doctrine that Christ died for all persons, whether elect or not.

Atonement, Vicarious The view that the atoning death of Christ was on behalf of sinners.

Attributes, Communication of *See* COM-MUNICATION OF ATTRIBUTES.

Attributes of God The characteristics or qualities of God that constitute him as what he is. They should not be thought of as something attributed to or predicated of him, as if something could be added to his nature. Rather, they are inseparable from his being.

Attributes of God, Absolute Those characteristics of God that are independent of, or irrespective of, his relationship to created objects and persons.

Attributes of God, Communicable Attributes of God for which corresponding characteristics can be found in human nature.

Attributes of God, Emanant Qualities of God that relate to his creation.

Attributes of God, Incommunicable Attributes of God for which no corresponding characteristics can be found in human nature.

Attributes of God, Moral *See* MORAL ATTRIBUTES.

Attributes of God, Natural *See* NATURAL ATTRIBUTES OF GOD.

Attributes of God, Transitive or relative Those attributes of God that are involved in his relationship to his creation.

Augsburg Confession The basic Lutheran confession of faith. Written by Philipp Melanchthon, it was presented to the Diet of Augsburg in 1530.

Augustine of Hippo (354-430) Bishop of Hippo. A great theological synthesizer and interpreter of the Christian faith, Augustine is generally considered the greatest theologian of the early church.

Augustinian-Donatist controversy *See* DONATISM.

Augustinianism A theological system emphasizing the depravity of human nature, the necessity of divine predestination, and the priority of faith over reason. To a large extent, Augustinianism involved a synthesis of Platonic philosophy and Christian theology.

Augustinian theodicy An attempt to explain evil as a part of the creation that is necessary for its greater good.

Aulén, Gustaf Emanuel Hildebrand (1879-1978) Swedish theologian and bishop associated with the Lundensian school of theology, which emphasizes the primacy of love. He is best known for *Christus Victor,* his restatement of what he calls the classic view of the atonement, an earlier form of which is the ransom theory.

Authentic existence In existentialism, a way of life that asserts one's own individuality and freedom. It is a secular equivalent of salvation.

Authenticity, Criteria of Criteria employed by form critics and redaction critics to assess whether words attributed to Jesus in the Gospels were actually spoken by him.

Authenticity, Question of The question of whether the words attributed to Jesus are actually from him.

Authoritarianism Forceful or dogmatic insistence upon blind adherence to a view or practice.

Authority The right to command belief or action.

Authority, Imperial The right to issue a decree because of the position that one holds.

Authority of the Bible *See* BIBLE, AUTHORITY OF THE.

Averroes (1126-1198) Islamic philosopher who attempted to recover the true essence of Aristotelian thought independently of theological considerations.

Averroism A view that seems to imply that a proposition true in theology may contradict one that is true in philosophy, and vice versa.

Azusa Street meetings Meetings held in a former Methodist church at 312 Azusa Street in Los Angeles in 1906 by a black holiness preacher named William I. Seymour. They are often considered the beginning of modern Pentecostalism.

Bb

Backsliding A temporary or partial diminution of one's spiritual commitment. It is less serious or major than apostasy.

Baillie, Donald (1887-1954) Scottish pastor and theologian who taught at the University of St. Andrews. His best-known work is *God Was in Christ*. Brother of John Baillie.

Baillie, John (1886-1960) Scottish theologian who taught at Auburn and Union (New York) theological seminaries, Emmanuel College (Toronto), and the University of Edinburgh. Among his best-known works are *A Diary of Private Prayer*, *Our Knowledge of God*, and *Invitation to Pilgrimage*. Brother of Donald Baillie.

Baptism An act of Christian initiation in which water is applied to a person by dipping, pouring, or sprinkling.

Baptism, Believers' Baptism in which a credible profession of faith is first required.

Baptism, Infant The practice of baptizing infants. Some who observe this practice understand it as effecting regeneration (Roman Catholics, Lutherans), while others see it as a sign of the covenant (Presbyterians, Reformed).

Baptism, Lay Administration of baptism by an unordained person.

Baptism, Modes of The manner in which water is applied to the candidate, whether by immersion (dipping or plunging), pouring, or sprinkling.

Baptism for the dead The practice of the Marcionites, Novatianists, and Mormons of baptizing a living person for the benefit of a dead person, generally an ancestor. Some believe they find an allusion to the practice in 1 Corinthians 15:29.

Baptism of the Holy Spirit A blessing that John the Baptist promised would accompany the ministry of Jesus (Matt. 3:11; Mark 1:8; Luke 3:16). It occurred at Pentecost, which Luke understood to be a fulfillment of Joel 2:28-32 (see Acts 2:16-21). Some teach that the baptism of the Spirit is a special act of the Spirit subsequent to regeneration, while others understand 1 Corinthians 12:13 as implying that all regenerate persons have undergone this baptism.

Baptismal formula A formal statement pronounced in connection with the administration of water baptism.

Baptismal regeneration The doctrine that baptism results in regeneration of the subject baptized. Usually based upon John 3:5 and Titus 3:5, this doctrine is found particularly in Roman Catholic and Lutheran theology.

Baptist A Christian who believes in such doctrines as a church membership composed solely of regenerate believers, believers' baptism by immersion, a congregational form of church government, separation of church and state, and the priesthood of all believers.

Barclay, Robert (1648-1690) The first major Quaker theologian.

Barclay, William (1907-1978) Scottish pastor and biblical scholar who taught at the University of Glasgow. A universalist in theology, he is best known for his *Daily Study Bible*.

Barth, Karl (1886-1968) Swiss theologian generally thought of as the founder of neoorthodoxy. He may well have been the most influential Protestant theologian of the twentieth century.

Basil the Great (ca. 330-379) Bishop of Caesarea and one of the Cappadocian theologians who developed a formula for the Trinity as consisting of one substance (*ousia*) in three persons (*hypostases*). The formula was adopted at the Council of Constantinople (A.D. 381).

Baur, Ferdinand Christian (1792-1860) German Protestant theologian at the University of Tübingen who exerted a strong influence on the development of the methods of historical criticism.

Bavinck, Herman (1854-1921) Dutch Reformed theologian who taught at the seminary at Kampen and the Free University of Amsterdam.

Baxter, Richard (1615-1691) A leading Puritan theologian and pastor. Among his most important works are *The Saint's Everlasting Rest*, *The Reformed Pastor*, and *A Call to the Unconverted*.

Beast, Mark of the *See* MARK OF THE BEAST.

Beatification In the Roman Catholic Church, the first step in the legal process leading to sainthood.

Beatific vision In Roman Catholic theology, direct knowledge of God by the believer.

Beelzebub A god of the Philistines (2 Kings 1:2). The name was used by New Testament Jews to refer to the prince of demons (Matt. 12:24).

Begging the question An informal logical fallacy consisting of assuming that which one is attempting to prove; a form of circular reasoning.

Begotten Fathered by or derived from. *See also* ONLY BEGOTTEN.

Behaviorism A twentieth-century school of psychology pioneered especially by John Watson that, instead of relying on introspection, gathers its content from experimentation and observation of behavior.

Being A property of everything that is; in a sense, the most basic metaphysical category.

Being, Analogy of *See* ANALOGY OF BEING.

Belial A name used for the devil (2 Cor. 6:15).

Believer An adherent to certain teachings, and in particular, a Christian.

Believers' baptism *See* BAPTISM, BELIEVERS'.

Bellarmine, Robert (1542-1621) Jesuit theologian who did much to establish Thomas Aquinas's *Summa Theologica* as the basic theological authority for Roman Catholicism.

Benediction A pronouncement of blessing.

Benevolence of God See GOD, BENEVOLENCE OF.

Bergson, Henri (1859-1941) French philosopher who taught a doctrine of creative or emergent evolution, according to which an *élan vital* (life force) within matter develops reality to new ends.

Berkeley, George (1685-1753) Irish theistic philosopher. A subjective idealist, Berkeley maintained that material objects exist only as perceived by us. He also argued that for these ideas to exist, God must exist.

Berkhof, Louis (1873-1957) Calvinist theologian who served for many years as professor of systematic theology and president of Calvin Theological Seminary. His best-known writing is his *Systematic Theology*.

Beyondness, Dimensional A concept used by Søren Kierkegaard to convey the idea of transcendence. Transcendence is thought of not as spatial distance, but as God's being in a different dimension altogether, or in a different realm of reality, from that in which we exist.

Beza, Theodore (1519-1605) John Calvin's successor as leader in Geneva. In some ways Beza took the concept of predestination further than had Calvin (hyper-Calvinism).

Bible, Authority of the The teaching that since God, the supreme authority, has given us the Bible by divine inspiration, it has derivatively the right to prescribe the belief and actions of Christians.

Bible, Canon of the The collection of books accepted by the church as authoritative.

Bible, Inerrancy and infallibility of the Terms referring to the complete truthfulness of the Bible in what it teaches. Inerrancy means that it teaches no error. Infallibility means that it will not fail to accomplish what it is meant to do. Some use the term *infallibility* only in reference to the Bible's truthfulness in matters of faith and practice.

Bible, Inspiration of the The act of the Holy Spirit upon biblical writers that ensured that what they wrote faithfully preserved divine revelation and made the Bible effectively the Word of God.

Biblical authority *See* BIBLE, AUTHORITY OF THE.

Biblical criticism Study that attempts to

determine the true meaning of the Bible by using techniques applied to other written documents.

Biblical numerics The study of the significance of numbers in the Bible.

Biblical theology Organization of theological teachings in terms of the portions of the Bible where they occur rather than by topic. Biblical theology makes no attempt to restate the biblical expressions in a contemporary form.

Biblical-theology movement A movement that arose, flourished, and declined between approximately 1945 and 1965. It emphasized the theological dimensions of the Bible and had close affinities with neoorthodoxy.

Biblicism A very strong and even unquestioning commitment to the authority of the Bible.

Bibliolatry Placing such a high estimation upon the Bible as virtually to worship or idolize it.

Bibliology The doctrine of Scripture.

Big-bang theory A cosmological theory according to which the universe began with all matter concentrated in one place. As a result of an explosion, matter became spread throughout what is now the universe, which is continuing to expand. The big-bang theory is also known as the superdense-state theory.

Binding and loosing A reference to Jesus' statements in Matthew 16:19 and 18:18. The Roman Catholic interpretation is that the Roman Catholic Church (through the priesthood and ultimately the pope) has the power to retain or remit sins.

Bioethics The study of ethical issues related to biological matters, particularly human life. It is often also termed biomedical ethics.

Biological evolution *See* EVOLUTION, BIOLOGICAL.

Birth, New *See* REGENERATION.

Bishop Literally, "an overseer," an official given responsibility for managing or guiding the work of the church (1 Tim. 3:1-7; Titus 1:5-9). In some types of church government, a bishop is an official charged with oversight of a geographical area containing several churches.

Bishop of Rome The bishop whose office came to possess supreme authority in the Roman Catholic Church: the pope.

Bitheism Belief in two gods.

Black theology A twentieth-century North American theology having considerable affinity with liberation theology. It regards God's concern for the salvation of humans as not being exclusively spiritually oriented, but as also pertaining to political, economic, and social deliverance. James Cone is the major theologian of the movement.

Blake, William (1757-1827) A mystical English poet and artist from whose thought the Death of God theologians, particularly Thomas J. J. Altizer, drew much of their inspiration.

Blasphemy Irreverent and insulting or slanderous expressions against God.

Blasphemy against the Holy Spirit A sin mentioned by Jesus in Matthew 12:31, Mark 3:28-29, and Luke 12:10. It will not be forgiven, he said. It appears not to be a single act, but a continued rejection of light and truth, leading to a state in which one is unable to distinguish between the working of the Holy Spirit and that of Satan.

Bless In reference to a human, to praise or thank God; in reference to God, to bestow some good upon a human.

Blessed hope The second coming of Christ (Titus 2:13). Some believe that the term refers to a secret coming of Christ to remove the church prior to the great tribulation.

Blessing Some particular good received.

Blik A concept developed by the philosopher R. M. Hare to refer to a way of viewing things that is not altered or affected by facts.

Blindness, Spiritual *See* SPIRITUAL BLINDNESS.

Bloch, Ernst (1885-1977) A German Marxist philosopher whose concept of hope in *The Principle of Hope* had a considerable influence upon Jürgen Moltmann's theology of hope.

Blood In the Bible, frequently a synonym of life. Thus the shedding of blood refers to the giving of one's life.

Bodily presence *See* PRESENCE, BODILY.

Bodily resurrection of Christ The idea that Christ's resurrection was of the physical body, not merely a spiritual manifestation.

Body The physical aspect of human nature or the materialized state of the person.

Body, Mortal The body that we have, which is susceptible to death.

Body, soul, and spirit *See* TRICHOTOMISM.

Body and soul *See* DICHOTOMISM.

Body of Christ Literally, Christ's physical nature; metaphorically, the church.

Boehme, Jakob (1575-1624) German Lutheran mystic and theosophist.

Boethius, Anicius Manlius Severinus (480-524) Theologian who sought to use reason to support faith and attempted to explain the Trinity by using Aristotelian philosophy.

Bogomils An eleventh-century Bulgarian group considered heretical by the Eastern Orthodox Church. In opposing the sacramental materialism of the church, they rejected water baptism and the use of bread and wine in the

Lord's Supper. They were dualistic in theology.

Bonaventura (1221-1274) Franciscan theologian and influential mystic.

Bondage of sin, the The power of sin to virtually enslave or dominate the sinner.

Bondage of the Will A writing of Martin Luther that reflected an Augustinian view of the human will. It opposed Erasmus' *On Free Will.*

Bonhoeffer, Dietrich (1906-1945) German Lutheran pastor and theologian whose most influential concepts are "cheap grace" and "religionless Christianity." Forbidden by the Nazis to speak publicly or publish, he became a member of the resistance, was imprisoned from 1943 to 1945, and was executed on a charge of treason.

Book of Common Order The liturgical handbook used by the Church of Scotland and associated Presbyterian churches.

Book of Common Prayer The book of services and prayers used by the Church of England and other Anglican communions.

Book of Concord See CONCORD, BOOK OF.

Book of life In ancient cities, a register of the names of citizens (see Ps. 69:28; Isa. 4:3). The idea was extended to a register of those who are citizens of the heavenly kingdom and possess eternal life (Dan. 12:1; Luke 10:20; Phil. 4:3; Heb. 12:23; Rev. 13:8; 17:8; 20:15; 21:27).

Booth, Catherine (1829-1890) "Mother of the Salvation Army." Daughter of a Wesleyan minister, she was expelled from that movement, whereupon she married William Booth and helped him found the Salvation Army.

Booth, William (1829-1912) Methodist minister who, taking a strong interest in meeting people's physical needs and combating social evils, founded in London's East End a rescue mission that eventually developed into the Salvation Army.

Born again *See* REGENERATION.

Born of God *See* REGENERATION.

Born of the Spirit *See* REGENERATION.

Bottomless pit A place that serves as the realm of the dead and the prison for Satan and certain demons from which the beast or Antichrist will come (Rev. 11:7; 17:8; 20:1-3). It is not the ultimate destination of the wicked.

Bowne, Borden Parker (1847-1910) Liberal Methodist philosopher who popularized personal idealism and strongly emphasized the immanence of God.

Bradwardine, Thomas (ca. 1290-1349) Professor of divinity at Oxford and archbishop of Canterbury. Emphasizing God's grace and irresistible will, he strongly opposed Pelagianism.

Brahma In Hinduism, the whole of reality.

Branch Davidians A cult, led by a claimed messiah, David Koresh, that built a compound outside Waco, Texas. After a long standoff with agents of the U.S. Bureau of Alcohol, Tobacco, and Firearms, the compound was destroyed by fire on April 19, 1993, taking the lives of most of the inhabitants.

Breaking bread *See* LORD'S SUPPER.

Breath of life A reference in Genesis 2:7 to God's conferring life upon the human.

Brethren of the Common Life Religious society in the Netherlands in the fourteenth to early seventeenth centuries. It emphasized religious zeal and moral purity and combined mysticism and philanthropy. Thomas à Kempis was perhaps the most famous member of the movement.

Bride of Christ A term for the church.

Brightman, Edgar Sheffield (1884-1953) Twentieth-century personalist philosopher who held to a view of God as finite.

British Israelitism A sect that teaches that the true Israel is the Anglo-Saxon people.

Brother A term sometimes used by Christians for one another.

Brotherhood of man A concept emphasizing that all humans are children of the same God and hence should treat one another in a brotherly fashion. *See also* UNIVERSAL BROTHERHOOD.

Brown, Raymond (1928-1998) Twentieth-century Roman Catholic New Testament scholar.

Brown, William Adams (1865-1943) American Presbyterian theologian who taught at Union Theological Seminary in New York. An influential liberal, he maintained that doctrines derive not from revelation, but from experience.

Bruce, F. F. (1910-1990) Conservative twentieth-century New Testament scholar who taught at the University of Manchester.

Brunner, Heinrich Emil (1889-1966) Swiss Reformed pastor and theologian who was second only to Karl Barth in influence within the neoorthodox movement.

Buber, Martin (1878-1965) Jewish philosopher best known for his stress on I-thou rather than I-it relationships.

Bucer, Martin (1491-1551) Lutheran Reformer who attempted to mediate the differences between the Lutherans and Zwinglians on the Lord's Supper. He also strongly emphasized the Holy Spirit and his work.

Buchman, Frank (1878-1961) Lutheran clergyman and founder of Moral Rearmament, earlier known as the Oxford Group.

Buddhism Eastern religion founded by Siddhartha Gautama (ca. 566-486 B.C.).

The goal of the Buddhist is to escape from the chain of reincarnation and karma to nirvana, where there is cessation of desire.

Building An image used of the church.

Bullinger, Heinrich (1504-1575) Swiss Reformer who became Zwingli's successor in Zurich in 1531.

Bultmann, Rudolf (1884-1976) German New Testament scholar at the University of Marburg who applied Martin Heidegger's existentialist philosophy to the construction of theology. Bultmann is best known for his pioneering work on form criticism of the Gospels and his method of demythologization.

Bundle theory *See* MIND, BUNDLE THEORY OF.

Bunyan, John (1628-1688) English Puritan preacher and writer best known for his *Pilgrim's Progress*.

Buried with Christ A reference to baptism (Rom. 6:4).

Burnt offering A sacrifice in which the entire victim was consumed on the altar.

Bushnell, Horace (1802-1876) American Congregationalist theologian who was one of the most influential forces in the construction of nineteenth-century American liberalism. He expounded the moral-influence view of the atonement.

Butler, Joseph (1692-1752) British bishop, theologian, and apologist who in his *Analogy of Religion* used an empirical argument to contend very effectively against deism.

Cc

Cabala *See* KABBALA.

Cadbury, Henry (1883-1974) American New Testament scholar and specialist in Lukan studies. A member of the Society of Friends, Cadbury warned against the twin dangers of modernizing Jesus and of archaizing our faith.

Caird, John (1820-1898) Scottish pastor, theologian, and philosopher. He was a neo-Hegelian and an authority on Spinoza.

Cajetan, Thomas de Vio (1469-1534) Dominican cardinal, theologian, and philosopher who defended the power and monarchical supremacy of the pope. Cajetan attempted to persuade Luther to recant on three successive days in Augsburg in 1518.

Call, calling God's summons of humans to salvation or to special positions of service.

Call, Effectual A call that is efficacious or results in a favorable response by the one called.

Call, Internal A call that comes through the inner working of the Holy Spirit.

Calovius, Abraham (1612-1686) A German Lutheran who was a defender of strict orthodoxy. He particularly opposed the teachings of the Syncretists and of George Calixtus, who advocated the union of the Lutheran, Reformed, and Roman Catholic churches.

Calvin, John (1509-1564) Reformer who gave the Reformed faith its most complete and systematic statement through his *Institutes of the Christian Religion*.

Calvinism The thought of John Calvin. The term is applied particularly to the doctrine of predestination, according to which God sovereignly chooses some to salvation not because of any merit or even foreseen faith, but simply by his free will and unmerited grace.

Cambridge Platonists An important English philosophical and theological movement in the seventeenth century. They interpreted Christianity from a general Platonic perspective, strongly emphasizing reason over experience.

Campbell, Alexander (1788-1866) One of the founders of the Christian Church (Disciples of Christ). A son of Thomas Campbell.

Campbell, Thomas (1763-1854) A Scottish-Irish minister who was one of the founders of the Christian Church (Disciples of Christ).

Campbellites Followers of Alexander Campbell.

Camp meetings Religious revival meetings held in the open air on the American frontier in the early part of the nineteenth century. Frequently there were dramatic conversion experiences involving emotional and even physical phenomena. Camp meetings were adopted especially by the Methodists.

Camus, Albert (1913-1960) Existentialist philosopher, novelist, and playwright whose concept of the absurdity in life has influenced some Christian thought.

Canon The collection of books deemed authoritative by the church.

Canonical Criticism *See* CRITICISM, CANONICAL.

Canonization The process of settling the canon of Scripture; also, the legal process in the Roman Catholic Church whereby one is made a saint.

Canon law The official rules of the church regarding its procedures and discipline.

Capitalism An economic system built upon private ownership of property.

Capital punishment Infliction of the death penalty for certain serious acts of wrongdoing.

Cappadocian theologians Three theologians in the province of Cappadocia in the latter half of the fourth century: Basil (the Great) of Caesarea, his brother Gregory of Nyssa, and Gregory of Nazianzus. They were largely responsible for enunciating the orthodox doctrine of the Trinity over against Arianism.

Cardinal A special high official of the Roman Catholic Church. Cardinals have special duties, most notable of which is the collective choosing of the pope.

Cardinal sin A designation for the major sins: pride, covetousness, lust, anger, gluttony, envy, and sloth.

Cardinal virtues, Seven The seven basic virtues upon which all other Christian virtues are considered to hinge: faith, hope, love, justice, prudence, temperance, and fortitude.

Carlstadt, Andreas Rudolf Bodenstein von (ca. 1480-1541) German Protestant Reformer. After joining the Reformation, Carlstadt took some matters of reform even further than had Luther, leading to a split between them.

Carnal Literally, "fleshly," an adjective usually applied to worldly or unspiritual Christians.

Carnap, Rudolf (1891-1970) Twentieth-century logical positivist.

Carnell, Edward John (1919-1967) A Protestant theologian and apologist who was one of the leaders in the new evangelicalism, a resurgence of evangelical scholarship after World War II. Carnell spent the major portion of his career at Fuller Theological Seminary. His best-known books include *An Introduction to Christian Apologetics*, *Christian Commitment*, and *The Case for Orthodox Theology*.

Casuistry The applying of moral laws or rules to specific cases.

Catechism A popular manual or summary of Christian beliefs.

Catechist One who gives instruction in the Christian faith.

Catechumen One being instructed in the Christian faith.

Categorical imperative In the thought of Immanuel Kant, a moral command that is unconditionally and universally binding.

Category transgression According to linguistic or analytical philosophy, a transition from one type of proposition or "language game" to another.

Cathari A term applied to several different groups in church history that have emphasized purity of life.

Catholic Universal or orthodox (from the Greek word *katholikos*, meaning "general").

Catholic Church, Roman *See* ROMAN CATHOLICISM.

Catholicism, Conventional Roman Roman Catholicism that holds to the traditional or conventional position as enunciated by the Council of Trent.

Catholicity Universality or all-inclusiveness.

Catholic modernism A small movement beginning in the nineteenth century in the Roman Catholic Church. It sought to modernize the statement of the faith. Names associated with Catholic modernism include Alfred Loisy, George Tyrrell, and Edouard Le Roy.

Catholics, Old *See* OLD CATHOLICS.

Causality, Method of A means of understanding God by investigating the creation and then attributing to him whatever characteristics were necessary to cause it.

Celibacy The state of being unmarried for religious reasons.

Ceremonial laws In contrast with moral laws, laws pertaining to religious practices such as the offering of sacrifices and purification.

Chafer, Lewis Sperry (1871-1952) Evangelist, theologian, and educator who in 1924 founded Dallas Theological Seminary, which he then served as president and professor of systematic theology. His *Systematic Theology* became the standard statement of dispensational premillenialism.

Chalcedon, Council of (451) Ecumenical council that, gathering up earlier pronouncements such as those made at the Council of Nicea, spelled out the definitive statement of orthodox Christology. The immediate occasion of the Council of Chalcedon was the teachings of Eutyches.

Chalcedonian Christology Christology that accords with the orthodox definition prescribed by the Council of

Chalcedon: Jesus Christ as fully God and fully human, two natures in one person.

Channing, William Ellery (1780-1842) Influential American Unitarian pastor and theologian.

Chaos theory A development in modern mathematical and scientific theory intended to provide a framework for understanding irregular occurrences in nature.

Charismata Spiritual gifts, as in 1 Corinthians 12:8-10. *See also* CHARISMATIC GIFTS.

Charismatic gifts Any spiritual gifts, but especially the unusual or miraculous ones such as speaking in tongues, healing, and raising the dead.

Charismatic movement A movement emphasizing the charismatic gifts, and especially a surge of such interest and practice beginning in the 1950s.

Charismatics Those who believe in and practice the charismatic gifts.

Chastening, chastisement Moral and spiritual discipline through instruction and correction.

Cheap grace Acceptance of forgiveness and of God's gifts without repentance and obedience. The concept was developed by Dietrich Bonhoeffer in *The Cost of Discipleship*.

Chemnitz, Martin (1522-1586) Second-generation Lutheran theologian and leader who was influential in consolidating Lutheranism after Luther.

Cherub, cherubim Invisible ministering spirits in God's immediate presence; probably a class of angels.

Chicago school of theology The liberal theology associated with the University of Chicago, especially in the early part of the twentieth century. There was a strong affinity with pragmatism and even more so with process philosophy.

Children of God In the New Testament, Christians. Also, a cultic group organized by David Berg in Los Angeles in 1967. Beginning as an evangelical group, it modified its teachings as new revelations were believed to have been received.

Childs, Brevard (1923-) Professor of Old Testament at Yale University Divinity School. Among the first to point out the decline of the biblical-theology movement, he is best known for his concept of canon criticism.

Chiliasm Belief in an earthly millennium; in particular, in the early centuries of the church a premillenialism that held a very vivid and imaginative view of conditions during the millennium.

Christ Literally, "the anointed one," the title designating Jesus as the Messiah.

Christ, Active obedience of Jesus' positive fulfillment of the Father's will.

Christ, Advent of The coming of Christ. When referring to Christ, the New

Testament uses the term (*parousia*) only of his second coming; but in second-century Christian writings, it is used to refer to both comings.

Christ, Blood of A reference to Christ's death and its atoning value.

Christ, Coming of The coming of Christ to earth, either the first or second time.

Christ, Deity of The idea that Christ is God as is the Father.

Christ, Doctrine of Teachings about the nature and significance of the person and work of Christ.

Christ, Exaltation of The several steps upward after Jesus' death and burial, including the resurrection, ascension, and resumption of his place at the right hand of God.

Christ, Follower of One who seeks to live by Jesus' teachings.

Christ, Humanity of The idea that Jesus was as fully human as we are, except that he was without a sinful nature and actual sin.

Christ, Humiliation of The stages of self-emptying that Jesus underwent, including his earthly life, suffering, death, and burial (some would also include a descent into Hades).

Christ, Identification with The believer's union with Christ. This doctrine is based upon the many biblical statements about the believer's being in Christ and Christ's being in the believer.

Christ, Imitation of The attempt of the Christian to live according to Christ's example. The idea has given rise to a whole collection of devotional literature, including Thomas à Kempis's *Imitation of Christ* and Charles Sheldon's *In His Steps*.

Christ, Impeccability of The idea that Christ was unable to sin.

Christ, Intercessory work of A reference both to Christ's atoning death and to his continuing work of pleading with the Father for us (Heb. 7:25).

Christ, Jesus A full reference, including both name and title, for Jesus of Nazareth, the incarnate Second Person of the Trinity.

Christ, Lordship of *See* LORDSHIP OF CHRIST.

Christ, Nature of A reference to who and what Christ was and is.

Christ, Offices of The threefold role of Christ as prophet, priest, and king.

Christ, Person of A reference to who Christ is, as contrasted with what he does.

Christ, Preexistence of The concept that the person who was born at Bethlehem as Jesus of Nazareth was the preexistent Second Person of the Trinity.

Christ, Preincarnate prophetic ministry of

The idea that prior to his incarnation Jesus ministered through the message of the prophets.

Christ, Reign of The rule of Christ, which is incomplete at present but will become complete at the time of his return.

Christ, Revelatory role of Christ's work of making known the Father and his will. This fulfills the office of prophet.

Christ, Second coming of *See* SECOND COMING OF CHRIST.

Christ, Two natures of The doctrine that Jesus was in one person both divine and human.

Christ, Vicarious death of The doctrine that Christ's death had a value on our behalf.

Christ, Work of What Christ did, as contrasted with who and what he was and is.

Christadelphians A small sect that originated in the United States about 1850. They are Unitarian and consider themselves brothers of Christ.

Christ as king A reference to one of the three offices of Jesus Christ; his ruling power.

Christ as priest A reference to one of the three offices of Jesus Christ; his atoning and intercessory work.

Christ as prophet A reference to one of the three offices of Jesus Christ; his work of revelation.

Christ as sacrifice The idea that Christ in his death played the part that animals did in the Old Testament sacrificial system.

Christ as substitute The idea that Christ's death was in our place.

Christendom The realm of Christianity; that is, the peoples among whom and the lands in which Christianity is the dominant religion.

Christ event The incarnation. The term is frequently used by those who conceive of revelation primarily as historical event rather than as disclosure of Christ's nature and attributes.

Christian One who believes in Christ and seeks to live according to his teachings.

Christian beliefs The concepts that make up the cognitive structure of Christianity.

Christian calendar The significant dates of the Christian year.

Christian doctrines Christianity's teachings about the nature of God, his work, and his relationship to his creation.

Christian ethics The teachings of Christianity on right and wrong.

Christian experience The experience of Christians. More than mere sensory experience, including religious experience, is in view.

Christian humanism *See* HUMANISM, CHRISTIAN.

Christianity The religion founded on the life and teachings of Jesus.

Christianity and culture The relationship between Christianity and culture, in terms of both Christianity's biblical roots and its contemporary practice and expression.

Christian liberty *See* LIBERTY, CHRISTIAN.

Christian perfection A life of sinlessness as a Christian's goal.

Christian Platonism An attempt to blend Christian theology and Platonic philosophy.

Christian Science (Church of Christ, Scientist) A religious system founded by Mary Baker Eddy in 1879. Her writings, especially *Science and Health with Key to the Scriptures*, are regarded by followers as the authoritative interpretation of the Bible. Christian Science is basically an idealism the major concepts of which are that sin and death are unreal, and so humans can avoid sickness and do not need atonement.

Christian socialism Any attempt by Christians to set up a system in which property is owned in common rather than by individuals.

Christian year The several important seasons of the year as determined by the church. Beginning with Advent, certain dates are designated for obser-vance of important events and truths of the Christian faith.

Christmas The day observed as the birth of Christ—December 25.

Christocentric Pertaining to any system of thought or practice in which Christ has the central or dominant place.

Christ of faith The Christ believed in and preached by the early Christians. The Christ of faith contrasts with the Jesus of history, who can be identified and investigated by historical research.

Christological Pertaining to the Christ, or more specifically the doctrine of Christ.

Christology The doctrinal study of the person and work of Christ.

Christology, Functional Christology that emphasizes what Jesus Christ did rather than what (or who) he was. Thus it may conceive of Jesus as someone who acted on behalf of God rather than as someone who was God. Generally claiming that the Bible makes only functional, not ontological, statements about Christ, functional Christology may then either limit itself to the biblical view or regard later ontological thinking as legitimate and consistent with the biblical view.

Christology, New Testament The doctrine of Christ as enunciated in the New Testament books.

Christology, Patristic The Christology of the church fathers.

Christology, Three-stage The teaching that the preexistent Second Person of the Trinity became incarnate as a human and later, at the time of the ascension, returned to heaven.

Christology, Word-flesh The teaching that the Word (the Second Person of the Trinity) took on a human physical nature, but not a human soul.

Christology, Word-man The teaching that the Word (the Second Person of the Trinity) took on full human nature.

Christology from above Christology that approaches the person of Christ from a doctrinal conception rather than through historical research.

Christology from below Christology that approaches the person of Christ through investigation of the historical Jesus.

Chrysostom, John (347-407) Preacher and theologian of the Eastern or Greek church who was known especially for his eloquent preaching.

Church, the Those who are true believers in Christ. The term is used in the New Testament both in a universal sense (all such believers) and in a restricted sense (a particular group of believers gathered in one place).

Church, Authority in the The right to determine the beliefs and practices within the church. In the ultimate sense this authority belongs to God, but there is a question as to whether it

is to be exercised by the clergy, by certain chosen lay leaders, or by all believers.

Church, Doctrine of the Principles concerning the nature, function, organization, and sacraments of the church.

Church, Local A group of believers in one locality who are organized into a worshiping and ministering fellowship.

Church, Rapture of the The idea that Christ at his second coming will catch up the church to be with him. Frequently the notion is that the church will be removed so as to be spared from the great tribulation. *See also* RAPTURE.

Church and state, Question of The question of the relationship between the authority of the church and that of the state. *See also* SEPARATION OF CHURCH AND STATE.

Church constitution A document spelling out the procedures governing the business of a church group.

Church councils Groups of representatives from individual churches or denominations who are called together to discuss issues of mutual concern.

Church discipline The church's active guidance of the conduct of its members. The term frequently carries a negative connotation—namely, either instruction aimed at correction or even excommunication.

Church extension The founding of new congregations by established churches.

Church fathers The church leaders of the period immediately following the New Testament era.

Church government The system by which churches are organized to carry out their business. The major types of church government (episcopal, presbyterian, congregational) differ as to where the authority in the church rests.

Church-growth movement A movement begun by Donald McGavran in 1961 to study and teach what causes congregations to grow.

Church membership Official affiliation with a church body, including certain responsibilities and privileges such as the right to vote.

Church of Christ, Scientist *See* CHRISTIAN SCIENCE (CHURCH OF CHRIST, SCIENTIST).

Church of Christ Uniting An ecumenical movement originally called the Consultation on Church Union (COCU). Its aim is actual organic merger of church fellowships.

Church officers Those who possess some particular authority, both intrachurch and interchurch, but especially the former.

Church offices Positions entailing authority in and giving structure to the church.

Church of Jesus Christ of Latter-day Saints *See* MORMONISM.

Church of South India A union formed in 1947 of the Methodist, Congregational, Presbyterian, and Anglican churches in south India.

Church planting The founding of new congregations.

Church purity The ideal that the church, as the body of Christ, should be pure just as he is. This may involve an insistence on regeneration as a prerequisite for church membership, the exercise of church discipline, or both.

Church renewal A twentieth-century version of what in earlier years was known as revival or awakening. It aims at a resurgence of vitality in the church.

Church universal All believers from all times and places.

Circumcision The act of removing the foreskin of the male; as a religious rite it signifies the membership of the individual within the Jewish community.

Circumcision, Physical Removal of a portion of the foreskin of the male. This contrasts with the spiritual or inward circumcision of which Paul speaks in Colossians 2:11, which is a matter of internal repentance and faith.

Circumcision of the heart Dedication of oneself to the Lord as a spiritual sign and act. *See also* INTERNAL CIRCUMCISION.

Civil disobedience An act of disobedience to the civil authority as a protest against a law deemed unjust.

Civil religion The blending of religious values with the values of a nation.

Civil righteousness The doing of good or humane acts that though not meritorious are nonetheless commendable; those positive moral virtues possessed even by non-Christians. Although such acts and virtues are genuinely good and pleasing to God, they in no sense qualify one for salvation.

Civil rights Fundamental rights guaranteed citizens by the state.

Cleanness A ceremonial status of purity. Hebrew law stipulated what made certain persons, places, and objects unclean as well as how one could be purified.

Clement of Alexandria (ca. 150-220) Greek theologian who was the first major figure of the school of Alexandria.

Clement of Rome (?-ca. A.D. 100) A late-first-century presbyter and bishop in Rome. He was the author of an early letter to the Corinthian church.

Clergy Those who have been ordained for religious service, as distinct from the laity.

Clergy, Secular Roman Catholic clergy not members of, or bound to, any particular religious order.

Closed continuum In the thought of Rudolf Bultmann and others, the idea that the universe is bound and governed by fixed and inviolable natural laws, so that miracles are impossible.

Coadjutor bishop A bishop who assists a diocesan bishop.

Cocceius, Johannes (1603-1669) German Reformed theologian who developed the idea of the covenants of works and grace.

COCU *See* CHURCH OF CHRIST UNITING.

Cohabitation The situation of persons who, although not married to each other, live together in a sexual relationship.

Coherentism A test for truth in which propositions are not justified by derivation from foundational propositions, but by their coherence with other propositions. In holism, the coherence is with all propositions.

Coherence theory of truth A view holding that the measure of the truth of propositions is their mutual coherence.

Coke, Thomas (1747-1814) Important Methodist preacher and leader in the generation following John Wesley.

Collective eschatology *See* ESCHATOLOGY, COLLECTIVE.

Collegialism The belief that the church and the state are voluntary, mutually independent associations created by their members.

Comforter The Holy Spirit (see, e.g., John 14:16).

"Coming for" A reference to the belief of pretribulationists that Christ's second coming will take place in two stages, the first of which will be removal of the church from the world before the great tribulation.

Commission, Great Christ's command to his disciples to evangelize the world (Matt. 28:19-20).

Common grace *See* GRACE, COMMON.

Common Order, Book of *See* BOOK OF COMMON ORDER.

Common Prayer, Book of *See* BOOK OF COMMON PRAYER.

Communal offerings In the Old Testament, a class of voluntary offerings not required as atonement for sin; for example, the peace offering.

Communicable attributes *See* ATTRIBUTES OF GOD, COMMUNICABLE.

Communication of attributes The teaching, found especially in Lutheran scholastic theology, that the attributes of Christ's deity are communicated to the humanity and vice versa, or that the attributes of each nature are attributes of the one person.

Communion A term for the Lord's Supper.

Communion, Holy The Lord's Supper.

Communion of saints A reference to the unity of all Christian believers, which may also emphasize the communion in Christ between living believers and those already dead.

Communism A social, political, and economic order in which the means of production are owned by the state, not by private parties.

Communitarianism The sharing of goods in the early church, a practice that led to some later instances of communal living and Christian socialism.

Community In postmodernism, since meaning is not inherent in the text, objectivity is provided by the interpretive community's conventions.

Comparative-religions criticism An approach explaining the history of the Judeo-Christian faith in terms of patterns of development believed to be common to all religions.

Compatibilistic freedom The idea that human freedom is not inconsistent with certainty of what will be done, either in terms of God's having rendered certain what is to happen or of his foreknowing what the person will choose to do.

Conception, Miraculous Usually a reference to the virgin birth of Christ.

Conciliarism A fifteenth-century reform movement in the Western church. It asserted the authority of general councils over the pope.

Concomitance In Roman Catholic theology, the teaching that both the body and blood of Christ are present in both the bread and the wine.

Concord, Book of A collection of the creeds and confessions generally accepted within the Lutheran church.

Concord, Formula of A doctrinal confession adopted by Lutheranism in 1577 after nearly thirty years of study and discussion. It was intended to settle the controversy between the Philippists (followers of Philipp Melanchthon) and the genuine Lutherans.

Concupiscence The tendency or inclination of human nature toward sin.

Concursus God's continuous action in conjunction with the action of his creatures.

Condemnation Negative judgment upon sin.

Conditional immortality A variety of annihilationism according to which immortality is a special gift to believers; unbelievers simply pass out of existence at death.

Conditional unity of the human person *See* UNITY OF THE HUMAN PERSON, CONDITIONAL.

Cone, James (1938-) A black theologian who is the major spokesman for black theology.

Confession The act of acknowledging one's sin or declaring one's faith.

Confession of 1967 A statement of faith that replaced the Westminster Confession as the primary doctrinal standard of the United Presbyterian Church in the United States of America.

Confession of sin The acknowledgment or admission of sin, whether to God or to other humans. In the Roman Catholic Church, confession must be made to a priest, who then remits the consequences of sin.

Confessional standard A creed or confession that serves as the official theological definition of a group.

Confessionalism Expressing Christian faith through the formulation of formal statements to which all agree.

Confessions of faith Formal statements of doctrinal beliefs.

Confirmation A sacrament of the Roman Catholic Church (and a few other groups) in which the person consciously and intentionally confirms or ratifies the faith testified to in baptism.

Congregational church A church or group of churches practicing the congregational form of church polity.

Congregational form of church government A form of church government emphasizing the autonomy, independence, and authority of the local church.

Congregationalism *See* CONGREGATIONAL CHURCH.

Congruism A form of Calvinism that holds that God renders certain what occurs, but that he does so by working with the human will, so that the human being freely chooses that which God intends.

Conscience The sense of being obligated to do the right and avoid the wrong; in some views, a virtual faculty of human nature.

Conscientious objection Refusal to serve in the military because of religious or philosophical objection to the taking of human life even in war.

Consecration The setting apart of a person, place, or object for special divine use.

Consecration of the host In the Roman Catholic mass, the act by which the wafer of the Eucharist is transubstantiated into the Lord's body.

Consequent nature In the thought of Alfred North Whitehead, the concrete actuality and activity of God in relation to the processes of the world.

Conservation *See* PRESERVATION.

Conservatives Those who endeavor to maintain or preserve that which has been; in theology, those who emphasize holding to the authority of the Bible's teachings.

Consistent eschatology *See* ESCHATOLOGY, CONSISTENT.

Constantine the Great (ca. 275-337) Roman emperor who in A.D. 313 accepted the legitimacy of Christianity and in effect established Christianity as the official religion of the Roman Empire.

Constantinople, First Council of (381) Ecumenical council that mainly reaffirmed earlier conciliar decisions, thus further establishing orthodox Christology.

Constantinople, Standing Synod of Standing synod that in November 448 condemned the views of Eutyches.

Constructive theology The attempt to synthesize or formulate a theology, and especially the work of a group of nonevangelical American theologians formed in the 1970s. Believing traditional or orthodox theology to be no longer tenable, they have attempted to reshape doctrines to suit the modern world.

Consubstantiation The idea, characteristic of Lutheran theology, that in the Lord's Supper the bread and wine are not transformed into the body and blood of Christ, but that the molecules of the flesh and blood are present "in, with, and under" the molecules of the bread and wine.

Consultation on Church Union *See* CHURCH OF CHRIST UNITING.

Consummation of the age The end of history, particularly as ushered in by the second coming of Christ.

Contemporary Roman Catholic theology

Roman Catholic theology especially as formulated since the Second Vatican Council. It contrasts with traditional scholasticism.

Contemporization A stating of timeless truths in up-to-date forms.

Contextualization of theology The attempt to adapt the expression of theology to a given time, place, culture, or audience.

Contingency argument for God One of Thomas Aquinas's cosmological arguments for the existence of God: For anything contingent to exist, there must be at least one being that (or who) is not contingent.

Contingent being Something that does not exist in and of itself but depends for its existence upon some other being.

Continuous creation *See* CREATION, CONTINUOUS.

Contradiction, Law of A principle of logic that states that a thing cannot be both A and non-A at the same time and in the same respect.

Contribution, Gift of A spiritual gift mentioned by Paul in Romans 12:8: the ability to give joyously to an unusual degree.

Contrition Sorrow for sin because it is an offense against God rather than because it may lead to unfortunate consequences for the sinner. (The latter is known in Roman Catholic theology as "attrition.")

Conventicle A religious group or a meeting for worship outside of, and to some degree in protest against, the established church.

Conventional Roman Catholicism *See* CATHOLICISM, CONVENTIONAL ROMAN.

Conversion The action of a person in turning to Christ. It includes repentance (renunciation of sin) and faith (acceptance of Christ).

Conversionistic Christianity Varieties of Christianity that emphasize the need of taking a definite step as one begins the Christian life.

Conviction of sin The persuasion that one is a sinner. According to Jesus in John 16:8-9, it is produced by the work of the Holy Spirit.

Convocation Literally, a "calling together," a gathering for worship or instruction.

Cooperation, Ecclesiastical Different denominational groups working together for common purposes.

Cornerstone, Christ as Part of the imagery of the church as a spiritual temple; it signifies how basic and crucial Christ is to the entire church (Isa. 28:16; Eph. 2:20; 1 Peter 2:6).

Corporate personality A reference to the idea that the human race is an organic whole rather than separate individuals. Thus Adam's sin was not an isolated act of an individual, but rather an act of the human race, so that consequences are experienced by the entire human race.

Corporate solidarity A reference to the idea that there is a unity of action and responsibility within the human race. *See also* CORPORATE PERSONALITY.

Correction A part of discipline in which erroneous ideas and actions are pointed out so they can be modified to what is true and right.

Correlation, Method of Paul Tillich's method of stating theology in the form of answers to questions implied in human existence.

Correspondence theory of truth A view holding that the truth of propositions is measured by their agreement with the reality they describe.

Corrupted nature Human nature as corrupted or polluted by the fall and sin.

Corruptible body Our present physical body, which is subject to death and decay.

Cosmic eschatology *See* ESCHATOLOGY, COSMIC.

Cosmic history The history of the whole creation.

Cosmological argument for God An argument for the existence of God: Since every existent thing in the universe must have a cause, there must be a God.

Cosmology The study of the origin and nature of the universe.

Cosmology, Naturalistic An explanation of the origin and nature of the universe in terms of physical laws or forces within it; there is no need of anything from outside.

Council, Church A meeting in which representatives of the church attempt to determine courses of action.

Council of Trent *See* TRENT, COUNCIL OF.

Counselor A reference to the Holy Spirit's role of guiding and encouraging the believer (John 14:16).

Counter-Reformation, the A sixteenth-century reform movement aimed at purifying and strengthening the Roman Catholic Church from within.

Covenant An agreement between God and humans in which God pledges to bless those who accept and commit themselves to him.

Covenant, New *See* NEW COVENANT.

Covenant, Old *See* COVENANT OF WORKS.

Covenant community A people brought into being by a divine covenant, whether the nation of Israel or the church.

Covenant nation of Israel A reference to the idea that God has chosen Israel to be the special object of his favor and deals with them on the basis of a compact made with them.

Covenant of grace God's offer of salvation through Christ's work to all who accept it.

Covenant of redemption The agreement made between God the Father and God the Son whereby the latter would give his life for the salvation of the human race.

Covenant of works The covenant between God and Adam that promised that obedience would be rewarded with eternal life and disobedience punished by eternal death.

Covenant people In the Old Testament, Israel; in the New Testament, the church.

Covenant relationship A relationship based upon a covenant between God and his people.

Covenant theology Theology that views the relationship between God and humanity as a type of agreement between them that governs the dealings of God with humans.

Covenantal view of baptism The idea that baptism is a sign of participation in the covenant. Hence only adult believers and the children of believing parents are to be baptized. In this view, baptism has in the new covenant the place that circumcision had in the old.

Covetousness The sin of desiring that which belongs to another.

Creatio de novo Creation without the use of preexisting materials. It is therefore genuine creation rather than a refashioning of what already exists.

Creatio ex nihilo Literally, "creation out of nothing," the idea that God created without the use of previously existing materials.

Creation That which God has brought into being.

Creation, Continuous The idea found especially in the thought of Karl Heim that the creation does not merely remain in existence, but is constantly passing out of existence and being recreated by God in each instant of time.

Creation, Development within The idea that there has been development or elaboration within the creation—parts of God's handiwork were not created in their final form.

Creation, Doctrine of Teachings regarding God's act of bringing into existence all that is.

Creation of humans God's act of bringing humanity into initial existence.

Creation, New That which God is bringing about in remaking or renewing the fallen creation, both in terms of individual regeneration and renewal of the entire cosmos.

Creation, Theology of Theology that emphasizes the doctrine of creation.

Creationism Belief that the universe and life (especially human life) originated from definite action by God rather than from chance factors.

Creationism, Progressive The teaching that God created *de novo* in several steps; that is, he created the first member of each "kind," which then developed (or evolved). The kinds, then, have not evolved from one another in an uninterrupted causal chain. This view, which is sometimes called microevolution (evolution within kinds) as opposed to macroevolution (evolution across kinds), puts emphasis upon the fact of creation rather than upon evolution. God created the human *in toto*, fashioning both the material and immaterial aspects of human nature *de novo*; he did not use an existing being that had evolved physically and modify it into a human.

Creationist view of the origin of the soul *See* SOUL, CREATIONIST VIEW OF THE ORIGIN OF THE.

Creative evolution The idea that God produces all that is by working immanently through laws of nature. This is a variation of theistic evolution.

Creator, the A reference to God in terms of his having brought into existence all that is. The term is often used popularly as a synonym for God.

Creator emeritus A reference to the basically deistic view that God, having begun the evolutionary process, does not directly involve himself in it.

Creature Any being that derives its existence from God.

Creature, New A person who has been regenerated or born again.

Creed A summary of the beliefs of a person or group, often a denomination.

Creedalism Insistence upon formal subscription to a statement of belief, in exactly those words.

Crisis theology A synonym for neo-orthodoxy; it was used especially in the early years of the movement.

Criteria of authenticity *See* AUTHENTICITY, CRITERIA OF.

Critical methodology A method that seeks to evaluate the evidence for the genuineness of a document or statement rather than merely taking it at face value.

Criticism, Canonical A method developed especially by Brevard Childs that, while not approaching the Bible uncritically, goes beyond standard critical study. It attempts to interpret the Bible as canon—that is, in terms of the authority that the traditions exerted within the believing community.

Criticism, Comparative-religions An approach explaining the history of the Judeo-Christian faith in terms of patterns of development believed to be common to all religions.

Criticism, Form (*Formgeschichte*) A method of biblical criticism that seeks to get behind the written sources to what was actually said and done. It attempts to identify and evaluate layers of material added to the tradition during the period of oral transmission.

Criticism, Historical A method of attempting to evaluate historical evidence, particularly for the biblical text. The ultimate aim is to determine what actually occurred.

Criticism, Literary-source A method of study that attempts to isolate the various written sources on which the present biblical text is based.

Criticism, Reader-response A theory of biblical interpretation, closely allied with postmodernism, in which the meaning of a text is not found in the original author's intention, but in what the text says to the reader.

Criticism, Redaction A method of biblical criticism that seeks to identify the writer's role in selection, modification, and perhaps even creation of material for inclusion.

Criticism, Source A discipline that attempts to isolate and identify the different written sources underlying the current form of the text.

Criticism, Structural Criticism that attempts to find certain generic elements of human existence and experience within the biblical text. It is also termed "structural exegesis."

Criticism, Textual Critical study that attempts to identify the exact form of the original text.

Cross, the The instrument of Christ's execution. The term is also used to represent his crucifixion, his death, and the atonement.

Cross, Theology of the *See* THEOLOGY OF THE CROSS.

Crown A headpiece signifying honor or high office. The term is used to symbolize the rewards Christians receive.

Crucified with Christ A reference to the believer's identification with Christ in his death (Gal. 2:20).

Crucifixion The most painful and shameful form of execution practiced by the Roman Empire. The person was nailed to a cross and left to hang vertically until dead.

Crypto-Calvinist A term leveled in accusation against Philipp Melanchthon and his followers for allegedly accepting too much of the teachings of Calvin and thus being secret Calvinists.

Cullmann, Oscar (1902-1999) Twentieth-century New Testament scholar at the University of Basel. He is best known for his book *Christ and Time* and for his concept of functional Christology.

Cults Groups that are heretical in one or more significant respects and that frequently practice strong social control over their members. They sometimes also engage in forms of brainwashing to gain and retain converts.

Culture The total pattern of human behavior and its products; a society's ways of life and thinking.

Curate A member of the clergy who assists the minister of a parish.

Curse Pronouncement of an expression wishing evil upon another.

Cusa, Nicholas of *See* NICHOLAS OF CUSA.

Cyclical view of history The idea that the events of history form a recurrent pattern so that no real progress is made.

Cyprian (ca. 200-258) Bishop of Carthage and theologian whose views contributed to the doctrine of the church.

Cyril of Alexandria (376-444) Patriarch of Alexandria and theologian who emphasized the unity of the person of Christ.

Dd

Damnation The pronouncement of a curse or judgment upon someone or something, especially the consignment of a person to hell.

Darby, John Nelson (1800-1882) An Irish minister who was an early leader in the Plymouth Brethren movement. He popularized dispensationalism.

Darkness A scriptural symbol of ignorance, evil, and destruction. *See also* OUTER DARKNESS.

Dark night of the soul Taken from the title of a book by John of the Cross, an expression referring to the seeming absence of God.

Darwinism The earliest general form of the theory of biological evolution as it was propounded by Charles Darwin in *The Origin of Species* (1859). It is often used as a synonym for evolution.

Davidic covenant The covenant in which God granted the kingdom to David and his descendants forever (2 Sam. 7; cf. 2 Chron. 13:5).

Davidic kingdom The earthly kingdom of Israel ruled by David and his successors.

Day In Scripture, the hours of daylight, a long era, or a specific period.

Day of the Lord A future day of judgment identified in the New Testament with Christ's second coming.

Day of wrath The day of the Lord's judgment.

Days, Last *See* LAST DAYS.

Deacon, deaconess An official of the local church. The term derives from a verb meaning "to serve." Qualifications for the office, the origin of which is apparently recorded in Acts 6:1-6, are found in 1 Timothy 3:8-13. That women served as deacons is indicated in Romans 16:1.

Dead, Abode of the The place to which persons go upon death until resurrection. *See also* INTERMEDIATE STATE.

Dead, Prayers for the The practice of praying for the dead. Found especially in Roman Catholicism, prayers for the dead are based in large measure upon the apocryphal text of *2 Maccabees 12:44*.

Dead in Christ Those who have died believing in Christ (see, e.g., 1 Thess. 4:16).

Dead Sea Scrolls A collection of writings found in caves near the Dead Sea and especially at Qumran. These scrolls, the first of which were discovered in 1947, were probably produced by an Essene community.

Death The cessation of physical life. *See*

also ETERNAL DEATH; SPIRITUAL DEATH.

Death, First Physical death.

Death, Second The final state of those who die apart from the salvation offered by God. The term is found in Revelation 2:11, 20:6, 14, and 21:8.

Death of God theology A theological movement that flourished briefly in the mid-1960s. The primary exponents were Thomas J. J. Altizer, William Hamilton, and Paul Van Buren. Although there were differences, the three agreed that a transcendent God was no longer a part of the experience of modern humans. The theology was also referred to as Christian atheism and secular theology.

Death penalty The practice of executing persons found guilty of certain heinous crimes, especially murder.

Decalogue, the The Ten Commandments.

Deceiver, the Satan.

Deconstruction A radical variety of postmodernism, in literary criticism and philosophy, associated with persons such as Jacques Derrida, Michel Foucault, and the Yale school of literary criticism. Derrida deconstructs by finding contradictory elements within any system. Foucault deconstructs by historical analysis (sometimes "fictive"), showing that those possessing power determine normativity, truth, and right.

Decrees, Eternal Decrees of God that were made in eternity.

Decrees of God The decisions of God that, made in eternity, render certain all that occurs within time.

Decretive will A reference to God's will as bringing certain things to pass; he is regarded as the initiator. This is in contrast to his permissive will, which is more of the nature of a passive compliance.

Deification The practice of treating a person (e.g., the Roman emperor) or object as divine.

Deism Belief in a God who created but has no continuing involvement with the world and events within it.

Deity A reference to God or the possessing of godhood.

Deliverance The act or state of being freed from some bondage, as from the slavery in Egypt, or more particularly, from the power of sin.

Deliverer A person who Old Testament believers expected would come and liberate them from oppression. The anticipation was fulfilled in the coming of Christ.

Delphi *See* ORACLE OF DELPHI.

Deluge, the The great flood of Genesis 7.

Demigod A semidivine being.

Demiurge In Greek thought, especially that of Plato, a being who fashioned the material world. The term is used once in the Bible (Heb. 11:10) to refer to God's role as Creator.

Demoniac A person who is demon-possessed.

Demonology The study of demons.

Demon possession A condition of being inhabited and dominated by demons.

Demons Fallen angels who now work evil under the leadership of their chief, Satan.

Demons, Casting out of The act of removing demons from demoniacs, usually by command. It is also known as exorcism.

Demythologization The theological method, found especially in the thought of Rudolf Bultmann, of interpreting the supernatural elements (the "myths") of Scripture not in a literal fashion, but in accord with the categories of existentialism.

Denomination A group of believers or churches united on the basis of a common set of beliefs and practices.

Denominationalism A dedication to, or enthusiasm for, one's denomination.

Depravity Sinfulness, corruption, or pollution of one's nature.

Depravity, Total The idea that sinfulness affects the whole of one's nature and colors all that one does; it does not necessarily mean that one is as sinful as one can possibly be.

Descartes, René (1596-1650) French philosopher who founded the modern school of thought known as rationalism. He taught that truth can be discovered simply by pure reasoning.

Descent into hell The teaching that Jesus between his death and resurrection descended into hell. Reference to a descent into hell is found in the writings of many early Fathers and in later versions of the Apostles' Creed. The biblical evidence usually appealed to includes Acts 2:31, Ephesians 4:8-10, and 1 Peter 3:18-20. The doctrine is usually understood literally by Roman Catholic and Lutheran theologians, figuratively by the Reformed.

Descent of man A reference to the concept that the human has evolved from other living species.

Despair A sense of hopelessness or anguish—a common theme in existential theology and philosophy.

Determinism The belief that all that happens is inflexibly caused and fixed.

Developmentalism A capitalist approach that seeks to solve the problems of poor peoples and nations by helping them develop their own economy.

Developmental psychology The study of the stages through which humans pass.

Development in fruition The idea, found especially in the thought of John Baillie, that although in heaven we will not progress beyond the perfection attained at death, we will continue to exercise that perfection. The concept contrasts with "development towards fruition."

Development within creation *See* CRE-ATION, DEVELOPMENT WITHIN.

Devil, the Satan—the supreme evil spiritual being, who rebelled against God and now is engaged in opposing him. In the last times the devil will be finally subdued.

Devotio moderna A fifteenth- and sixteenth-century devotional movement within the Roman Catholic Church.

Devotions, Personal The practice of Bible study, meditation, and prayer as an act of personal or private worship.

Dewey, John (1859-1952) Philosopher and educational theorist; one of the major pragmatists and the primary architect of progressive education.

DeWolf, L. Harold (1905-1986) Methodist theologian at Boston University School of Theology and Wesley Theological Seminary who championed the use of reason in religion.

Diachronic approach The study of the development of a concept through successive periods of time. This approach contrasts with the synchronic—the study and comparison of several simultaneous concepts.

Diachronic semantics Semantical or linguistic study that emphasizes development through periods of time. *See also* DIACHRONIC APPROACH.

Diadem A crown; a symbol of royalty.

Dialectical materialism The philosophical basis of Marxist communism. An adaptation of Hegelianism, dialectical materialism substitutes a reference to matter wherever Hegel speaks of the spiritual or ideal.

Dialectical theology A term used as a synonym for neoorthodoxy, especially in its earliest years.

Diaspora A term for Jewish communities outside Palestine.

Dichotomism A view of human nature that regards it as consisting of two components, usually a material and a spiritual element (i.e., body and soul).

Dichotomy The division of anything into two parts. *See also* DICHOTOMISM.

Dictation theory *See* INSPIRATION, DICTATION THEORY OF.

Didache An early manual of instruction regarding the Christian life and church government.

Didactic material Material of a teaching or instructional nature; in particular, the instructional prose portions of the

Bible, as contrasted with the narrative portions.

Dimensional beyondness An aspect of Søren Kierkegaard's concept of transcendence: God is not simply far removed spatially, but is in an entirely different realm of reality beyond our dimensions of space and time.

Diocese In Roman Catholic, Eastern Orthodox, and Anglican churches, a geographical unit headed by a bishop.

Dionysius the Areopagite, Pseudo- A writer who probably lived in Syria in the fifth or early sixth century. Initially identified with Dionysius the Areopagite (Acts 17:34), pseudo-Dionysius attempted to blend Christian theology and neo-Platonic thought.

Dioscorus Patriarch of Alexandria from 444 to 451; opponent of Nestorianism and supporter of Eutyches.

Dipolar theism *See* THEISM, DIPOLAR.

Discerning of spirits The ability to evaluate what is said by prophets (1 Cor. 14:29).

Disciple A learner or follower of another. The term is used especially of Jesus' twelve closest followers.

Discipline Instruction particularly involving correction.

Discrimination Treating certain persons unfairly because of their membership in a particular racial or social group.

Disembodied state The condition of persons between death and resurrection.

Dispensation A stewardship or management of affairs. In the theological system known as dispensationalism, it refers to a period of time in which God deals with the human race in a distinct way.

Dispensation of innocence In dispensationalism, the period of God's dealing with Adam and Eve prior to the Fall.

Dispensation of law In dispensationalism, the period of God's dealing with the human race from the giving of the Law to Moses at Sinai until the New Testament era.

Dispensationalism A system of biblical interpretation and of theology that divides God's working into different periods that he administers on different bases. It involves a literal interpretation of Scripture, a distinction between Israel and the church, and a premillennial, pretribulational eschatology.

Dispensationalism, Progressive A variety of dispensationalism that emphasizes less strongly the distinctions between Israel and the church.

Distinctiveness A criterion of authenticity in critical study of the Gospels. The term is used by Reginald Fuller in reference to teachings that are not found in Judaism or the church, and thus are assumed to be authentically from Jesus.

Distinguishing of spirits *See* DISCERN-ING OF SPIRITS.

Divination The attempt to gain super-natural knowledge, especially of the future, by such means as omens or mediums.

Divorce Legal dissolution of a valid marriage.

Docetism The belief that the humanity of Jesus was not genuine—he merely seemed to be human.

Doctrine A belief or teaching regarding theological themes; that is, a tenet regarding the nature of God and his works.

Doctrine, Rule theory of A view, origi-nated by George Lindbeck of Yale University, that doctrines, rather than being first-level or truth claims, are sec-ond-level and resemble grammatical rules in providing guidance for the faith community.

Documentary hypothesis The theory that the Pentateuch is a compilation of sev-eral different written sources, gener-ally labeled J, E, D, and P.

Dodd, C. H. (Charles Harold) (1884-1973) British Congregational minister and New Testament professor at Oxford, Manchester, and Cambridge who is known particularly for his concept of realized eschatology.

Dogma A doctrine, usually in the form of an official or authoritative ecclesias-tical declaration.

Dogmatics The systematic study of doc-trine; synonymous with systematic theology.

Dogmatism The quality of being opin-ionated and categorical in one's beliefs; it is often unwarranted.

Dominican order An order founded in 1216 for defense of the faith. Including such members as Albertus Magnus and Thomas Aquinas, it contributed sig-nificant works to theology and apolo-getics. It played a significant role in the Inquisition.

Dominion-having A reference to God's command to Adam in Genesis 1:28 to have dominion over the rest of cre-ation. Some theologies see the exercise of dominion as the image of God in the human race.

Dominions A term in Ephesians 6:12 that is thought by some to refer to spir-itual beings, by others to refer to forces within the structures of society.

Donation of Constantine A document purporting to have been executed by Constantine, giving the western part of his empire to Pope Sylvester I. Nicholas of Cusa and Laurentius Valla demonstrated that it was a forgery.

Donatism An African separatist move-ment that objected to the reinstatement of Christians who had surrendered the Scriptures under persecution. In oppo-sition to the Donatists, Augustine developed the concept of the invisible church.

Donum superadditum The idea of a supernatural addition to human nature, adding what was lost in the fall, leaving human nature intact. According to medieval Catholic theology, it was the likeness of God (the *donum superadditum*) that the human lost, whereas the image of God was unaffected by the Fall.

Doomsday philosophy The belief that history will come to some disastrous end.

Dooyeweerd, Herman (1894-1977) Dutch Reformed philosopher whose major work was the four-volume *New Critique of Theoretical Thought* (1953-1958).

Dorner, Isaak August (1809-1884) German theologian who taught at Tübingen, Kiel, Königsberg, Bonn, Göttingen, and Berlin. His chief idea was that Christ's incarnation was a gradual and progressive matter.

Dort, Synod of (1618-1619) An international church assembly convoked to deal with theological and ecclesiastical issues within the Reformed Church in the Netherlands. Its major lasting accomplishment was the promulgation of the Canons of Dort, which articulated the Reformed position on election and related matters.

Double predestination The teaching that God has chosen not only some to be saved, but also others to be lost.

Doubt, Religious Uncertainty about the truthfulness of certain propositions, or a lack of consistent commitment to the object of religious trust. It is not to be confused with unbelief.

Doxology Declaration of praise to God. The term often refers to certain fixed expressions, all of which take the form "Glory [be] to God . . ."

Dread In the thought of Søren Kierkegaard, an existential state that is the precondition of sin. It is an anxiety about life itself, stemming from the tension between finitude and freedom.

Dream A series of thoughts, images, or emotions occurring during sleep. In biblical times God used dreams to reveal himself to humans. Dreams contrast with visions, which are similar revelations taking place in the conscious state.

Dualism Any view of reality based upon two fundamental principles, such as matter and spirit, nature and supernature, or good and evil.

Dulia Honor that can be given to persons other than God; for example, to Mary or the saints.

Duns Scotus, John (ca. 1266-1308) Franciscan scholastic born in Scotland and educated at Oxford and Paris. He taught at Oxford, Paris, and Cologne. In opposition to Thomas Aquinas, he held that faith is primarily a matter of will, not of reason, and therefore is not established by rational proofs.

Duty That which one is morally obligated to do.

Dwight, Timothy (1752-1817) Congregational clergyman, theologian, and educator. From 1795 until his death, he was president and professor of divinity at Yale University. A defender of conservative Calvinism, he exerted influence upon the Second Great Awakening. His major writing was a five-volume set of sermons, *Theology Explained and Defended*.

Dynamic presence A reference to the view that the body and blood of Christ are present in the Lord's Supper not literally and physically, but spiritually and influentially.

Dysteleological An entity or event apparently noncontributory to or contradictory to a rational or constructive purpose.

Ee

Early church The church of the earliest period of the Christian Era—also called the New Testament church, the church of the book of Acts, and the first-century church.

Earth, New The completely redeemed universe of the future; it is referred to as "new heavens and a new earth" (2 Peter 3:13).

Earthly body The body that humans have in their earthly life (see 1 Cor. 15:42-50).

Earthly kingdom The kingdom of God as it is manifested upon the earth. The phrase sometimes refers to the future millennial rule of Christ.

Earthly reign of Christ A reference to the millennium. *See also* EARTHLY KINGDOM.

Easter The Sunday on which the resurrection of Christ is celebrated.

Eastern Orthodoxy A designation of the Eastern or Greek churches that separated from the Western churches in A.D. 1054.

Eastern religions Religions originating in Asia, such as Hinduism, Buddhism, and Taoism.

Easy believism A popular approach akin to "cheap grace." It stresses that to be saved, one has but to believe—there is no need for a real commitment.

Ebionism An early Christological heresy that thought of Jesus as human but not divine.

Ecclesiastical separation *See* SEPARATION, ECCLESIASTICAL.

Eck, Johann (1486-1543) German theologian best remembered for his opposition to Martin Luther, especially at the Leipzig disputation.

Eckhart, Meister (ca. 1260-1328) German Dominican mystic and theologian who taught that God is not known through any of the normal means of human knowledge but through a direct spiritual uniting with him.

Ecology The study of the interrelatedness of the universe, and particularly of the preservation of the environment and natural resources.

Economic view of the Trinity An approach to the Trinity by Hippolytus and Tertullian that emphasized the differing manifestations and functions of the three persons.

Ecstatic utterances Audible expressions not ordinarily understood by the hearers.

Ecumenical councils Church councils

convened to attempt to resolve disputed issues, usually matters of doctrine.

Ecumenical movement, Modern A modern-day movement that has attempted to bring about the unity of believers. It began in 1910 as a result of international missionary conferences.

Ecumenism The attempt to bring about unity among believers. It may take the form of either cooperation between separate groups or actual merger into one organism.

Ecumenism, Early Early attempts to arrive at unified beliefs through councils that sought to formulate official doctrinal statements.

Eddy, Mary Baker (1821-1910) Founder of the Church of Christ, Scientist (Christian Science) and author of *Science and Health with Key to the Scriptures*.

Eden, Garden of *See* GARDEN OF EDEN.

Edification Literally "building up"; the strengthening of the spiritual life of Christians and congregations.

Edwards, Jonathan (1703-1758) Congregational minister and major theologian of the First Great Awakening. His most important pastorate was at Northampton, Massachusetts, where he preached the celebrated sermon "Sinners in the Hands of an Angry God." He served as president of the College of New Jersey (Princeton University) for only a few weeks before his death.

Effectual calling God's special working upon the elect so that they respond in faith.

Egotism An excessive sense of one's own importance; conceit.

Eisegesis The practice of reading meaning into a biblical text, as opposed to the practice of drawing out the meaning that is already there (exegesis).

El A basic name for God.

Élan vital In the thought of Henri Bergson, a vital force, immanent in all organisms, that causes the evolutionary developments that occur.

Elder A leader in the synagogue, in the early church, or in a local congregation of some denominations today. The qualifications for the office are stated in 1 Timothy 3:1-7 and Titus 1:5-9.

Elect Those specially chosen by God. The term can refer either to the nation Israel or to individuals designated for salvation or for special positions of service.

Election God's decision in choosing a special group or certain persons for salvation or service. The term is used especially of the predestination of the individual recipients of salvation.

Elements In the Bible, the fundamental principles of any system or body of knowledge, especially the letters of the alphabet.

Elkesaites A sect of early Jewish Christians that derived from Ebionism and contributed to the rise of Islam. It was syncretistic, theosophical, and legalistic.

Elohim A very common Hebrew name for deity, generic in nature, so that it is applied both to heathen gods and to the true God of the Israelites.

El Shaddai A name for God that emphasizes his power.

Emanent attributes *See* ATTRIBUTES OF GOD, EMANANT.

Emanation An outflow, usually associated with the idea that the creation did not originate from nothing, but as an outflow from God's own nature.

Emergent evolutionism *See* EVOLUTIONISM, EMERGENT.

Eminence, Method of A method of attempting to know God by taking qualities in human nature that reflect God and elevating them to a supreme degree.

Emmanuel A name for Jesus that means "God with us" (also "Immanuel").

Empirical Pertaining to the senses or that which can be known through sense perception.

Empirical approach A theological methodology that gains knowledge through sense perception.

Empirical church The church as actually found in history and human experience.

Empirical theology A theology based upon sense data; natural theology.

Empiricism A philosophical theology that holds that all knowledge comes through sensory perception.

Encyclical A circular letter, especially a papal document in modern times.

Encyclical letter A letter (e.g., Ephesians) that is intended to circulate from one congregation to the next.

End of the world The conclusion of earthly history. In Christian thought, it will be brought about by the second coming of Christ.

Endurance The ability of the Christian, by God's help, to persevere through trials, temptations, and afflictions.

English Reformation The break of the English churches from Rome when Parliament in 1534 declared Henry VIII the supreme head of the Church of England. This was an ecclesiastical and financial break from the Church of Rome. Doctrinally, however, the Reformation proceeded in varying degrees over a period of time.

Enlightenment, The A philosophical movement of the eighteenth century, especially in Germany and France. It was rationalistic and often hostile to religion.

Enthymeme A logical argument in which one of the premises is suppressed or unexpressed, and thus often untested.

Ephesus, Council of (431) An ecumenical council that condemned the teachings of Nestorius and affirmed the unity of the person of Christ.

Epicureanism A Greek ethical view that emphasizes that good consists in pleasure.

Epiphany From a Greek word meaning "manifestation," it refers to the first or second coming of Christ. It also is a festival of the Christian year (January 6).

Episcopacy The system of church government placing major authority in the office of bishop; also, the office itself.

Episcopal church government A form of church government that places primary authority in the office of bishop.

Episcopalians Persons belonging to Episcopal churches or subscribing to Episcopal beliefs.

Episcopius, Simon (1583-1643) Dutch theologian and leader of the Remonstrants, banished by the Synod of Dort. His incomplete four-volume statement of Arminianism, *Institutiones Theologicae*, was published posthumously.

Epistemology A theory of knowledge or an inquiry into how we gain knowledge.

Equiprobablism In casuistry, the position that if the arguments for two courses of action are equally cogent, one is justified in following either one.

Erasmus, Desiderius (1466-1536) Leading Christian humanist of the Reformation period who sought to reform the church by scholarship. At first he sided with Luther, but broke with him over the issue of freedom of the will.

Erastianism Named for Thomas Erastus (1524-1583) and deriving from his thought, the view that the state has authority over the church in all matters.

Erigena, John Scotus (ca. 810-877) Irish philosopher under whom European thought began to shift from Platonism to Aristotelianism. Although Scripture was his main authority, he also stressed the role of reason in discovering its meaning. He maintained that the best interpretation of Scripture is that which most closely agrees with reason.

Eschatological parable A parable dealing with the last things, such as those found in Matthew 25.

Eschatology The study of the last things or of the future generally.

Eschatology, Collective Eschatological events involving the whole of the universe or all of the human race.

Eschatology, Consistent The view of Albert Schweitzer and others that Jesus' actions and teachings were thoroughly eschatological.

Eschatology, Cosmic The study of the last things as they affect the entire human race or the entire creation collectively.

Eschatology, Individual The study of future events with respect to individuals; in particular, study of their death, intermediate state, and resurrection.

Eschatology, New Testament The teaching of the New Testament regarding the last things.

Eschatology, Old Testament The teaching of the Old Testament regarding the last things.

Eschatology, Realized The view of C. H. Dodd and others that the eschatological passages in the Bible do not refer to the future, but to matters occurring and fulfilled within the biblical period, and especially by Jesus' life and ministry.

Eschatomania An excessive interest in, or preoccupation with, the last things.

Eschaton The future culmination.

Eschatophobia A fear of, or avoidance of, discussing or studying the last things.

Essence of God *See* GOD, ESSENCE OF.

Essenes An ascetic Jewish sect that flourished from the second century B.C. to the end of the first century of the Christian Era.

Essential humanity Humanity as intended and created by God, in contrast to human nature as it exists after the Fall.

Essential man *See* ESSENTIAL HUMANITY.

Eternal condemnation Condemnation that lasts beyond this life into eternity.

Eternal consequences of sin The results of sin that are unending, in contrast with the temporal results, which cease at death.

Eternal death The finalization of spiritual death; the permanent separation of the sinner from God.

Eternal destiny The future state of the person, whether in heaven or hell, with God or apart from him.

Eternal destruction The endless future punishment of the wicked.

Eternal generation An understanding of the relationship among the members of the Trinity according to which the sonship of the Second Person is prior to the Incarnation (John 1:18; 1 John 4:9).

Eternal life The life given to the believer; it surpasses natural life in quality and also extends beyond this life to eternity.

Eternal punishment The endless nature of the punishment sinners will experience beyond this life.

Eternal redemption A phrase used in Hebrews 9:12 to indicate that unlike the Old Testament sacrifice of animals, the effect of which was limited, the redeeming death of Christ has an eternal effect.

Eternal security of the believer The doctrine that truly regenerate believers will never lose their salvation.

Eternal state *See* FINAL STATE.

Eternal will of God What God has willed or chosen from all eternity.

Eternity A transcendence of time; without beginning or end, it is also qualitatively superior to the temporal.

Ethical code Regulations defining right and wrong conduct, attitudes, or choices.

Ethical kingdom A reference to God's rule over the moral conduct of believers.

Ethical purity Living in strict conformity to a moral code; it may connote asceticism.

Ethical system, Christian A system of right and wrong based on Christian principles and teachings.

Ethical teaching Teaching that pertains to the way life is to be conducted; in particular, Jesus' instruction on morality.

Ethics The study of right and wrong to determine what one ought to do or what is good for the human.

Ethics, Biblical A system of right and wrong based upon, or found in, the Bible.

Ethics, Consequentialist view of An ethic that measures the goodness or rightness of an action by the consequences that follow from it.

Ethnic Israel Israel as a national rather than religious group.

Ethos A pervading set of ideas, values, or sentiments characterizing a particular time and place.

Eucharist The Lord's Supper. The term is used especially by sacramentalists.

Eudaemonism An ethical theory that evaluates actions in terms of their ability to produce happiness or personal well-being. Its emphasis is on a life controlled by reason rather than the pursuit of pleasure.

Euthanasia Literally, "good death," an attempt to prevent the process of death from being unduly prolonged and painful. It may involve either the omission of treatment (passive euthanasia) or direct acts aimed at terminating life (active euthanasia).

Eutyches (ca. 375-454) Archimandrite of a monastery in Constantinople. Having been condemned and deposed by the standing Synod of Constantinople (448), he was supported by the Robber Synod of Ephesus (449) and then finally condemned by the Council of Chalcedon (451).

Eutychianism The teaching that Jesus had only one nature.

Evangelical One who holds to the beliefs and practices of evangelicalism.

Evangelicalism A movement in modern Christianity emphasizing the gospel of forgiveness and regeneration through personal faith in Jesus Christ, and affirming orthodox doctrines.

Evangelical Lutherans in Mission A Lutheran group that developed primarily out of the Lutheran Church-Missouri Synod.

Evangelical theology Theology that affirms the traditional doctrines of orthodox Christianity, with an emphasis upon the need for individual personal regeneration.

Evangelism The presentation of the gospel with the goal of bringing the hearer to faith in Jesus Christ and thus to salvation.

Evangelism, Gift of One of the spiritual gifts, an unusual effectiveness in the presentation of the gospel. In Ephesians 4:11 evangelists are mentioned among the gifts God gives to the church.

Evangelistic crusades Organized evangelistic efforts usually aimed at reaching an entire city or large area. They often involve the cooperation of several churches.

Evangelists In the early church, those who first brought the Good News. They were mentioned as one of God's gifts to the church (Eph. 4:11). The writers of the four Gospels were also referred to as evangelists. Today the term refers to anyone doing the work of spreading the gospel, but especially to professionals who do not serve any one particular church, but give their entire ministry to evangelism.

Eve The first woman, wife of Adam; she was made by God from Adam's rib (Gen. 2:21-22).

Evening prayer, evensong In the Anglican church, an evening service.

Everlasting life *See* ETERNAL LIFE.

Everlasting punishment *See* ETERNAL PUNISHMENT.

Evidences of Christianity Factual data supporting the claims of Christianity; such data include fulfilled prophecy, miracles, and some archaeological discoveries.

Evil That which is morally bad or harmful.

Evil, Moral *See* MORAL EVIL.

Evil, Natural *See* NATURAL EVIL.

Evil, Problem of The question of how to reconcile the existence of evil in the world with the existence of a loving and all-powerful God.

Evil angels Angels who rebelled against God and thus fell. Under their leader Satan they now engage in opposing God's work. They are also known as demons.

Evil one Satan.

Evil spirits Demons.

Evolution The process of development from one form into another; in particular, the biological theory that all living forms have developed from simpler forms by a series of gradual steps.

Evolution, Biological The development of more complex biological forms from less complex forms.

Evolution, Naturalistic The idea that evolution has proceeded by means of immanent laws within the physical universe; it is simply a matter of atoms, motion, time, and chance.

Evolution, Theistic The view that God began the creation with a *de novo* act and then worked from within the process of evolution to produce the desired results. He has intervened within the process to modify what was emerging, but has never again created *de novo*. In particular, he created the human's spiritual nature (or soul) directly and then infused it into a previously existent physical form.

Evolutionary naturalism The idea that nature grows and develops over time, producing new forms through evolutionary processes.

Evolution debate The conflict between those who hold to creationism and those who hold to the theory of evolution. It was particularly prominent between conservative Christians and scientists in the first part of the twentieth century.

Evolutionism, Emergent The idea that new entities are arising from within the evolutionary process because of creative forces therein.

Exaltation of Jesus Christ *See* CHRIST, EXALTATION OF.

Ex cathedra Literally, "from the throne," a designation of statements made by the pope in his official capacity. Dealing with matters of faith and morals, these statements are regarded as infallible.

Excluded middle, Law of The logical principle that a thing must be either A or non-A; in other words, a proposition must be either true or false.

Excommunication The cutting off or expulsion of a person from the fellowship of the church.

Exegesis The obtaining of the meaning of a passage by drawing the meaning out from, rather than reading it into, the text.

Exegetical method The technique of exegesis.

Exhortation The strengthening of a believer through warning, advice, or encouragement.

Exhortation, Gift of One of the spiritual gifts mentioned in Romans 12:8: special ability to strengthen others through warning, advice, or encouragement.

Existence The state or quality of being.

Existence of God, Arguments for the Rational evidences marshaled to prove that God exists.

Existential, Supernatural *See* SUPERNATURAL EXISTENTIAL.

Existential estrangement In the thought of Paul Tillich, the human condition of being dependent upon the ground of being for existence and yet estranged from the ground of being by virtue of not being what one essentially is and ought to be.

Existential humanity Human nature as found in the current state of human beings. Existential humanity contrasts with essential humanity—that is, human nature as God originally intended and created it.

Existentialism A philosophy that emphasizes existence over essence; that is to say, the question "Does it exist?" is more important than "What is it?" Among the other themes of existentialism are human freedom, subjectivity, and irrationality.

Existential man *See* EXISTENTIAL HUMANITY.

Existential theology Theology that is based on an existential philosophy.

Ex lege The idea that God is above or outside the law and therefore not subject to it.

Ex lex See EX LEGE.

Ex nihilo, Creatio See CREATIO EX NIHILO.

Ex opere operato The Roman Catholic doctrine that sacraments operate "from the work done." That is, provided that no obstacle is placed in the way, a sacrament is efficacious by virtue of the act of the administrant and apart from the inward qualifications of the recipient.

Exorcism The casting of evil spirits out of a person.

Exorcist One who engages in exorcism.

Expediency The quality of being advantageous or suited to the end in view; especially, subordination of moral principle to facilitate a purpose.

Experience, Theology of Theology based primarily on one's own individual experience rather than some external authority.

Expiation The cancellation of sin. Expiation contrasts with propitiation, which is the appeasing of divine wrath.

Explicit opportunity, Universal *See* UNIVERSAL EXPLICIT OPPORTUNITY.

Exposition Interpretation, explanation, and clarification of a biblical passage.

External calling A summons or invitation that comes through external means, such as the preaching of the Word, rather than through an internal influence by God.

External circumcision Literal or physical circumcision.

External grounds Independent means of evaluating a theological concept or biblical passage. It may be another passage of Scripture or another theological concept. In the thought of Emil Brunner, the term refers to empirical considerations (e.g., the evidence of natural science) as they bear on the doctrine of creation.

Extrabiblical Pertaining to material not found in the Bible.

Extrabiblical sources Sources other than the Bible.

Extra-Christian sources Materials produced by non-Christians.

Extranatural Pertaining to that which falls outside of (but not necessarily on a higher plane than) the physical universe.

Extreme unction A sacrament of the Roman Catholic Church. Also known as last rites, it consists of an anointing with oil at the time of death.

Ff

Fairbairn, Andrew Martin (1838-1912)
British theologian whose major contribution was his work on the consciousness of Christ.

Faith Belief in and commitment to something or someone. Christian faith is specifically a complete trust in Christ and his work as the basis of one's relationship to God.

Faith, Confession of A public declaration of faith, whether one's personal statement, as in believers' baptism, or a formal listing of doctrines, as in the Augsburg or Westminster Confessions.

Faith, Gift of One of the spiritual gifts mentioned in 1 Corinthians 12:9. It involves an unusual or remarkable ability to exercise faith.

Faithfulness God's loyalty to his people on the basis of the covenant commitments that he has made, and a similar fidelity of God's people to their commitment to him.

Faith healing The practice of trusting God to miraculously heal the sick or injured on the basis of a faith that he will do so.

Fall Adam and Eve's initial sin of disobe-dience as a result of which they lost their standing of favor with God (Gen. 3).

Fall, Effects of the Results, such as guilt and corruption of nature, issuing from the Fall.

Fall, Literal view of the Belief that the Fall was an actual space-time event that happened to two historical persons.

Fall, Mythical view of the Belief that Genesis 3 does not describe an actual event but is rather a symbolic or representative account.

Fallen humanity The human race in its condition after the Fall.

Falling away *See* APOSTASY.

False Christs Persons who, in the last times, will falsely claim to be the Christ (Matt. 24:5, 24; Mark 13:22).

Farrar, Frederic William (1831-1903) Liberal Anglican minister and theologian who questioned the doctrine of eternal punishment.

Farrer, Austin (1904-1968) Anglican philosopher, theologian, and pastor who spent most of his active ministry at Oxford.

Fast, fasting Voluntary total or partial abstinence from food for a limited time. It is usually undertaken for spiritual benefit.

Fatalism The belief that all that happens is controlled by an impersonal force. It is generally a pessimistic philosophy.

Fate An impersonal power thought to rule over human lives.

Father, God the The First Person of the Trinity.

Father, Work of the Those activities of God particularly associated with the Father, such as hearing prayers.

Fatherhood of God A reference to the fact that God has given life to all humans and relates to them much as a human father relates to his children.

Father of lies A reference to Satan (John 8:44).

Fathers, the Those leaders and thinkers in the early centuries of the Christian Era who gave particular shape to the Christian movement.

Fathers, Church The leading theologians of approximately the first six centuries of the Christian Era.

Fear A negative experience of anticipation of pain or great distress; also, a reverence and respect for someone or something, particularly for God.

Feasts, Christian Days of celebration commemorating special events in the Christian year.

Feasts, Old Testament Three annual festivals for which the Hebrews assembled at Jerusalem in special celebration: Passover (the Feast of Unleavened Bread), the Feast of First Fruits (the Feast of Weeks), and the Feast of Tabernacles (Booths) (Deut. 16:16).

Febronianism An eighteenth-century German theological movement begun by Johann Nikolaus von Hontheim, who wrote under the pen name of Justinus Febronius. The major contention of Febronianism was a contesting of the doctrine of papal infallibility; it was maintained that groups of Christians, such as the bishops acting as a whole, had more power than did the pope.

Federal Council of Churches The original name of the conciliar movement among churches in the United States; it was later renamed the National Council of the Churches of Christ.

Federal headship A reference to the view that when Adam sinned, he was acting as the representative of the human race; consequently, the whole race suffers the consequences of Adam's first sin.

Federal theology A theological school of thought especially identified with Johannes Cocceius (1603-1669). It held that Adam represented the human race in the covenant of works established by God.

Feeling, Theology of A theology, most completely represented by Friedrich Schleiermacher, that regarded human feelings rather than belief or moral action as the locus of religion and basis of theology.

Fellow man The whole human race regarded as united in common experience.

Fellowship The sense of community that Christians share as they work and pray together, encouraging and comforting one another.

Fellowship with God A relationship between a believer and God that involves sharing of common concerns, interests, and values.

Feminist theology Theology that lays heavy emphasis upon the status and liberation of women.

Ferré, Frederick (1933-) American philosopher of religion who has made special contributions to understanding the nature and function of theological language. Son of Nels F. S. Ferré.

Ferré, Nels F. S. (1908-1971) Swedish-American theologian who emphasized love as the central interpretive principle of theology. The major portion of his teaching career was spent at Andover Newton Theological School and Vanderbilt University. His best-known works are *Christ and the Christian* and *The Christian Understanding of God*.

Festivals Special occasions of celebration, usually in commemoration of a significant event.

Feuerbach, Ludwig (1804-1872) Nineteenth-century German philosopher who contended that the idea of God is a human projection: The human creates God in his own image.

Fiat creationism The belief that God created by a direct act. It frequently also includes the ideas that creation took place in a brief period of time and that there has been no natural development of intermediate forms.

Fideism The view that the objects of religious belief and commitment must be accepted by faith rather than proved by reason.

Filioque Literally, "and from the Son," a term in the Latin or Western versions of the Nicene Creed. It refers to the concept that the Holy Spirit proceeds both from the Father and from the Son. Not in the original form of the creed, *filioque* appears to have been first inserted at the local Council of Toledo (589). The Eastern or Greek church did not accept this teaching, and that difference was the main doctrinal point in the separation of the Eastern from the Western church in 1054.

Filling of the Holy Spirit The Holy Spirit's occupation and control of the total life of the Christian. The filling of the Holy Spirit can be repeated and frequently needs to be. It is to be distinguished from the baptism of the Holy Spirit, which occurs at the time of regeneration.

Final body The body received at the resurrection.

Final consummation The end of history; the fulfillment of God's plan in the second coming and the events following it.

Final form In progressive revelation,

the last and definitive expression of a doctrine.

Final state The state of the individual following the resurrection, whether in heaven or hell.

Finite God A reference to the idea that God is limited. Edgar S. Brightman and others used the concept as a solution to the problem of evil: Evil exists because God is unable to prevent it.

Finiteness, Anxiety of *See* SIN, ANXIETY-OF-FINITENESS THEORY OF.

Finitism Belief in a limited (or finite) God.

Finney, Charles Grandison (1792-1875) American pastor, evangelist, theologian, and professor and president of Oberlin College. He taught an Arminian system of theology and a perfectionist view of sanctification.

Firmament In Hebrew thought, the apparent void in which the clouds and lights of heaven are found.

Firstborn The oldest legitimate son. By ancient custom the firstborn received a special inheritance (in some cases, everything; in others, a double portion). In the New Testament the term designates Christ as the heir of the Father.

Firstborn of all creation A reference to Christ (Col. 1:15; Heb. 1:6).

Firstborn of the dead A reference to Christ as the first to be raised (Col. 1:18; Rev. 1:5).

First day of the week Sunday or the Lord's Day. Christians observe Sunday as their day of worship because the Lord's resurrection took place on that day.

First death Physical death.

First fruits Old Testament offerings from the first harvestings of the year. They were given to the Lord in recognition that the land and all that it produces come from and belong to him.

First Person of the Trinity God the Father.

First resurrection *See* RESURRECTION, FIRST.

First Vatican Council *See* VATICAN COUNCIL I.

Fixed feast A Christian holiday that is always observed on the same date; for example, Christmas. A movable feast falls on different dates in different years; for example, Easter.

Flacius, Matthias (1520-1575) Lutheran theologian born in Croatia who was the leader of a group called Gnesio-Lutherans ("true Lutherans"). They opposed Philipp Melanchthon and his followers (the Philippists) for being too conciliatory to the Roman Catholics.

Flesh Human nature. In the Bible the term has both a literal and figurative meaning: It is used of the physical nature and also of the sinful nature of human beings.

Fletcher, Joseph (1905-1991) Twentieth-century Episcopalian clergyman and prime advocate of situation ethics, the view that good is relative to the situation. The only real measure of the goodness or rightness of an action is whether it is the most loving thing to do under the given circumstances. In his later years, he turned away from religion as a basis for ethics.

Flew, Antony (1923-) Twentieth-century philosopher of the analytical school, which maintains that the role of philosophy is to analyze language.

Flood, the In the time of Noah, the great downpour of rain that lasted for forty days and forty nights and resulted in the death of all living creatures except those within the ark. Some scholars hold that the flood waters covered the entire world (the universal-flood theory), while others maintain that the flood occurred only in the area in which Noah lived (local-flood theory). Biblical and other forms of evidence have been cited in support of each theory.

Flood theory The belief that the great flood created unusual geological conditions that account for the apparent great age of the earth.

Followers of the Way Apparently a Christian self-designation. The Christian faith is referred to as "the Way" in Acts 9:2; 19:9, 23; 22:4; and 24:14, 22.

Foot washing A practice in biblical times. If a host especially wished to honor his guests, he would personally wash their feet. Jesus washed the disciples' feet (John 13:1-17) as a sign of humility and love. Some Christian groups practice foot washing as a demonstration of the same qualities.

Forbearance Long-suffering, patience, or self-restraint—a quality of God that is also to be found in believers.

Forbidden tree The tree of the knowledge of good and evil from which Adam and Eve were forbidden to eat (Gen. 2).

Forces of evil Satan, his demons, and all others who do his will, whether individuals or structures of society.

Foreknowledge God's prescience or foresight concerning future events.

Foreknowledge, limited The teaching that God knows some, but not all, future events. The usual form of the theory is that God does not know free human actions in advance of their occurrence.

Foreknowledge, exhaustive The doctrine that God knows from eternity all that will ever happen, including free human actions. It may or may not include the idea that he knows every possibility that could have occurred.

Foreordination God's rendering an event certain before it occurs.

Forgiveness Pardon of sin. God practices

forgiveness and also expects his followers to do so.

Forgiveness of sins Pardon of wrongdoing. Forgiveness entails cancellation of any penalty sin may have incurred and of any ill feeling it may have aroused.

Form In Plato, form is the real essence of a thing; it exists independently of individual concrete entities. In Aristotle, the form of something is the principle by which it is organized; form contrasts with that which is organized—namely, the matter. *See* also GOD, FORM OF.

Form Criticism *See* CRITICISM, FORM.

Forms, Platonic The unchanging pure essences of things; they exist independently of any specific empirical instances. Examples are "humanness," "whiteness," and "chairness."

Formula of Concord A doctrinal statement drawn up in 1577 in an attempt to unite the Philippists (the followers of Philipp Melanchthon) and the Gnesio-Lutherans (genuine Lutherans).

Fornication In the broadest sense, sexual immorality of all kinds; in a narrower sense, voluntary sexual intercourse between unmarried people. The narrower sense contrasts with adultery, which is similar action by a married person with someone other than his or her spouse.

Forsyth, Peter Taylor (1848-1921) British evangelical Congregationalist theologian.

Fortitude One of the seven cardinal virtues: strength of mind that enables a person to bear adversity with courage.

Fortunate fall (*felix culpa*) The idea that God's permitting the Fall was a good thing because it has allowed him to reveal more of his basic nature through the work of redemption.

Fosdick, Harry Emerson (1878-1969) American theologian, preacher, and author who did much to popularize liberalism. He taught at Union Theological Seminary (New York) and served as pastor of Riverside Church of New York City.

Fourfold sense of Scripture The medieval idea that the Bible has four senses: (1) literal, (2) moral, (3) allegorical, and (4) anagogical.

Foundationalism A view of knowledge in which certain beliefs are not justified by any other propositions, and all other propositions are justified by derivation from these. In classical foundationalism the foundations provide certainty by being either indubitable, incorrigible, or evident to the senses, and the other propositions are derived from them by deduction.

Four Gallican Articles Articles drawn up by an assembly of French clergy in Paris in 1682 to spell out the respective roles and powers of the king, the pope, and the French bishops.

Four spiritual laws The basic truths of the gospel as stated by Bill Bright, president of Campus Crusade for Christ: (1) God loves and has a wonderful plan for each human; (2) humans are sinful and separated from God; (3) Jesus Christ is God's only provision for the remission of human sin; (4) each person needs to individually receive Jesus Christ as Savior and Lord.

Fourth Gospel The Gospel of John.

Fox, George (1624-1691) Englishman who founded the Society of Friends (Quakers).

Francis of Assisi (1182-1226) A medieval Catholic saint who emphasized imitating Christ through absolute poverty, humility, and simplicity and had a great love and appreciation for nature.

Franciscan order A Roman Catholic order founded by Saint Francis of Assisi in the thirteenth century. Members of the order practiced poverty and ministered to the needy. Contrary to Francis's spirit, they supported the Inquisition.

Francke, August Hermann (1663-1727) A leader of Lutheran Pietism. Pastor, professor at the University of Halle, and author, Francke also founded various educational and charitable institutions.

Frankl, Viktor (1905-1997) Jewish psychiatrist who was imprisoned in a German concentration camp and while there discovered the central place of hope in human life. He developed his system of logotherapy out of these experiences.

Free churches Churches that are not allied with any state structure and have traditionally opposed such affiliations.

Freedom, Compatibilistic See COMPATIBILISTIC FREEDOM.

Freedom, Human The concept that humans freely determine their own behavior and that no external causal factors can adequately account for their actions.

Freedom, Noncompatibilistic or Incompatibilistic The view that the freedom of an act is incompatible with any certainty of its occurrence. On this view, the action of a moral agent cannot both be foreknown by God and be genuinely free.

Freedom of the Will A treatise written by Erasmus in 1524 to refute Luther.

Free will The concept that human choices and actions are self-determined. It has been used as a solution to the problem of evil: Evil is understood as resulting from human misuse of the freedom God gave.

Freewill offering In the Old Testament, a voluntary offering made as part of a request to God or in gratitude for what he has done. Because of the voluntary nature, an imperfect sacrificial animal could be offered (Lev. 22:23).

Freewill Theism See OPEN THEISM.

Freudianism Both the psychological

theory of human personality and the form of psychotherapy devised by Sigmund Freud (1856-1939). It divides the human psyche into id, ego, and superego and sees sexual energy as the driving force of human personality.

Friend A name used of Christians in Acts 27:3 and 3 John 15. The designation apparently relates to Jesus' statement in John 15:13-15, where Jesus calls his followers "friends."

Friends, Society of (Quakers) A group founded in the seventeenth century by George Fox. They emphasize simplicity of life, pacifism, democracy in church government, and an "inner light" of revelation that God gives to individuals.

Fruit of the Spirit A group of spiritual virtues referred to by Paul in Galatians 5:22-23; for example, love, joy, and peace.

Fruits of righteousness The good works of the Christian life (Phil. 1:11).

Full inerrancy See INERRANCY, FULL.

Fullness of the Holy Spirit See FILLING OF THE HOLY SPIRIT.

Fullness of time A reference to the time of Christ's first coming (Gal. 4:4); it is generally thought of in the twofold sense of the time established by God and the readiness of world conditions for Christ's coming.

Functional analysis A type of philosophical linguistic analysis that, rather than prescribing one "right" way language is to be used, describes the various ways it actually is used. Functional analysis is also known as "ordinary language philosophy," as opposed to "ideal language philosophy."

Functional Christology See CHRISTOLOGY, FUNCTIONAL.

Functionalism An aspect of philosophical pragmatism according to which the meaning or truth of a proposition is the consequences that follow from it. Functionalism emphasizes that which occurs (verbs) rather than the nature of things (nouns and adjectives).

Functional subordination The idea that Christ, the Second Person of the Trinity, while not ceasing to be equal with the Father in what he was, made himself subject to the Father in what he did.

Functional theology A theology based upon functionalism.

Fundamentalism A conservative theological movement that began in the United States in the late nineteenth century and remained influential well into the twentieth century. It insisted that certain basic doctrines or "fundamentals," such as the inerrancy of Scripture and the virgin birth of Christ, must be maintained. In later years the term came to be associated with a particular mind-set of separation, legalism, and even obscurantism.

Fundamentals, The A twelve-volume

series of articles expounding the basic doctrines of the Christian faith. Published between 1910 and 1915 and associated with fundamentalism, the series defended Protestant orthodoxy against liberalism.

Future body The resurrection body that the believer will have.

Future kingdom That aspect of the kingdom of God that will be most fully inaugurated by the Lord's second coming.

Future life The condition and place of existence of the human being following death.

Future punishment Punishment that will be administered as a result of the coming judgment.

Future state The condition of persons after this life, including both the intermediate state and the final state (heaven or hell).

Futurism Interest in, and study of, the future.

Futuristic Pertaining to the future, or modern or progressive in nature.

Gg

Gaebelein, Arno Clemens (1861-1945) Bible teacher and conference speaker who was a major contributor to the development of the fundamentalist movement. He was especially known for his interest in and work on prophecy and Israel.

Gallican Articles, The Four *See* FOUR GALLICAN ARTICLES.

Gallicanism A French movement that aimed at decreasing papal authority and increasing the power of the state over the church.

Gallic Confession A statement of religious belief drawn up by French Protestants in 1559.

Gap theory The belief that Genesis 1:2a should be translated, "The earth became without form and void"; verse 3, then, begins a description of the re-creation or re-forming of the earth. Virtually all of geological time is thus placed in the gap between God's original creative act in verse 1 and his subsequent re-creation of the world.

Gaps, God of the A reference to God's being the answer to the mysteries of nature or the gaps in human knowledge.

Garden of Eden The place in which God set the first man and woman and from which they were driven after their sin. Some scholars have attempted to identify the approximate location of the garden, which, from the description in Genesis 2:10-14, is thought to have been somewhere in Mesopotamia.

Gehenna Transliteration of the Hebrew for the valley of Hinnom (2 Kings 23:10). It came to represent the final spiritual state of the ungodly (Matt. 10:28; Mark 9:43).

General Assembly The highest governing body of the Presbyterian church; it is made up of lay and clergy representatives from all of the presbyteries.

General Association of Regular Baptists A group of conservative Baptists who withdrew from the Northern Baptist Convention in 1932 in protest over perceived theological liberalism within that group.

General calling God's invitation to all humans to accept Jesus Christ and be saved.

General confession In Roman Catholicism, the confession in a private prayer of all or part of the sins of one's life even though one may believe that some of them have already been forgiven. In the Anglican *Book of Common Prayer*, it is a prayer said by minister and congregation at the beginning of matins and evensong.

General faith A belief in a statement or set of statements; it contrasts with vital faith, which is placing one's trust in a person.

General redemption The doctrine that the death of Christ was intended to include all of humanity, whether or not all believe. It is also referred to as unlimited atonement.

General resurrection The resurrection of all humanity in distinction from the resurrection of Christ, Lazarus, or other isolated individuals.

General revelation *See* REVELATION, GENERAL.

Generation The act of begetting; also an age in time, a group of individuals living at one time, or a group of individuals at the same stage of descent from a common ancestor.

Genetic conditioning A reference to the idea that a human's behavior is determined by hereditary factors.

Genetic determinism A reference to the idea that a human being's beliefs and actions are determined by his or her genetic makeup.

Genetic fallacy The mistaken belief that once we have explained what causes an idea to be held, we have determined its truth or falsity.

Genevan Catechism A catechism by John Calvin that was published in Geneva in French in 1537 and in Latin in 1538.

Genre A distinctive type or category of literary composition.

Gentile One who is not by race a Jew.

Geographical conditions Topographical and climatic factors that affect the behavior of a group of people, including their religious practices. In a dry climate, for example, prayer for rain might be common.

Gerhard, Johann (1582-1637) Important Lutheran theologian whose influence on Lutheranism some scholars see as exceeded only by Martin Luther and Martin Chemnitz. His major work was a system of dogmatics, *Loci Theologici*.

"Germ theory" of the origin of sin The idea that for someone to sin, the substance of sin must already exist; that is to say, sin is "caught" from a preexisting source.

Geschichte A German word for "history" that Rudolf Bultmann used to refer to "significant history," or the subjective inner effect upon a person. *Geschichte* contrasts with *Historie*, or mere history, which is the objective fact of an event's occurrence.

Ghost, Holy *See* HOLY GHOST.

Gifford Lectures Endowed lectureships at four ancient Scottish universities since 1888. The aim of the series is "promoting, advancing, teaching, and diffusing the study of natural theology, in the widest sense of that term, in other words, the knowledge of God," including "the foundation of ethics."

Gifts, Spiritual Special endowments of the church by the Holy Spirit, whether unusual abilities, spiritual qualities, or gifted individuals. Four lists of spiritual gifts are found in Scripture—Romans 12:6-8, 1 Corinthians 12:4-11, Ephesians 4:11, and 1 Peter 4:11.

Gilkey, Langdon (1919-) Theologian at the University of Chicago Divinity School. Among his better-known works are *Shantung Compound*, an account of life in a World War II prison camp, and *Naming the Whirlwind*, a discussion of religious language.

Gill, John (1697-1771) Eighteenth-century Baptist pastor in England. Largely self-educated, he was a voluminous writer and a hyper-Calvinistic theologian.

Giving, Gift of A gift of the Holy Spirit (Rom. 12:8) that involves special generosity in contributing one's financial resources to the cause of Christ.

Gladden, Washington (1836-1918) Congregationalist minister who did much to popularize liberal theology and the social gospel.

Glastonbury A town in Somerset, England, that was a major center of pilgrimage in the Middle Ages because of the claim that its abbey had been founded by Joseph of Arimathea.

Glorification The final step in the process of salvation; it involves the completion of sanctification and the removal of spiritual defects.

Glorification of God The act of giving praise and glory to God.

Glorification of the body Glorification in terms of receiving a new and indestructible body.

Glorification of the soul Glorification in terms of future perfection of one's spiritual qualities.

Glorified body The resurrection or perfected body of the future.

Glorified with Christ A reference to the fact that those who suffer with Christ will also be glorified with him (Rom. 8:17). Glorification, like the other facets of salvation, is a result of union with Christ.

Glory Originally, brightness, greatness, or splendor, which is one of the attributes or qualities of God.

Glory, Theology of *See* THEOLOGY OF GLORY.

Glossolalia The practice of speaking in tongues. It is mentioned in Acts 2 and 1 Corinthians 12 and 14. Some Christians consider it a gift of the Holy Spirit to be practiced even today.

Glossolalist One who believes in and practices speaking in tongues as a gift of the Holy Spirit.

Gnesio-Lutherans A group in the sixteenth century who believed themselves to be the true followers of Martin Luther, or the "genuine Lutherans," as contrasted with the Philippists, the followers of Philipp Melanchthon, whom they considered to be too ready to compromise with Roman Catholicism.

Gnosticism A movement in early Christianity, beginning already in the first century, that (1) emphasized a special higher truth that only the more enlightened receive from God, (2) taught that matter is evil, and (3) denied the humanity of Jesus.

God, Absoluteness of A reference to the doctrine that God is perfect and thus unchanging.

God, Acts of The actions of God within human history. The biblical-theology movement thought of the major events, such as the Exodus and the "Christ event," as the virtually exclusive locus of divine revelation.

God, Anger of The wrath of God; his righteous reaction to unrighteousness.

God, Aseity of A reference to the fact that the basis of God's life is within himself and is not caused by anything external.

God, Attributes of *See* ATTRIBUTES OF GOD.

God, Being of God's essence, or what he is.

God, Benevolence of An aspect of God's love: his concern for, and desire to do good to, his children.

God, Breath of A reference to God's giving life to humanity by breathing into Adam (Gen. 2:7).

God, Changelessness of A reference to the fact that there is no change, either quantitative or qualitative, in God. He is what he always has been and always will be.

God, Children of In the New Testament, Christians; also, the name of a cultic group growing out of a house church organized by David Berg in Los Angeles in 1967.

God, Compassion of God's feeling of and for the condition of his creatures; it leads to merciful action on their behalf.

God, Consequent nature of In the thought of Alfred North Whitehead, the founder of process theology, God's concrete action in the world—God's responsiveness to and receptivity of the processes in the world.

God, Decretive will of God's decisions that actually bring to pass every event that occurs.

God, Dependability of The constancy of God's nature; as a result, we can rely on what he does and promises.

God, Doctrine of Teachings about the nature and works of the Supreme Being, the Creator of all else that is.

God, Essence of The full nature of what

God is. In the thinking of some theologians, especially in the past, the essence was distinguished from the attributes of God, as if it were some sort of underlying substratum.

God, Eternity of The fact that God has no beginning and will have no end. He always has been and always will be.

God, Faithfulness of God's fidelity to his promises—he always fulfills what he says he will do.

God, Fatherhood of A characterization of God's special relationship with his chosen people, whether Israel or Christians. He treats them as an earthly father treats his children. Whether God is to be regarded as the Father of all humans, however, has long been a matter of debate.

God, Foreknowledge of God's knowledge of all that will come to pass before it occurs. The term connotes not merely passive cognizance but active will.

God, Form of The essential nature of God, which, according to Philippians 2:6, Jesus manifested prior to the incarnation.

God, General will of God's overall intentions, the basic values with which he is pleased.

God, Genuineness of A reference to the fact that God, unlike false gods, is an actual living being.

God, Glory of The splendor, greatness, and magnificence of God.

God, Goodness of The moral character of God; his moral attributes, such as love and faithfulness. The goodness of God contrasts with the greatness of God—his power, knowledge, and eternality.

God, Good pleasure of God's sovereign will or his doing that which he chooses without reference to external considerations and without coercion; in particular, his will with respect to humans (see, e.g., Eph. 1:5; Phil. 2:13).

God, Government of The aspect of God's providence that controls and directs whatever occurs.

God, Grace of God's dealing with his people not on the basis of what they deserve, but simply in terms of his goodness and generosity relating to their needs.

God, Greatness of God's natural attributes, such as his power, knowledge, and eternality.

God, Holiness of God's separateness from all else and particularly from all evil.

God, Image of That which distinguishes humans from the rest of God's creatures. Some theologians believe the image refers to substantive qualities resident within human nature, others view it as a relationship into which the human enters, while still others see it as something that the human does.

God, Immanence of God's presence and

activity within the created world of nature.

God, Immateriality of A reference to the fact that God is spirit, not having any material or physical nature.

God, Immeasurability of A reference to the fact that God, being infinite, exceeds all finite human measures and standards.

God, Immensity of God's transcendence of all spatial limitations and locations.

God, Immutability of The doctrine that God is unchanging. In some Greek thought this teaching became virtually a static view of God. Properly understood, however, it is simply an emphasis upon the unchanging character and dependability of God.

God, Incomprehensibility of A reference to the fact that the greatness of God results in our never being able to understand him fully.

God, Independence of A reference to the fact that God does not need anything outside himself for his existence.

God, Infinity of God's greatness of nature that has no limits and cannot be limited.

God, Integrity of The set of God's attributes relating to truthfulness. Integrity includes genuineness (being true), veracity (telling the truth), and faithfulness (proving true).

God, Interdependence of *See* INTERDEPENDENCE OF GOD.

God, Invisibility of A reference to the fact that God, being spiritual, cannot be seen unless he chooses to manifest himself in some form.

God, Justice of God's administering his kingdom in accordance with his law.

God, Kingdom of *See* KINGDOM OF GOD.

God, Knowledge (as an attribute) of God's awareness of all truth (a result of his having originated all that is).

God, Law of That which God has established as right and good.

God, Life of A reference to the fact that God is a living being, not a lifeless idol, and that he is the source or cause of his own existence.

God, Love of God's concern and action for the welfare of his creatures. Many theologians consider love to be the most basic or fundamental of God's attributes.

God, Loving-kindness of God's faithful and persistent love toward his creatures.

God, Majesty of The greatness and glory of God.

God, Mercy of God's compassionate concern for his people; his tenderhearted treatment of the needy.

God, Moral purity of God's freedom

from anything wicked or evil; his purity includes the dimensions of holiness, righteousness, and justice.

God, Nature of What God is, as contrasted with what he does.

God, Omnipotence of God's ability to do all things that are proper objects of power.

God, Omnipresence of A reference to the fact that God is everywhere present and has access to all portions of reality.

God, Omniscience of God's knowing all things that are proper objects of knowledge.

God, Oneness of The fact that God, although three persons, is yet one in essence.

God, Perfection of The absolute completeness and fullness of God. He does not lack anything or have any moral imperfection.

God, Persistence of God's continuation in his loving treatment of his creatures. He does not abandon or give up on them.

God, Personality of A reference to the fact that God is not an impersonal force, but a personal being capable of thought, feeling, will, and interaction with other persons.

God, Plan of A reference to the decrees of God determining all the things that shall occur and bringing them to reality.

God, Power of God's ability to do all things that are proper objects of power.

God, Preceptive will of That which God commands to be done.

God, Primordial nature of In Alfred North Whitehead's theology, the unchanging abstract essence of God.

God, Righteousness of The holiness of God as applied to his relationships to other beings.

God, Self-existence of That attribute of God whereby he exists simply of himself without the need of any external force or cause.

God, Son of Jesus Christ, the second person of the Trinity.

God, Sovereignty of God's supremacy and control over all that occurs.

God, Specific will of God's intention and decision regarding a particular issue, in contrast to his general preference or pleasure.

God, Spirit of The Holy Spirit, the Third Person of the Trinity.

God, Spirituality of The immaterial, nonphysical nature of God.

God, Splendor of The majesty or glory of God.

God, Transcendence of God's separation from and superiority to the creation and history.

God, Unity of A reference to the fact that God is one God, not many.

God, Veracity of God's unwavering truthfulness and representation of things as they actually are.

God, Will of Generally, God's intention for a particular person or group of persons.

God, Wisdom of That attribute of God by virtue of which he always acts with full knowledge and correct values.

God, Wrath of God's displeasure with evil; it is expressed in judgment and punishment.

God Almighty A translation of the Hebrew name *El Shaddai*, which emphasizes God's power.

God-breathed A reference to the divine inspiration of the Bible (2 Tim. 3:16).

Godhead The full Trinity.

Godliness Likeness to God in moral and spiritual character.

God-man The incarnate Second Person of the Trinity, Jesus Christ.

God-spirited A reference to the Scriptures as being inspired or "God-breathed" (2 Tim. 3:16).

Gogarten, Friedrich (1887-1968) German theologian who moved from liberalism to neoorthodoxy to a defense of Rudolf Bultmann's demythologization. His criticisms of Bultmann have been followed by some post-Bultmannians.

Golden Rule Jesus' statement, "Do to others what you would have them do to you" (Matt. 7:12, NIV).

Gomarus, Franciscus (1563-1641) Dutch Calvinist theologian who opposed the views of Arminius. He played a prominent part in the Synod of Dort but was unable to convince the synod to adopt his supralapsarian variety of Calvinism.

Good, goodness That which is morally excellent or, in the Christian framework, accords with God's nature.

Good Friday The Friday before Easter Sunday; it is celebrated as a commemoration of Christ's death.

Good News The gospel.

Good pleasure of God *See* GOD, GOOD PLEASURE OF.

Good Shepherd A self-designation of Jesus (John 10:11).

Good Spirit According to Nehemiah 9:20, that which God gave to instruct his people in the wilderness. This is often thought of as an Old Testament reference to the Holy Spirit.

Good works The acts of obedience that the believer does by God's grace (Matt. 5:16; Eph. 2:10). The term is also used of human efforts done in one's own strength, which are considered unacceptable by God.

Gospel The message of salvation offered by God to all who believe; also, one of the first four books of the New

Testament, which recount the life and teachings of Jesus.

Gospel, Social Implications of the *See* SOCIAL IMPLICATIONS OF THE GOSPEL.

Gospel of Christ A Pauline term for the message of salvation (Rom. 15:19; 1 Cor. 9:12; 2 Cor. 2:12; 9:13; 10:14; Gal. 1:7; Phil. 1:27; 1 Thess. 3:2).

Gottschalk (ca. 805-869) Theologian and monk who apparently was the first person to teach double predestination.

Governing assembly A group chosen to give direction to and make decisions for a particular church or denomination.

Government, Divine God's providence in terms of his directing all things to the ends that he has chosen.

Government, Gift of One of the spiritual gifts (1 Cor. 12:28): the ability to administer.

Grace God's dealing with humans in undeserved ways; it is simply an outflow of God's goodness and generosity.

Grace, Cheap *See* CHEAP GRACE.

Grace, Common Grace extended to all persons through God's general providence; for example, his provision of sunshine and rain for everyone. In the thought of John Wesley, the term may refer to a prevenient grace coming to all persons and restoring them to the point where they are capable of believing.

Grace, Covenant of *See* COVENANT OF GRACE.

Grace, Efficacious A reference to the fact that those whom God has chosen for eternal life will unfailingly come to belief and salvation. Some use the term *irresistible grace*, but that is a more negative concept.

Grace, Free An expression used by John Wesley to emphasize that God's universal gift of grace in no way depends on human merit. Also used in the late twentieth century by Zane Hodges to maintain that repentance and obedience are not required for salvation.

Grace, Irresistible *See* GRACE, EFFICACIOUS.

Grace, Means of Channels by which God conveys his blessings to humans; for example, the sacraments or, more informally, prayer and Bible study.

Grace, Prevenient In Wesleyanism or Arminianism the belief that although all persons begin life with a sinful nature, God restores each individual to the point where there is sufficient ability to believe.

Grace, Sanctifying *See* SANCTIFYING GRACE.

Grace, Special The grace by which God redeems, regenerates, and sanctifies his people.

Grace, Sufficient A reference to the fact that God's grace is adequate to save the person who believes.

Grammaticohistorical exegesis Interpretation of the Bible that emphasizes that a passage must be explained in the light of its syntax, context, and historical setting.

Great Awakenings Two religious revivals in the United States, approximately 1735-1743 and 1795-1830.

Great Commission, the Christ's command to the church to preach the gospel throughout the entire world (Matt. 28:19-20).

Great dragon The devil (Rev. 12:3).

Greatness of God *See* GOD, GREATNESS OF.

Great tribulation An unparalleled period of great anguish and trouble at the end of time.

Grebel, Conrad (ca. 1498-1526) Founder of the Swiss Anabaptist movement and of the first Free Church congregation.

Greek The Indo-European language in which the New Testament was written (the particular dialect utilized was Koiné).

Greek dualism The tendency in Greek philosophy to distinguish sharply between the material and the immaterial—for example, the body and the soul.

Greek Fathers Early church fathers of the Eastern branch of Christianity.

Greek metaphysics Ancient Greek thought on the ultimate nature of reality. Plato emphasized ideas or pure essences, Aristotle the form-matter relationship. The influence of Greek metaphysics upon the construction of Christian theology often resulted in dualism—for example, the dualism of body and soul.

Gregory I (the Great) (ca. 540-604) Pope from whose papacy (590-604*)* the beginning of the medieval period of the church is generally dated.

Gregory of Nazianzus (ca. 330-389) One of the Cappadocian theologians whose formulation of the doctrine of the Trinity came to be adopted as the orthodox view.

Gregory of Nyssa (ca. 330-395) One of the Cappadocian theologians whose formulation of the doctrine of the Trinity came to be adopted as the orthodox view.

Gregory Palamas *See* PALAMAS, GREGORIUS.

Groningen theology A theological movement in the Dutch Reformed Church in the mid-nineteenth century. Centered at the University of Groningen, its aim was a revitalized theology combined with a humanism like that of Erasmus. The Groningen school denied the Trinity and claimed that Jesus had only a spiritual or divine nature that is shared by God and humans.

Grotius, Hugo (1583-1645) Dutch jurist and statesman. His major contribution to theology was in developing the governmental theory of the atonement, which holds that the major point of the atonement was to demonstrate the seriousness of the law and of sin.

Ground of being Paul Tillich's conception of God not as one being among many, nor even as the Supreme Being, but as the ground of all being, the force or power within all things that causes them to be.

Guardian angel The particular angel supposedly assigned to watch over an individual. The concept has little scriptural support, the passages most frequently appealed to being Matthew 18:10 and Acts 12:15.

Guilt Liability to punishment for wrongdoing. The term is also sometimes applied to feelings of culpability that may have no objective basis.

Guilt offering In ancient Israel a payment of damages or restitution for a violation of the law (Lev. 5:14—6:7; 7:1-7).

Gutierrez, Gustavo (1928-) Latin American Catholic theologian considered the major voice in liberation theology.

Guyon, Madame (1648-1717) French mystic who emphasized the importance of striving for spiritual perfection, understood as a disinterested love of God and complete obedience to him.

Hh

Hades Greek word used in the Septuagint for the Hebrew *Sheol*, the place of the dead. In Matthew 11:23, Luke 10:15, and Luke 16:23, it represents the place of punishment of the wicked.

Hades, Descent into In later forms of the Apostles' Creed, a teaching that between Jesus' death and resurrection he descended into Hades and preached there. The biblical evidence cited includes Psalm 16:10, Ephesians 4:8-10, 1 Timothy 3:16, 1 Peter 3:18-19 and 4:4-6. Some theologians, however, believe that these passages do not refer to a descent into Hades, but either to Jesus' descent to earth and his preaching during his lifetime or to his being delivered from death.

Halfway Covenant A compromise worked out by American Puritans in 1662: Second-generation Puritans who had not themselves made a profession of faith were permitted to have their children baptized. No one in this second or third generation could, however, participate in the Lord's Supper or have the privileges of church membership until they gave personal testimony of regeneration. The opposition of Jonathan Edwards resulted in elimination of this arrangement.

Hallelujah A Hebrew word meaning "praise the Lord."

Hallow To set something apart as holy or to consecrate for religious use. That which has been thus treated is referred to as "hallowed."

Halloween The name given to October 31, the eve of the festival of All Saints' Day.

Hamilton, William (1924-) One of the best-known advocates of the Death of God (or secular) theology, which flourished briefly in the middle 1960s.

Happiness A sense of well-being or pleasure.

Hardening (hardness) of heart The act (or state) of resistance to and rejection of the Word and will of God.

Hare, R. M. (Richard Mervyn) (1919-) Twentieth-century British analytical philosopher.

Harmonistic school A group of theologians and biblical scholars who attempt to harmonize biblical passages that contain apparent discrepancies.

Harnack, Adolf von (1851-1930) German Lutheran liberal theologian and New Testament scholar who taught at Leipzig, Giessen, Marburg, and Berlin. His most influential work was *What Is Christianity?* (1901).

Hartshorne, Charles (1897-2000) Student of Alfred North Whitehead and process philosopher who contributed a great deal to the formation of process theology. He taught at the University of Chicago, Emory University, and the University of Texas.

Hate The opposite of love; a feeling of intense dislike or opposition.

Head The part of the body that is most prominent and exercises control over the rest. Hence Christ is spoken of as the head of the church and of all things (Eph. 1:10, 22-23).

Healing The restoration of health, whether physical, mental, or spiritual.

Healing, Gift of One of the more miraculous spiritual gifts (1 Cor. 12:9) exercised by the apostles and by the early church: the ability to restore to health.

Heart In biblical psychology, the center of the human emotions and even of the person.

Heaven The future abode of believers. A place of complete happiness and joy, it is distinguished especially by the presence of God.

Heavenlies, the The place where God, Christ, and believers exist together.

Heavenly body An astronomical object, such as a star, moon, or planet.

Heavenly Father The First Person of the Trinity. The expression is often used in prayer.

Heavenly gift A problematic expression in Hebrews 6:4. Apparently some who have tasted of the heavenly gift later fall away. Arminians hold that the heavenly gift is salvation; many Calvinists say it is simply an enlightenment.

Heave offering That part of the peace offering that was reserved for the use of the priest (Lev. 7:32, 34).

Hebraic Pertaining to the Hebrews.

Hebrew The earliest name for Abraham and his descendants; also, the language they spoke.

Hebrew mentality The Hebrew people's typical way of thinking. At an earlier period, their mentality was thought to be very nontheoretical and functional in nature, but recent studies have seriously challenged or even disproved this conception.

Hebrew psychology The way in which the Hebrew people and particularly the Old Testament writings understood human nature.

Hebrew thought *See* HEBREW MENTALITY.

Hedonism A philosophy of life that sees pleasure as the supreme good.

Hegel, Georg Wilhelm Friedrich (1770-1831) German idealistic philosopher whose views inspired both absolute idealism, which is the theory that all of reality is mental and organic in nature, and dialectical materialism.

Hegelianism The philosophy of Georg Hegel and his followers; in particular, the view that history is determined by innate patterns of thesis, antithesis, and synthesis. It also includes the idea that all of reality and all of history are organic in nature and that reality is basically one great mind.

Heidegger, Martin (1889-1976) Twentieth-century German existentialist philosopher who had considerable influence on theology.

Heidelberg Catechism A catechism drawn up by the theological faculty of Heidelberg at the request of Frederick III and adopted by a synod there in 1563. It was at some points Reformed in theology rather than Lutheran, particularly in its treatment of the sacraments (specifically the Lord's Supper).

Heilsgeschichte A German word meaning "salvation history." Certain twentieth-century theologians—for example, Oscar Cullmann and Gerhard von Rad—see the Bible as basically "salvation history," the ongoing story of God's redemptive activity. Instead of using specific texts as proofs for doctrines of theology, they interpret Scripture in a general or organic way.

Heim, Karl (1874-1958) German Lutheran theologian who taught at Halle, Münster, and Tübingen. His particular contributions were in the area of relating theology and Scripture to science.

Heir One who is entitled to receive the property of a decedent.

Heirs with Christ *See* JOINT HEIRS WITH CHRIST.

Heisenberg Principle *See* UNCERTAINTY PRINCIPLE.

Hell The place of future punishment of wicked or unbelieving persons; it is a place of great anguish from which God is totally absent.

Hellenistic Pertaining to the practices or ways of thinking of the Greeks, especially after Alexander the Great.

Hellenistic world The world of Greek thought, politics, and culture.

Helps, Gift of One of the spiritual gifts mentioned in 1 Corinthians 12:28: a spiritually conferred ability to give aid to others.

Helvetic confessions Confessions drawn up in Switzerland. The First Helvetic Confession (1536) is the same as the Second Confession of Basel. The Second Helvetic Confession (1566) is an extended treatise on Christian doctrine.

Henotheism Belief in one god without rejecting the existence of other gods; basically, the belief that there are different gods for different peoples or nations.

Henry, Carl F. H. (1913-) Baptist theologian who was one of the founders of the New Evangelicalism and is regarded by many as the leading evangelical theologian of the second half of the twentieth century. He was the first editor of *Christianity Today*.

Heresy A belief or teaching that contradicts Scripture and Christian theology.

Heresy, Christological A view that deviates from the orthodox formulation regarding the person and work of Christ.

Heretical Pertaining to any view that has been officially condemned by an authoritative body.

Hermeneutic, New *See* NEW HERMENEUTIC.

Hermeneutic of suspicion An approach that looks for hidden motives in writings and actions.

Hermeneutical circle A set of tenets and assumptions that makes a given hermeneutic a consistent or coherent system.

Hermeneutical method An approach to interpretation of the Bible.

Hermeneutics The science of interpretation of the Scripture.

Hermetic books A group of mystical writings dealing with various religious and philosophic subjects and incorporating Platonic, Stoic, neo-Pythagorean, and Eastern religious thought. Dating from the second or third century A.D., the books are associated with Hermes Trismegistus, a designation of the Egyptian god Thoth.

Herrmann, Wilhelm (1846-1922) Nineteenth-century liberal German scholar who spent most of his career at Marburg.

Hesychasm A Christian monastic movement that developed a series of spiritual exercises intended to produce a mystical encounter. The adherents of hesychasm assumed a contemplative posture that included directing one's gaze toward the region of the navel. Accordingly, they were dubbed "navel gazers."

Hibbert Lectures A series of lectures established in 1878 to promote antitrinitarian perspectives and, in general, liberal views of religious subjects.

Hick, John (1922-) Twentieth-century philosopher of religion who is perhaps best known in theological circles for his editing of *The Myth of God Incarnate* and for his advocacy of religious pluralism.

Hierarchy A system of church government that has a series of levels, with more authority being invested at the higher levels.

High Church A segment of the Anglican church that emphasizes liturgy and has a strong affinity with Roman Catholicism.

Higher criticism A method of biblical interpretation that seeks to determine the authorship and date of books, the literary documents underlying them, and their historical dependability. Higher criticism contrasts with lower criticism, which concerns itself with questions of the correct reading of the text.

High priest Originally, simply the chief priest among the brethren (Lev. 21:10). In later Judaism, however, the position came to involve special prestige and power in Israel.

High-priestly prayer of Jesus Jesus' intercession for his followers in John 17.

Hinduism An Eastern religion that includes among its teachings reincarnation, karma, and nirvana—that is, absorption of the individual into the whole of reality. This absorption ends the cycles of birth and rebirth.

Hinnom, Valley of A valley south and west of Jerusalem. In the days of the evil kings of Judah, it was the site of child sacrifice. Accordingly, the transliteration of the Hebrew name (Gehenna) has come to represent the place of everlasting punishment.

Hippolytus (ca. 170-236) A Greek-speaking presbyter in the church of Rome who led a schism against Bishop Callistus. His most significant writings were *A Refutation of All Heresies*, *The Apostolic Tradition*, and a commentary on Daniel.

Historic Christianity The traditional views and teachings of Christianity.

Historical Pertaining to events that have occurred.

Historical account In a general sense, a synonym of narrative; in a more specific sense, a factual report of what has actually occurred.

Historical authority The reliability of the Bible in telling us that which actually occurred or was normative for people in biblical times. It contrasts with normative authority, the Bible's right to declare what is actually binding upon us today.

Historical criticism *See* CRITICISM, HISTORICAL.

Historical events Actual objective occurrences in the past.

Historical Jesus A reference to the person of Jesus as he lived on earth and can be investigated by the methods of historical research. The historical Jesus contrasts with the Christ of faith, the risen Christ believed in and preached by the apostles and the early church; that is, the Christ who appears in the theologizing of Paul and the other New Testament writers.

Historical Jesus, Search for the An attempt in the latter part of the nineteenth century to determine precisely what the historical Jesus said and did.

Historical method The techniques employed by the discipline of history.

Historical research Scholarship pertaining to what occurred in the past.

Historical roots The historical situation

from which a given institution or belief originated.

Historical semantics Study of the chronological development of the meanings of words. It is also referred to as diachronic semantics.

Historical theology Study of the chronological development of theological thought; in the case of Christianity, the study of the development of Christian theology from biblical times to the present.

Historicism, New A variety of postmodernism. In contrast to older historicism that sought to reconstruct exactly what had happened in the past, the new historicism may recreate history by a creative rewriting, to fit present beliefs.

Historie A German word for "history." Rudolf Bultmann and others of his school used the term to refer to that which actually occurred and can be investigated by the historical method.

Historiographer One who engages in the writing or study of history.

History-of-religions school A school of thought that studies the development of religions. Areas of interest include interpreting the Judeo-Christian faith in terms of the historical development through which religions typically go.

Hocking, William Ernest (1873-1966) American idealistic philosopher who sought to extend philosophy beyond the academic world, particularly into the realm of religion. His contention that missionaries should engage in social work involved him in the liberal-conservative debates. His major works on religion were *The Meaning of God in Human Experience, Human Nature and Its Remaking*, and *Living Religions and a World Faith*.

Hodge, Archibald Alexander (1823-1886) Nineteenth-century Reformed theologian who taught at Princeton Seminary, carrying on the Reformed tradition expounded by his father Charles.

Hodge, Charles (1797-1878) Nineteenth-century systematic theologian at Princeton Seminary. His three-volume systematic theology enunciated a thoroughgoing Reformed theology.

Hofmann, Johann Christian Konrad von (1810-1877) German Lutheran theologian often regarded as the most significant of the Erlangen school. He focused on what later came to be known as *Heilsgeschichte*.

Holiness A condition of purity or freedom from sin or of being set apart to special service.

Holiness, Christian The sanctification or actual godliness of the believer.

Holiness movement, American A movement in the tradition of John Wesley that emphasized total sanctification and Christian perfection. It originated in the United States in the mid-nineteenth century.

Holiness movements, Modern Movements within Christianity that strongly emphasize total sanctification and a life of separation and godliness.

Holiness of God God's separateness from all else and particularly from all evil.

Holism A variety of coherentism in which the measure of the truth of a proposition is its coherence with all other propositions.

Holocaust, the A reference to the persecution and genocide of Jews by Nazi Germany during World War II.

Holy angels *See* ANGELS, HOLY.

Holy Ghost A term for the Holy Spirit used particularly in the *King James Version*.

Holy mutability An expression used by Karl Barth to refer to the idea that God is free to correct, suspend, or replace his decrees.

Holy nation A particular nation especially chosen and designated by God for fellowship with and use by him. The term is applied to Israel and also by some modern-day people to their own nation.

Holy of Holies The inner part of the tabernacle or temple. Only the high priest could enter it, and then only once a year on the Day of Atonement to offer sacrifice for cleansing.

Holy One of Israel A name for God, especially in Isaiah.

Holy orders *See* ORDERS, HOLY.

Holy Place The larger outer part of the tabernacle or temple. It contained the incense, the altar, the table for showbread, and the golden lampstand.

Holy Saturday The day between Good Friday and Easter Sunday.

Holy Spirit The Third Person of the Trinity, fully divine and fully personal.

Holy Spirit, Deity of the A reference to the fact that the Holy Spirit is divine in the same sense as are the Father and the Son.

Holy Spirit, Ministry of the The work of the Holy Spirit.

Holy Spirit, Personality of the A reference to the fact that the Holy Spirit is not a mere force, but a person capable of interacting with other persons.

Holy Spirit, Promise of the Jesus' promise that after his departure he would send the Holy Spirit (e.g., John 15:26).

Holy Spirit, Witness of the The work of the Holy Spirit in testifying to the human heart concerning the divinity and truth of Scripture. The doctrine was developed by Augustine and most fully expounded by Calvin.

Holy Spirit baptism *See* BAPTISM OF THE HOLY SPIRIT.

Holy Week The week between Palm Sunday and Easter.

Homiletical Pertaining to preaching or the study of preaching.

Homiletics The science and art of the preparation and delivery of sermons.

Homoiousios An expression used by the semi-Arians maintaining that Jesus was not the same as God but was similar in nature to God.

Homologoumena Those New Testament writings universally recognized by the church as canonical. The term contrasts with *Antilegomena,* those writings about which there was some dispute.

Homoousios A term used by orthodox Christians, particularly Athanasius and his followers, to insist that Jesus is of the very same nature as the Father.

Homosexuality Sexual attraction to persons of the same sex. This is homosexual orientation. A person who actually participates in physical sexual acts with someone of the same sex is engaged in homosexual practice.

Honesty Truthfulness, openness, and fairness in all of one's representations and business dealings.

Honor Respect and esteem accorded to a person, organization, or object.

Hooker, Richard (ca. 1554-1600) Anglican theologian and apologist who responded to the Puritans on behalf of Anglicanism. His most significant work was *Laws of Ecclesiastical Polity.*

Hope The expectation of good things in the future; in the Christian setting, faith regarding the matters that are yet to be.

Hope, Theology of A twentieth-century theology associated especially with the thought of Jürgen Moltmann. It emphasizes the future dimension of God rather than the past.

Horrible decree An expression used by some, including Calvin himself, of the doctrine of reprobation—that is, the doctrine that God predestined some to eternal damnation.

Hosanna The Greek form of a Hebrew salutation meaning "Save now, we beseech thee." All six occurrences in the New Testament are in connection with the triumphal entry of Jesus into Jerusalem.

Host The wafer or bread that in the Lord's Supper is believed to become the body of Christ.

Host, Consecration of the *See* CONSECRATION OF THE HOST.

Hosts, Lord of A name for God that depicts him as the head of the heavenly forces. It does not appear in the Pentateuch, but probably originated in the period of the conquest or shortly thereafter.

Host (of heaven) The angels of God.

House church An informal group of believers who meet in private homes rather than church edifices for prayer, study, worship, and fellowship. The house church may sometimes be part of a larger fellowship that meets as a whole at other times.

House of God The tabernacle or temple; the term is also used of modern-day churches.

Household baptism The baptism of an entire household, as in Acts 16:33. It is thought by some to include infants and children.

Household salvation A situation in which an entire household is saved, as in Genesis 17 or Acts 16:15, 33.

Hubmaier, Balthasar (ca. 1480-1528) German Reformer and writer who was one of the early Anabaptists. He was tortured, imprisoned, and eventually executed for his belief in and preaching of believers' baptism.

Human behavior The activities of human beings.

Human beings The highest creation of God; humans were made in his image and likeness (Gen. 1:26) and were given dominion over the rest of creation.

Human condition The state in which the human race finds itself; generally, the fallen, sinful state of human beings apart from Christ.

Human effort The limited achievements that human beings can accomplish for themselves or on behalf of one another; it contrasts with the work of God in them or on their behalf.

Human freedom *See* FREEDOM, HUMAN.

Humanism Study of and interest in humanity. Humanism may refer to a philosophy that humans are the highest beings, in which case it is in effect a form of atheism. Or it may refer to a philosophy that although there is a higher being, humans are to be emphasized and valued more than the higher being.

Humanism, Christian The idea that, on the basis of the teachings of Christianity, human beings are to be highly valued.

Humanity The entire human race, or the essence of human nature.

Humanity of Christ A reference to the fact that Jesus Christ took on full, though unfallen, human nature.

Humankind A generic term for the entire human race.

Human nature The universal makeup of the human person. It is often appealed to as an explanation for certain typically human activities.

Human race The entire collection of human beings.

Human soul An entity believed to be the source of human psychological and spiritual life. When referring to Jesus, the expression designates that his nonmaterial as well as his material nature was human.

Hume, David (1711-1776) Scottish philosopher of the empiricist school. His effect on religion is most fully seen in his criticism of the proofs for the existence of God and his denial of the possibility of miracles.

Humiliation of Jesus Christ The stages of self-emptying that Jesus underwent, including his earthly life, suffering, death, and burial (some would also include a descent into Hades).

Humility The quality of not regarding oneself more highly than one should, nor being excessively concerned about one's welfare or reputation.

Husserl, Edmund (1859-1938) German philosopher who was a major exponent of phenomenology.

Hyperdulia In Roman Catholic theology, veneration offered to the Virgin Mary as the mother of God.

Hypocrisy From a word meaning "play acting," representing oneself as different and better than one is.

Hypostasis From a Greek word for "substance" or "nature," the real or essential nature of something as distinguished from its attributes. In Christian thought the term is used in reference to any one of the three distinct persons in the Trinity, and especially Christ, the Second Person of the Trinity, in his divine and human natures.

Hypostatic union The union of Jesus' divine and human natures in one person.

Hypothesis A proposition the truth of which remains to be tested.

Hypothetical universalism The idea that Jesus died for the sins of all persons and that all are capable of believing. Theoretically, then, all persons might be saved, though in practice that may not be the case.

Ii

"I am" sayings Sayings of Jesus such as "I am the way, and the truth, and the life," and "I am the good shepherd." They are thought by some to be reflections of the statement in Exodus 3 where God identifies himself as "Yahweh" or "I AM." In actuality, only Jesus' statement "Before Abraham was, I am" (John 8:58) is grammatically parallel to Exodus 3:14.

Ibn-Rushd Another name for Averroes.

Iconoclasm Literally, "image breaking," the practice of destroying images in an effort to eradicate idolatry. In 754 the Council of Constantinople gave legal sanction to iconoclasm. The Reformation practiced a more positive form of iconoclasm by emphasizing the Scriptures and the priesthood of believers. The term is also used figuratively of opposition to commonly held views.

Ictic A reference to instantaneous action in contrast to process.

Idealism Any philosophy that emphasizes the mental or spiritual dimension as being more real than the material.

Idealism, Berkeleian A philosophy that holds that all reality is but a collection of thoughts or ideas in the mind.

Idealism, Hegelian Also known as absolute idealism, a philosophy that all of reality is organic: it is like one great mind.

Idealism, Lotzean or Leibnitzean Also known as personal idealism, a philosophy that reality is personal or social; only persons or selves are real.

Idealism, Platonic A philosophy that maintains that abstractions or values are more real than specific instances or entities.

Idealistic evolutionism A view that sees evolution as taking place as a result of the spiritual or mental nature of reality.

Idealist interpretation of eschatology An approach that regards the apocalyptic material in the Bible as relating not to specific events within history but to timeless truths. It is also referred to as the symbolic view of eschatology or of the book of Revelation.

Ideal-time theory A theory that the apparent age of something created may be greater than its actual age. Thus Adam one minute after his creation was actually one minute old, but he may have had an ideal or apparent age of perhaps twenty years. This theory was first propounded by Philip Henry Gosse in 1857.

Ideas, Platonic The abstract universals or pure essences, such as whiteness and humanness, after which existing things are patterned.

Identification with Christ The believer's union with Christ. The doctrine is based on the many biblical statements about the believer's being in Christ and Christ's being in the believer.

Identity, Law of The logical principle that A is A.

Ideological theologians Theologians whose views are related to, derived from, and concerned with the defense of a particular ideology. James Fowler uses the term to refer to the more extreme liberation theologians who see only good in their view and only evil in opposing views.

Idol Anything less than God that is given the worship due only to him.

Idolatry The worship of an idol or idols.

Ignatius of Loyola (1491-1556) The founder of the Society of Jesus (Jesuits). His mystical experiences became the basis of his *Spiritual Exercises*, a manual of spirituality.

Ignorance Lack of knowledge. In Scripture, ignorance is a form of and basis of sin, but of a less culpable variety than deliberate sin.

Illumination The work of the Holy Spirit giving understanding when the Scripture is heard or read.

Illumination theory *See* INSPIRATION, ILLUMINATION THEORY OF.

Illuminative way The second of the three stages of the mystical experience; it is intermediary between the purgative way (cleansing from sins) and the unitive way (mystical union with God). The concept is found particularly in the writings of John of the Cross.

Illyricus Latinized name for Matthias Flacius.

Image of God That which distinguishes human beings from the rest of God's creatures: The human is created in God's own image (Gen. 1:26).

Image of God, Formal In the writings of Emil Brunner, the idea that although sinners are turned from God, they are still related to him or stand before him. They are rational beings, responsible and free. The formal image contrasts with the material image, the acts of response to God—that is, the human's being molded by God into a finished state.

Image of God, Functional view of the The conception that the image of God is not something intrinsic in human nature but is something that the human does.

Image of God, Relational view of the The idea that the image of God is not inherent in the person, but is present when the person stands in a particular relationship.

Image of God, Structural or substantive view of the The idea that the image of God is some quality or set of qualities, physical or psychological, in the person.

Images, Veneration of The practice of directing honor to God, angels, or saints by means of visual representations.

Imago Dei Latin term for "image of God."

Imitation of Christ The attempt of the Christian to live according to Christ's example. The idea has given rise to a whole collection of devotional literature, including Thomas à Kempis's *Imitation of Christ* and Charles Sheldon's *In His Steps.*

Immaculate conception, the The Roman Catholic doctrine that Mary was preserved from original sin, although she experienced the temporal effects of Adam's sin. The Scripture references usually appealed to are Genesis 3:15 and Luke 1:28. The dogma was proclaimed by Pope Pius IX in 1854.

Immanence God's presence and activity within the creation and human history.

Immanentism A belief in divine immanence.

Immanuel Literally, "God with us," a Hebrew name applied to Jesus Christ (Isa. 7:14). (Also "Emmanuel.")

Immateriality of God *See* GOD, IMMATERIALITY OF.

Immeasurability of God *See* GOD, IMMEASURABILITY OF.

Immensity of God *See* GOD, IMMENSITY OF.

Immersion A form of baptism in which a person is lowered into the water so as to be completely covered.

Imminence The condition of something that could happen at any time or is about to happen. When applied to the second coming, the term means that Christ could return at any time. (Some who hold this view maintain, however, that a sequence of events may be involved in the Second Coming.)

Imminent posttribulationism The belief that while the second coming of Christ will follow the tribulation, it could happen at any time. This view entails the presupposition that we may already be in the tribulation.

Immortality The condition of being able to live forever.

Immortality, Conditional The idea that Adam and Eve before the Fall, provided that they fulfilled God's stipulations and obeyed his commands, had the potential of living forever.

Immutability of God *See* GOD, IMMUTABILITY OF.

Impanation A reference to the view that in the Eucharist the bread is not transubstantiated into the flesh of Christ, but Christ is embodied in the bread. Thus the communicant receives both the body of Christ and the bread. This doctrine was taught especially by Guitmund of Aversa and John of Paris.

Impassibility, Divine A reference to the

idea that God is unaffected by whatever happens in the world; in particular, he does not experience suffering or pain.

Impeccability of Christ *See* CHRIST, IMPECCABILITY OF.

Imperial authority The right to issue decrees because of the office one holds.

Implication, Logical A relationship between two propositions such that if the former is true, the latter must be also.

Implicit faith The doctrine that one, without an explicit knowledge of Jesus Christ, may, on the basis of general revelation, exercise saving faith by believing the outlines of the gospel.

Implicit trinitarianism Indirect biblical evidences of the Trinity.

Imprecatory psalms Psalms in which the author invokes the curse of God upon enemies.

Imputation The attribution or transfer of one person's sin or righteousness to another.

Imputation, Doctrine of Either the justification of believers on the basis of Christ's righteousness or the condemnation of unbelievers on the basis of Adam's sin.

Imputation of Christ's righteousness God's act of crediting the righteousness of Christ to sinners who believe and accept his gift.

Imputation of guilt The declaration that a person is guilty on the basis of the action of another.

Imputation of sin, Conditional The idea that the sin of Adam in the fall is imputed to his descendants but becomes effective only when they ratify it by their own sin or by failure to repudiate their own sinful nature.

In Adam A reference to the idea that all persons are in Adam and thus Adam's sin was in some sense our sin (see, e.g., Rom. 5, particularly v. 12).

Inauthentic existence In existential thought, unwillingness to accept responsibility for oneself. It may entail simply conforming to the crowd or excusing one's behavior on the basis of some genetic, psychological, or social conditioning.

Incarnate Christ The state of Christ since the time of his becoming a human being.

Incarnation A reference to the doctrine that the Second Person of the Trinity, without giving up his deity, became a human being.

Incarnation, Dynamic The idea that Christ was not ontologically deity but that the power or influence of God was active and operative within him. This idea is found in dynamic monarchianism, an early trinitarian heresy, and in twentieth-century writings such as Donald Baillie's *God Was in Christ*.

Incarnational theology A theology affirming that the Second Person of the Trinity actually became human in the person of Jesus Christ; also, in popular twentieth-century thought, the idea that each of us is to represent Christ in the world.

Incense, Offering of *See* OFFERING OF INCENSE.

In Christ Jesus A reference, frequent in Paul, to the fact that the believer is identified with, and affected by, Christ (see, e.g., Gal. 2:20).

Incommunicable attributes *See* ATTRIBUTES OF GOD, INCOMMUNICABLE.

Incomplete state A condition short of the final version. The term is applied particularly to the intermediate state after death. It is not the final and eternal condition of the person, since it does not involve full bodily existence.

Incomprehensibility of God A reference to the fact that God cannot be understood by his creatures.

Incorruptible Not subject to death, destruction, or decay.

Independence of God *See* GOD, INDEPENDENCE OF.

Indeterminism The philosophy that human behavior is not (completely) caused by predisposing physical and psychological factors: Our actions are basically a matter of our will.

Indian theology An attempt to express

Christian theology in Indian, rather than Western, categories.

Indigenization Developing theologies out of the local culture, rather than by importing categories.

Individual eschatology *See* ESCHATOLOGY, INDIVIDUAL.

Individualism Emphasis upon the situation, actions, and will of the individual rather than the group.

Individualistic approach to Christianity Any variety of Christianity that stresses the individual's personal relationship to God to the neglect of the group or collective dimension.

Individual piety A reference to emphasis on the individual's personal relationship to God or to Jesus Christ.

Inductive approach The process of reasoning from a variety of experiences or observations to a conclusion. It contrasts with deduction, the application of general principles to specific instances. The inductive approach to inerrancy examines the actual nature of Scripture rather than the biblical teaching on the subject. The inductive approach to human sinfulness investigates the lives of actual persons rather than doctrinal abstractions on the matter.

Indulgence In Roman Catholicism, remission of the temporal (especially purgatorial) consequences of previously forgiven sins.

Indwelling The presence of Christ or the Holy Spirit within the life of the believer.

Inerrancy A reference to the variously interpreted doctrine that the Bible is free from error.

Inerrancy, Absolute The view that the Bible speaks specifically and conclusively on all matters and is fully truthful in all areas.

Inerrancy, Abstract approach to The position that the problematic phenomena of Scripture need not be explained. It is based on the belief that the evidence for inspiration and consequent inerrancy is overwhelming.

Inerrancy, Doctrine of The variously interpreted teaching that the Bible contains no error in that which it affirms.

Inerrancy, Full The view that the Bible is completely truthful in all that it teaches, but that not all of its allusions need be regarded as assertions.

Inerrancy, Harmonistic approach to Attempts to resolve the difficulties that apparently conflicting or inaccurate passages present for the doctrine of scriptural inerrancy.

Inerrancy, Limited A reference to the belief that the inerrancy of the Bible is limited in some way. A common version says that the Bible is inerrant in its theological or salvific references, but not in its references to matters of history and science.

Inerrancy, Moderate harmonization approach to Attempts to reconcile difficult or apparently conflicting passages of Scripture where this can reasonably be done with the data at hand; if there do not seem to be sufficient data, no explanatory effort is made.

Inerrancy of purpose The view that the Scripture will not fail to accomplish its purposes, even if factual errors are involved at some point.

Infallibility A reference to the doctrine that the Bible is unfailing in its purpose. In some usages of the term the Bible's authority may be restricted to matters of salvation.

Infallibility, Papal The Roman Catholic doctrine adopted in 1870 that when speaking in his official capacity (*ex cathedra*) on matters of faith and practice, the pope is unerring.

Infant baptism The practice of baptizing infants, even though they cannot give a credible testimony of personal faith.

Infant salvation The doctrine that infants who die are saved.

Infidelity *See* UNFAITHFULNESS.

Infinite being A reference to God as unlimited in all positive attributes. By contrast humans are limited in such attributes as knowledge, power, and presence.

Influential presence A reference to the idea that even if God is not personally present, his spiritual influence is present.

Informational revelation *See* REVELATION, INFORMATIONAL VIEW OF.

Infralapsarianism A form of Calvinism that teaches that the decree of the Fall logically preceded that of election. The order of God's decrees, then, is: (1) to create human beings; (2) to permit the Fall; (3) to save some and condemn others; and (4) to provide salvation only for the elect.

Inheritance Possessions received by an heir as a result of a will or legal process.

Inheritance of Adam's sin A reference to the idea that because of Adam's sin (the original or first sin), all persons are now guilty. This doctrine is also referred to as the imputation of Adamic sin.

Iniquity A term for sin emphasizing deviation from a correct course. It may thus refer to injustice, failure to fulfill the standard of righteousness, or lack of integrity.

Injustice Failure to render to someone that which is rightfully deserved.

Inner light An expression used by the Quakers to refer to guidance or revelation from God through an inward illumination.

Inner man The locus of divine regeneration in the human (Rom. 7:22; 2 Cor. 4:16; Eph. 3:16).

Inscripturation God's preserving his revelation in writing through the process of inspiration by the Holy Spirit.

Insensitivity An increasing resistance to the appeals and claims of Christ as one continues in sin.

Inspiration A reference to anything that moves or excites a person; in particular, the act of the Holy Spirit upon the biblical writers that ensured that what they wrote was the Word of God.

Inspiration, Concursive The process by which God revealed truth simultaneously with the Scripture author's being moved to write.

Inspiration, Dictation theory of The view that God actually dictated the exact words the biblical writers recorded.

Inspiration, Dynamic theory of The view that God guided the biblical writer to the concepts that were to be recorded, but not to the actual choice of words.

Inspiration, Illumination theory of The idea that the Holy Spirit's work of inspiration merely heightened the normal powers of the authors of Scripture. He gave them no specific guidance in what they wrote.

Inspiration, Intuition theory of The idea that inspiration involves simply a high degree of religious insight.

Inspiration, Plenary The view that all of Scripture, not simply certain books or certain portions of books or certain types of material, is inspired.

Inspiration, Verbal theory of The doctrine that the Holy Spirit so guided the biblical writer that even the words and details are what God intended to be written.

Instantaneous resurrection The doctrine that immediately upon death we will receive our future body. There is, then, no future bodily resurrection.

Instant reclothing *See* INSTANTANEOUS RESURRECTION.

Institutes of the Christian Religion The theological treatise written by John Calvin that became the great doctrinal standard of the Reformed church.

Institutional church, the The formal, visible, organized church. It contrasts with the spiritual church, which consists of all true believers, whether identified as such or not.

Instrumentalism In pragmatic philosophy, the belief that ideas are valid only if they lead to useful action.

Integrity of God *See* GOD, INTEGRITY OF.

Intelligence A quality of human nature that is part of the structural image of God, the ability to know and understand truth.

Intelligent design A movement, led by intellectuals such as law professor Phillip E. Johnson and William A. Dembski, that criticizes the logical and methodological basis of traditional evolutionary theory.

Intercession, Coextensiveness of A principle that says that since Christ's various works are coextensive, he intercedes for all those for whom he atoned, and vice versa. It is used in dealing with the question of limited or unlimited atonement.

Intercession of Christ A reference to the doctrine that Christ's current ministry on behalf of believers includes mediating for them before the Father.

Intercessory prayer Prayer offered on behalf of other persons.

Intercessory work of the Holy Spirit The concept that the Holy Spirit intercedes for us when we do not know how to pray (Rom. 8:26-27).

Interchurch association In the broadest sense, any collection or affiliation of congregations or denominations; in churches practicing a congregational polity, the organizational grouping of congregations sometimes referred to as a convention or conference.

Intercongregational organizations Either denominations or interdenominational fellowships.

Interdenominational fellowship Cooperative affiliation of individuals and churches of different denominations.

Interdependence of God In process theology, God's relatedness to the world and involvement with it: He is not impassive, detached, and immutable.

Intermediate state The condition of persons between the time of their death and the resurrection.

Internal call *See* CALL, INTERNAL.

Internal circumcision A reference to the idea that salvation as conversion and regeneration is an internal equivalent of what circumcision was externally and formally in Judaism (Rom. 2:29).

Internal communion The relationship among the three members of the Trinity.

Internal grounds Evidence or considerations within a given passage or conception that relate to its validity; for example, consistency and coherence (or lack thereof). External grounds, on the other hand, consist of evidence from outside data.

Internal testimony of the Holy Spirit The Holy Spirit's work witnessing to, and convincing the human heart and mind of, the divine origin and authority of Scripture.

International Council of Christian Churches Organization that united churches of varying denominations in protest against the World Council of Churches. It was brought into being through the leadership of Carl McIntire.

International Missionary Council A movement that stemmed from the 1910 missionary conference at Edinburgh. It merged with the World Council of Churches in 1961.

Interpretation A way of understanding or explaining a passage of writing or a concept.

Interpretation of tongues, Gift of A spiritual gift that involves the ability to understand and thus give the meaning of what has been spoken in a tongue (1 Cor. 12:10, 30; 14:13, 26-28). It may be possessed by the one speaking in a tongue or by another.

Interpretics A term used by Frederick Ferré to refer to the relationship between units of language ("signs") and the interpreter. This is similar to Charles Morris's use of the term *pragmatics*.

Inverted theology The tendency of human beings to place themselves over God and regard him as serving and pleasing them; in effect, it makes humans God and makes God the servant of humans.

Invisibility of God *See* GOD, INVISIBILITY OF.

Invisible background of creation Expression used by Hendrikus Berkhof speaking of the powers that were created by God as instruments of his love and that form the framework within which service must be carried out.

Invisible church, the All true believers of all times. It is invisible because it does not gather or meet (at least not until the eschaton) and because we cannot distinguish true believers from unbelievers who make a profession of being believers.

Invisible fellowship The relationship that exists among believers simply by virtue of their having the same faith. It does not require any formal connection or organization.

Invisible presence A reference to the idea that Christ, though unseen, is present among believers.

Invocation of the saints Requests to believers in heaven to intercede on behalf of the petitioner.

Inward nature The actual condition of the person in terms of subjective holiness. It contrasts with one's external relationship with God, the objective status of being justified or condemned by him.

Ipsissima verba The actual words spoken by Jesus.

Ipsissima vox The substance or sense of the words spoken by Jesus; it contrasts with the *ipissima verba,* the exact words of Jesus.

Irenaean theodicy Irenaeus' suggestion that evil is part of God's process of soul making, of the spiritual formation of the human being.

Irenaeus (ca. 130-200) An early Greek father who was in later life bishop of Lyons. He proposed the doctrine of recapitulation, according to which Christ took human nature and by his obedience restored what was lost through Adam's disobedience. That is, he summed up (recapitulated) what God had intended humanity to be.

Irish Articles A collection of 104 articles of belief adopted by the Irish Episcopal Church at its first convocation in 1615.

Ironside, Henry Allen (H. A.) (1876-1951) Evangelist, Bible teacher, author, and pastor of Moody Memorial Church (Chicago) from 1930 to 1948. He had a significant role in popularizing dispensationalism.

Irrationalism Any philosophy that values negatively the powers of human reason. In some forms, such as the existentialism of Søren Kierkegaard, it may actually involve placing a positive value upon the paradoxical.

Irresistible grace The idea that those whom God has chosen for eternal life will come to faith and thus to salvation. The doctrine is sometimes also referred to as efficacious grace.

Irreverence Lack of respect for the sacred.

Irving, Edward (1792-1834) Evangelical minister who, while pastoring in London, did much to popularize premillennialism. When he became a charismatic in 1830, he was forced to leave the Church of Scotland. His followers organized the Catholic Apostolic Church.

Islam The religion founded by Mohammed and based on his teachings.

Israel Those who are descended from Abraham. The term usually refers to physical Israel, those who are Jews by birth, or to national Israel, the modern state organized in Palestine. It also refers to spiritual Israel, believers who have the faith that Abraham had.

Israel, National Israel thought of as a specific national group.

Israel, New The church.

Israel, Political The political entity or nation of Israel.

Israel, Restoration of The idea that literal or national Israel will at some point be restored to the position of special status with God that it formerly experienced, a position currently accorded to the church.

Issy, Articles of A set of thirty-four articles of belief drawn up by a commission of the Catholic church meeting at Issy, near Paris, in 1695. The articles condemned the teachings of Madame Guyon.

Jj

Jah (or Yah) A shortened form of Yahweh (Exod. 15:2; 17:16).

Jansen, Cornelius (1585-1638) Flemish Catholic theologian who was a vigorous defender of the Augustinian view of predestination.

Jansenism A movement based upon the teachings and writings of Cornelius Jansen. In the nineteenth century one group of Jansenists in the Netherlands became part of the Old Catholic Church.

Jaspers, Karl (1883-1969) Leading German existentialist philosopher.

Jealousy Positively, a zeal for something; negatively, envy of someone. In the former sense, it is often attributed to God.

Jehovah *See* YAHWEH.

Jehovah's Witnesses Founded by Charles Taze Russell in the 1870s, a movement that rejects the doctrine of the Trinity and the traditional view of the person and work of Christ. At some points it follows extremely literal interpretations of the Bible. The name Jehovah's Witnesses was adopted in 1931.

Jerome (ca. 340-420) Biblical scholar who sought to introduce the best Greek learning to the Western or Latin church. His most important achievement was the Vulgate, a Latin translation of the Bible.

Jerusalem, New In Revelation 3:12 and 21:2, a reference to the ultimate state of the church.

Jerusalem council In Acts 15, a council held in Jerusalem to discuss the question of whether Gentile believers had to be circumcised and obey the law of Moses. The church of Antioch had sent Paul, Barnabas, and other believers to get a definitive answer from the apostles.

Jesuits Members of the Society of Jesus, which was founded by Ignatius of Loyola.

Jesus, Deity of *See* CHRIST, DEITY OF.

Jesus, Humanity of *See* CHRIST, HUMANITY OF.

Jesus, Twofold state of *See* STATES OF JESUS CHRIST.

Jesus Christ A compound name for the incarnate Second Person of the Trinity: "Jesus" refers to the man from Nazareth, and "Christ" is Greek for "Messiah," which means "anointed." In Acts 5:42 he is referred to as Jesus the Christ; apparently this was abbreviated to the form "Jesus Christ."

Jesus of Nazareth The name given to the child born to the Virgin Mary, who had conceived under the influence of the Holy Spirit.

Jesusologies Doctrinal understandings of Jesus that focus on his earthly life; particularly, nineteenth-century searches for the historical Jesus, which made him little more than a human being.

Jesus religion A popular, experience-centered form of Christianity in the latter half of the twentieth century.

Jew Either a person of Hebrew descent or a practicing adherent of Judaism (or both).

Jewish believers Persons of Jewish ancestry who came to believe in Jesus as the Messiah.

Jewish Christianity Christianity as found among persons in churches that were primarily Jewish.

Jewish law The law given through Moses together with interpretations and expansions added by Jewish rabbis.

John of Antioch (died 441) Patriarch of Antioch who succeeded in obtaining a compromise after the Council of Ephesus (431), which had condemned Nestorianism.

John of Damascus (ca. 675-749) Last of the great Eastern fathers. His best-known work is his *Fount of Wisdom* (or *Sources of Knowledge*).

John of the Cross (1542-1591) Christian mystic best known for his *Dark Night of the Soul*.

Joint heirs with Christ A reference in Romans 8:17 to one of the aspects of the believer's union with Christ: If we suffer with him, we will also be glorified with him.

Joy A sense of satisfaction and delight that is not affected by circumstances. In Scripture it is part of the fruit of the Spirit (Gal. 5:22).

Judaic Pertaining or related to the Jews or Judaism.

Judaism The religion and culture of the Jewish people.

Judaizers People who attempted to impose the standards and laws of Judaism upon Christianity. Some of the early Christians, for example, would have required Gentile converts to be circumcised and keep the Mosaic law. Paul's letter to the Galatians was written in part to refute this position.

Judaizing movements Groups that advocate retaining the Jewish background to Christianity. They have appeared at various periods, both within biblical history and within the subsequent history of the church.

Judgment Condemnation, or evaluation of one's guilt or innocence.

Judgment, Last *See* LAST JUDGMENT.

Judgment of the nations Christ's verdict on the extant Gentile nations following his second coming. Amillennialists tend to make it part of the one great final judgment. Premillennialists, particularly of the pretribulational variety, tend to make it a separate judgment.

Judgment seat The platform upon which a civil magistrate sits during judicial proceedings. The term is used of the final judgment to be rendered by Jesus Christ.

Judicial authority The capacity to decide the meaning or the truth of something. It contrasts with legislative authority, the right to determine the content of our beliefs.

Judicial union That aspect of the believer's union with Christ by virtue of which the sin of the human is borne by Christ and the righteousness of Christ is reckoned to the believer.

Julian of Eclanum (ca. 380-455) The most systematic exponent of Pelagianism; in some ways he even went beyond Pelagius.

Juristic view of sin The view that sin is morally wrong, violates the law, and thus incurs punishment. The juristic view contrasts with the aesthetic view, which defines sin as whatever is ugly, inharmonious, and thus repulsive.

Justice God's faithful administration of his kingdom in accordance with his law; his official righteousness and requirement that humans adhere to the standards he has set. In humans, justice is the concern that each person receive that which is rightfully his or hers.

Justification In the doctrine of salvation, the declaration that the human has been restored to a state of righteousness in God's sight.

Justification (philosophy) The strategy of establishing the truth of propositions.

Justification by faith Declaration that the person has been restored to a state of righteousness on the basis of belief and trust in the work of Christ rather than on the basis of one's own accomplishment.

Justin Martyr (ca. 100-165) Christian apologist who sought to show that Christianity expresses the noblest and highest concepts of Greek philosophy and thus is the supreme truth.

Justitia civilis See CIVIL RIGHTEOUSNESS.

Kk

Kabbala A mystical form of Judaism that developed in the Middle Ages. Among its doctrines was reincarnation. Among its esoteric practices was the assignment of numerical values to the letters of the Hebrew alphabet. These numerical values were then used to discover hidden meanings in the words of the Hebrew Scriptures.

Kähler, Martin (1835-1912) German Protestant theologian whose book *The So-Called Historical Jesus and the Historic Biblical Christ* (1896) drew the distinction between *Historie* and *Geschichte* that was to play a major role in twentieth-century Gospel research and Christology. Its separation of the Jesus of history from the Christ of faith greatly influenced the thought of Rudolf Bultmann.

Kalam cosmological argument An argument for the existence of God based on the principle of efficient causation and the impossibility of an infinite regress of events.

Kansas City prophets A group that teaches that the New Testament gift of prophecy is for today and practices that gift.

Kant, Immanuel (1724-1804) German philosopher who sought to unite philosophical rationalism and empiricism.

Kantianism A philosophy stemming from Immanuel Kant, particularly an epistemology that holds that all knowledge derives its content from sense experience, but its structure or form from categories of intellectual understanding found within the human mind.

Karma A doctrine found in several Eastern religions, saying that one's actions have inexorable results in one's condition, both in this life and in succeeding lives.

Käsemann, Ernst (1906-1998) Twentieth-century post-Bultmannian.

Keble, John (1792-1866) A founder of the Tractarian or Oxford movement.

Kempis, Thomas à *See* THOMAS à KEMPIS.

Kenosis Christ's emptying himself of equality with God (Phil. 2:7), thus becoming functionally subordinate to God, without giving up the attributes of deity.

Kenotic theology A theology that emphasizes the self-limitation of Christ or his giving up of divine prerogatives and attributes; in particular, a late-nineteenth-century British movement with this emphasis.

Kerygma The content of the early Christian message that must be believed by faith in order to receive salvation. The term is a transliteration of a Greek word meaning "proclamation."

Kerygmatic Christ The Christ who was preached in the sermons of the apostles; by contrast, the historical Jesus is the person historical research can verify actually lived and taught.

Keswick Convention An annual summer Bible conference held at Keswick in the Lake District of England. The term has also been used of similar conventions held in other places, for example, the United States.

Keys of the kingdom An expression used by Jesus to refer to certain authority that Peter (and possibly the other apostles) was to exercise (Matt. 16:19).

Kierkegaard, Søren (1813-1855) Danish existentialist philosopher and theologian. His writings had relatively little acceptance in his day, but have had considerable influence upon twentieth-century existentialism and neoorthodox theology.

King A male sovereign. In Scripture, the term may refer either to a human authority or to Christ.

King, Christ as *See* CHRIST AS KING.

King, Martin Luther, Jr. (1929-1968) Black American clergyman and civil-rights leader who organized the Southern Christian Leadership Conference and advocated nonviolent action against racial segregation. A recipient of the Nobel Peace Prize in 1964, he was assassinated in Memphis, Tennessee, on April 4, 1968.

King of glory A reference to God that emphasizes his greatness and splendor (Ps. 24:7-10).

Kingdom of Christ The kingdom of God. The term stresses Christ's sovereignty.

Kingdom of God The reign of God, whether internally within the heart of humans or externally. It is not a specific realm.

Kingdom of heaven Matthew's term for the kingdom of God.

Kingsley, Charles (1819-1875) Anglican clergyman, writer, and social reformer who held to Darwinism and attempted to integrate Christianity and science, even in his best-selling children's book *The Water Babies* (1863). He disapproved of asceticism and opposed the Oxford movement. Kingsley was of the Broad Church or liberal party but became more theologically conservative in his latter years.

Kneel To bend or bow the knee, usually as an act of worship or of homage.

Knowability of God The degree to which God can be understood or encountered. One's view of revelation will determine one's view of the knowability of God.

Knowledge That which is recognized and understood, whether of God, of other persons, or of other parts of the creation.

Knowledge, Fullness of An aspect of the glorification of the believer (1 Cor. 13:12).

Knowledge, Gift of One of the spiritual gifts mentioned in 1 Corinthians 12:8 and 13:8.

Knox, John (ca. 1514-1572) Scottish clergyman who introduced the Reformed theology of Calvin to Scotland. The most influential Reformer in Scotland, Knox served as pastor of St. Giles Church in Edinburgh. He viewed the state and the church as essentially the same community.

Koinonia A Greek word for "fellowship." See FELLOWSHIP.

Koran, the The holy book of Islam. Muslims believe its 114 chapters were virtually dictated to the prophet Mohammed by the angel Gabriel.

Küng, Hans (1928-) Swiss Roman Catholic theologian who advocated many of the reforms carried out by the Second Vatican Council but went beyond them by insisting that the true Catholic position on justification is basically similar to the Protestant. Also critical of the doctrine of the infallibility of the pope, Küng has been deposed from his official status as a Roman Catholic teacher.

Kuyper, Abraham (1837-1920) Dutch theologian, pastor, and politician. He was a leading formulator of classical Dutch Calvinistic theology.

Ll

Laity From a Greek word meaning "people," the whole people of God. The term has come, however, to refer to those who are not specifically set apart or ordained to the ministry.

Lake, Kirsopp (1872-1946) British biblical scholar and authority on the book of Acts and early Christianity. Some of his writings were controversial in nature, including an attempt to cast doubt on the story of the empty tomb.

Lake of fire The place of eternal punishment for the wicked. It is mentioned six times in the book of Revelation (19:20; 20:10; 20:14 [2]; 20:15; 21:18), being also referred to as "the fiery lake" and "the lake of burning sulphur."

Lamb of God, the A reference by John the Baptist to the work of Christ in taking away the sin of the world (John 1:29, 36).

Landmarkism A view held by a number of Baptists, particularly in the United States, that only the visible local church conforms to the New Testament model. The idea of a universal spiritual church is rejected. Communion is restricted to members of the local assembly. It also maintains that a sort of apostolic succession via baptism can be traced from John the Baptist to modern Baptist churches.

Last day(s) In the Old Testament, a future time of judgment and redemption; in the New Testament, either the period immediately preceding or the period inaugurated by Christ's coming.

Last judgment The evaluation of each individual that Christ will make after his second coming.

Last Supper The initial event establishing the Lord's Supper.

Last times *See* LAST DAY(S).

Latimer, Hugh (ca. 1485-1555) English Protestant preacher and martyr. Consecrated bishop of Worcester in 1535, he acknowledged the catholic church but denied the claims of the Church of Rome.

Latitudinarianism An attitude or mentality favoring freedom of thought, especially in religion; in particular, the position of a group of seventeenth-century Anglican clergymen who emphasized reason, tolerance, and an antidogmatic spirit.

Latourette, Kenneth Scott (1884-1968) Baptist missionary, scholar, and church historian, particularly of the history of missions. He taught in China and then at Yale University.

Latria In Roman Catholicism, the adoration given to God alone; it contrasts with *dulia,* honor that can be given to persons other than God—for example, to Mary or the saints.

Latter days, the The last days.

Laud, William (1573-1645) Archbishop of Canterbury and adviser to Charles I. He was imprisoned by Parliament in 1641 and executed for treason in 1645, in part as a result of his attempt to impose the Prayer Book upon Scotland.

Lauds In Roman Catholicism and Anglicanism, one of the prescribed daily offices or services of worship. Following matins, it is the first service of the day hours.

Law The Mosaic Old Testament law; it contrasts with the new covenant or the covenant of grace.

Law and grace A reference to the highly disputed question of the relative roles of law and grace.

Lawism The concept that ethical requirements can be expressed in laws or rules without the attitudinal dimensions and punctiliousness associated with legalism.

Lawless one, the The Antichrist (2 Thess. 2:8).

Law of reversal Ethelbert Stauffer's concept that God permits some sins to occur but directs them in such a way that good comes from them. This is a special adjunct of the doctrine of providence.

Lay baptism The administration of baptism by an unordained person.

Lay elders Officers who hold positions of leadership but are not formally ordained ministers. In presbyterian types of church government they, together with the clergy, form the session or consistory.

Laying on of hands The practice of ceremoniously touching a person being consecrated or ordained.

Lay person Anyone who is not ordained.

Leaven Yeast. Scripture often uses the term to represent evil. This is not always the case, however (Matt. 13:33 uses it in reference to the kingdom of God).

Left-wing liberalism In theological contexts, an extreme form of liberalism in which the distinctiveness of Christianity and of Jesus Christ is lost, being dissolved into religion in general.

Legalism A keeping of the law, particularly in a formal sense, and a regarding of obedience as meritorious.

Legends Tales coming down from the past; in form criticism, stories about prominent personages in the Judeo-Christian tradition.

Legislative authority The right to determine the content of belief or practice.

Leibnitz, Gottfried Wilhelm von (1646-1716) German philosopher and epistemological rationalist who argued that God has created the best of all possible worlds.

Leipzig disputation Debate held from

June 27 to July 15, 1519, at the University of Leipzig, involving Johann Eck, Martin Luther, and Andreas Carlstadt.

Lent The period of forty fast days (i.e., forty weekdays or forty-six calendar days) from Ash Wednesday to the Saturday immediately preceding Easter. It is intended to be a time of abstinence, prayer, and works of charity.

Leo I (the Great) (ca. 400-461) Pope from 440 to 461. Leo advanced the idea of papal supremacy over the imperial authority. In 452 he persuaded Attila the Hun to stop his raid on the city of Rome.

Lessing, Gotthold Ephraim (1729-1781) German philosopher, critic, and dramatist who rejected biblical revelation and explained Christianity's origin naturalistically. Although not a theologian, he prepared the way for critical study of the Bible, especially of the New Testament, and for liberal theology.

Levites In the broadest sense, members of the tribe of Levi. The priests were taken from the Levites; the remainder of the tribe were support staff assisting in the work of the temple. It is this latter group that is usually in view when the term *Levites is* used.

Levitical system The system of sacrifices and ceremonial law found in the Old Testament.

Lewis, C. S. (Clive Staples) (1898-1963) British novelist and lay theologian whose popular writings as an apologist

for Christianity have had considerable influence among intellectuals.

Lex talionis Retribution or punishment in kind; the idea of "an eye for an eye and a tooth for a tooth."

Liberal capitalism Capitalism that includes certain elements of the welfare state. Rather than a purely competitive approach, there is a measure of public provision for human needs.

Liberal Catholicism A growing movement within Roman Catholicism that gives significant place to biblical criticism, process philosophy, and similar modern conceptions.

Liberal evangelicalism A rather imprecise movement among evangelicals that, while stressing the authority of Scripture and the need for a personal relationship with Christ, is open to modern intellectual developments, particularly toward biblical criticism and views of the atonement other than the penal-substitution theory.

Liberal Jesus The picture of Jesus drawn by liberalism, usually as a good teacher who made no claim to being divine.

Liberalism Any movement that is open to redefining or changing the traditional doctrines and practices of Christianity.

Liberalism, Classical Theological liberalism that flourished in Europe in the nineteenth century and in the United

States in the late nineteenth and early twentieth centuries.

Liberalism, Theological Theologies that redefine or modify traditional doctrines.

Liberal Jesus The picture of Jesus constructed by liberal searchers for the historical Jesus. The Jesus they find is often a reflection of their own beliefs and teachings.

Liberation Deliverance from anything that would restrict or enslave.

Liberation theology A collection of theological movements (Third-World liberation movements, feminist theology, and black theology) that put more emphasis on deliverance of human beings from various types of temporal bondage—economic, political, and social—than on personal redemption from sin. It tends to draw upon social sciences rather than biblical and theological bases.

Libertarianism A type of antinomianism; emphasis on liberty as contrasted with the keeping of rules.

Liberty, Christian The freedom to choose courses of action that, instead of being compelled by other human beings, grow out of one's commitment to Christ and the Scriptures.

Liberty, Religious Freedom to worship according to the dictates of one's conscience without political or other coercion.

Licentiousness A form of antinomianism or self-indulgence that rejects or casts off all rules; particularly, permissiveness in sexual matters.

Liddon, Henry Parry (1829-1890) An Anglican minister who was a leader of the later Oxford or Tractarian movement.

Lie The active conveying of a falsehood with the intent to deceive someone to whom the truth is owed.

Life The state of being alive. The term may refer to physical life, which is biological in nature, or to spiritual life, which is a state of being alive, responsive, and active in the spiritual realm.

Life, Everlasting *See* ETERNAL LIFE.

Life in the flesh The life of humans under the control of their depraved nature. It contrasts with life in the Spirit, which is motivated and given impetus by the Holy Spirit. Paul compares the two in Galatians 5:13-26.

Life in the Spirit The life of the Christian under the control of the indwelling Holy Spirit (Gal. 5:13-26).

Life-of-Jesus movement An effort, particularly by nineteenth-century liberal scholars, to construct a picture of the historical Jesus.

Life setting (*Sitz im Leben*) The original setting in which an event took place or a teaching was introduced.

Light Illumination coming from the sun or an artificial source. In Scripture, the term is used to refer to God and the good that comes from him. By contrast evil is associated with darkness.

Likeness of God Usually a synonym for the image of God. However, some theologians, including Irenaeus, thought it to be something separate from the image. Medieval Catholicism regarded the likeness as a spiritual holiness added to the natural qualities of personality and reason.

Limbo A term used by medieval theologians to refer to the supposed location of souls who after death do not deserve to go to either heaven or hell. There are two limbos: *limbus patrum* and *limbus infantium.*

Limbus infantium In Catholic theology, a place where unbaptized infants go upon death. They do not experience pain and punishment, nor do they experience salvation and the enjoyment derived from God's presence.

Limbus patrum In Catholic theology, a place where the souls of Old Testament saints resided until Christ descended into hell to free them.

Limited atonement A reference to the view that Christ's atoning death was only for the elect.

Limited inerrancy *See* INERRANCY, LIMITED.

Linguistic analysis A twentieth-century form of philosophy that, rather than making normative judgments about whether something is true or false, right or wrong, emphasizes the meaning of language.

Linguistic semantics Word study that is concerned with the identification and description of meaning in existing languages; it contrasts with logical semantics, which is concerned with the relationship of signs and symbols to their referents.

Literalism Biblical translation or interpretation that takes the meaning of language in its plainest, most obvious, and often most concrete sense.

Literal Israel Israel as a national or ethnic group.

Literal meaning The plainest or most direct meaning of language.

Literal sense of Scripture *See* LITERALISM.

Literary-framework theory *See* PICTORIAL-DAY (LITERARY-FRAMEWORK) THEORY.

Literary-source criticism *See* CRITICISM, LITERARY-SOURCE.

Liturgical year *See* CHRISTIAN YEAR.

Liturgy Prescribed forms of worship, including language, vestments, and paraphernalia.

Living being In Genesis 1—2, an expression used to refer to various forms of life. The human is said to have become a living being when God breathed into him (Gen. 2:7).

Living hope The glorious expectations that the regenerated believer has as a result of the resurrection of Christ (1 Peter 1:3).

Living sacrifice A term Paul uses to urge his readers to present themselves as offerings to God (Rom. 12:1).

Local church, local congregation The body of believers organized in one specific place for fellowship, worship, evangelism, and related activities.

Local evangelism Witnessing done directly in one's home territory rather than in foreign fields.

Locke, John (1632-1704) English philosopher often thought of as the first of the modern empiricists. Educated in theology, chemistry, and medicine, he taught that the human mind is a blank sheet that achieves knowledge through sense impressions written on it.

Logia A collection of sayings of Jesus believed to have been used by Matthew and Luke. It is often identified with the document "Q."

Logical empiricism See LOGICAL POSITIVISM.

Logical positivism A twentieth-century philosophical movement that maintains that a synthetic statement is meaningful only if there is a set of sense data that would verify or falsify it. Logical positivism tends to restrict

meaningfulness to analytical statements and empirical observations.

Logocentrism A term used by the French deconstructionist philosopher Jacques Derrida to refer to a view of language in which the meaning or truth of language is based on an objective structure of reality, independent of the language.

Logos A Greek term for "Word" used in the prologue to the Gospel of John to refer to Christ. In later theology, it is used of reason or the reason of God.

Logotherapy A system of psychotherapy developed by Viktor Frankl that helps people find a reason or purpose in life.

Loisy, Alfred Firmin (1857-1940) Biblical scholar regarded in many ways as the founder of French Roman Catholic modernism.

Lombard, Peter See PETER LOMBARD.

Lord A translation of Yahweh or Jehovah. The term is also used of Jesus Christ by believers.

Lord of hosts See HOSTS, LORD OF.

Lord's Day The first day of the week or Sunday.

Lordship of Christ Jesus Christ's authority and rule over the life of the Christian.

Lordship theology The teaching that saving conversion requires repentance of sin and acceptance of Jesus Christ as Lord as well as Savior.

Lord's Prayer, the A model or paradigm prayer given by Jesus (Matt. 6:9-13).

Lord's Supper, the The sacramental practice of eating bread and drinking wine or grape juice in commemoration of Jesus' death. It follows the pattern of his Last Supper with the disciples on the eve of his crucifixion.

Love One of the supreme attributes of God—concern for and action to bring about the welfare of another. There are a number of Greek terms for love, including *eros* (sexual passion) and *philia* (friendship); but the highest form of love is that which seeks the welfare of others (*agape*).

Love feast A common meal shared by the members of the early church. In some instances it occurred prior to observance of the Lord's Supper (1 Cor. 11:20-21).

Love of God Either God's love for us (in which case the genitive is subjective) or our love for God (in which case the genitive is objective).

Love of man Either human love or love for one's fellow human beings.

Loving-kindness Mercy or steadfast love for another.

Low Church The segment of the Anglican church that is relatively evangelical and does not stress liturgy or apostolic succession.

Lucifer A term used of the king of Babylon in Isaiah 14:12-14 and occasionally used to refer to Satan. Some theologians believe that the passage in Isaiah refers to both the king of Babylon and Satan.

Lundensian school A school of theological thought associated with the University of Lund, Sweden, and emphasizing divine love as the central motif of theology.

Lust A strong desire or craving for something. Although it could originally be understood either positively or negatively, the term has now come to mean a bad desire, particularly, inordinate sexual passion.

Luther, Martin (1483-1546) The major figure in the German Reformation. A Roman Catholic monk who as a result of study of Scripture came to differ with the Catholic church on many points and especially on the doctrine of justification. Luther was eventually excommunicated by the church. While his intention was only to reform or purify the church, his action led to the creation of a new denomination separate from Roman Catholicism.

Mm

Macdonald, George (1824-1905) Scottish theologian and writer best known for his fairy tales and fantasies.

Macedonianism The views about the Holy Spirit held by the Pneumatomachians ("Spirit-fighters"). The sect took its name from Macedonius, Arian bishop of Constantinople.

Macedonians Also known as Pneumatomachians ("Spirit-fighters"), a fourth-century radical Christian group that opposed the doctrine of the full deity of the Holy Spirit.

McGiffert, A. C. (Arthur Cushman) (1861-1933) Church historian at Union Seminary in New York who was a prominent force in the promulgation of theological liberalism. His theology was greatly affected by his contention that a "scientific" history, which excludes the supernatural, is more objective than a history that allows for divine involvement in the world. He was also an advocate of the social gospel.

Machen, J. (John) Gresham (1881-1937) A conservative American Presbyterian theologian who taught at Princeton Seminary until the reorganization of that school in 1929 led to his departure together with Cornelius Van Til, Oswald T. Allis, Robert Dick Wilson, and others to form Westminster Seminary in Philadelphia. Machen was known as an excellent New Testament scholar, apologist, and persuasive proponent of evangelical Christianity. Although he did not call himself a fundamentalist, his thought was much employed by fundamentalists.

M'Cheyne, Robert Murray (1813-1843) Scottish minister who was noted for his personal piety, prayer, compassion, and evangelism. He died at the age of twenty-nine while serving a pastorate in Dundee.

McIntire, Carl (1906-) The major force behind the American Council of Christian Churches.

Mackintosh, Hugh Ross (1870-1936) Scottish theologian and writer whose major position was as professor of systematic theology at New College, University of Edinburgh, from 1904 to 1936. He was a moderate liberal who introduced German scholarship to the British scene. His doctrine of the person of Christ includes a kenotic theory of incarnation. He opposed the penal-substitution theory of the atonement.

McPherson, Aimee Semple (1890-1944) Pentecostal revival preacher and radio speaker. She served as pastor of the Angelus Temple in Los Angeles and helped found the International Church of the Foursquare Gospel.

Macroevolution Evolution in the comprehensive sense: All organisms have derived by evolution from the simplest form or the earliest variety of life.

Macrointerpretation Interpretation that attempts to explain a large number of biblical passages or concepts in terms of one basic concept.

Magnificat, the Mary's hymn praising the Lord for choosing her to be the mother of the Messiah and for honoring his covenant with Israel (Luke 1:46-55).

Maimonides, Moses (1135-1204) A leading Jewish medieval philosopher. His *Guide to the Perplexed* sought to relate theology to philosophy.

Mainz, Synod of Synod of bishops in Mainz, Germany, which in 848 condemned Gottschalk's doctrine of predestination.

Majesty of God The greatness and glory of God.

Majoristic controversy A controversy in Lutheranism between the Philippists and the Gnesio-Lutheran ("true Lutheran") party over concessions made by the Philippists to the teachings of Georg Major (1502-1574), a professor at the University of Wittenberg and pupil of Melanchthon, that good works are necessary to salvation. One of the Gnesio-Lutherans, Nikolaus von Amsdorf, stated that good works (i.e., works performed for the express purpose of attaining salvation) are in fact harmful to salvation.

The Formula of Concord (1577) settled this issue.

Major orders The senior or higher ranks of ordained clergy. In the Roman Catholic Church there are three: priesthood (including the episcopacy), diaconate, and subdiaconate.

Major Prophets The prophetical writers Isaiah, Jeremiah, Ezekiel, and Daniel.

Maker, the A popular reference to God as the Creator.

Mammon An Aramaic word for "riches" or "wealth."

Man The highest of God's earthly creatures—man alone was made in God's image. The term is also used of the male human being in distinction from woman, the female human being.

Man, Age of A reference to the question of how long genuinely human forms have existed upon the earth.

Man, Composite nature of A reference to the idea that human nature is made up of both material and immaterial components.

Man, Divinity of A reference to the idea found particularly in religious liberalism that each human has an element of the divine within.

Man, Doctrine of The theological understanding of human nature and destiny.

Man, Essential nature of The human as

originally created; it contrasts with the human as now found in the fallen state.

Man, Fall of *See* FALL.

Man, Immaterial nature of That part or aspect of human nature that survives death.

Man, Intraspecific development of A reference to the idea that there has been growth and development within the human species; it contrasts with the idea of development from or to another species.

Man, Material nature of That part or aspect of human nature that undergoes physical death.

Man, Modern *See* MODERN MAN.

Man, Natural The human in the unredeemed condition, outside of salvation in Jesus Christ.

Man, Naturalistic view of The idea that the human is simply a part of nature.

Man, New A term used by Paul of the regenerate human being (Eph. 4:22-24; Col. 3:9-10).

Man, Old A term used by Paul of the unregenerate human being or the human apart from salvation in Christ (Rom. 6:6; Eph. 4:22-24; Col. 3:9-10); it contrasts with the new man.

Man, Question of the origin of The question of whether the human was directly created by God or descended from some other living form either in the entirety of human nature or in physical nature.

Mandaeans Present-day adherents to Gnosticism who live in southern Iraq.

Mandaeism Basically Gnostic thought that includes, in syncretistic fashion, elements of Persian dualism, Platonism, astrology, Judaism, and ancient Babylonian and Egyptian teachings.

Manduction A reference to the idea that Jesus' body is actually eaten in the Lord's Supper.

Mani (ca. 216-277) Persian philosopher who combined Persian, Christian, and Buddhist ideas to form Manichaeism, a dualistic religion.

Manichaeism A dualistic philosophy that became a major religion in the ancient world. There was a strong emphasis on asceticism as a means of salvation.

Man of lawlessness The Antichrist (2 Thess. 2:3).

Man of sin A translation sometimes given of Paul's reference in 2 Thessalonians 2:3 to the Antichrist. "Man of lawlessness" is a better translation.

Manson, Thomas Walter (1893-1958) British biblical scholar and author who taught at the University of Manchester. His major emphasis was on the life and teachings of Jesus.

Maranatha An Aramaic expression found in 1 Corinthians 16:22 that may be translated either as an exhortation ("Our Lord, come") or as an indicative ("Our Lord has come").

Marburg Colloquy Meeting held between the Lutherans and the Zwinglians in 1529 to try to resolve the differences between them. While agreement was reached on fourteen of the fifteen articles, there was irreconcilable difference on the question of whether the body and blood of Christ are actually present in the bread and wine. The colloquy led to separation rather than agreement.

Marcel, Gabriel (1889-1973) French Christian existentialist philosopher.

Marcion (died ca. 160) Second-century heretic who distinguished sharply between the Creator God in the Old Testament and the Redeemer God in the New Testament. He substantially modified the New Testament to fit his views.

Marcionism The theological views taught by Marcion emphasizing the difference between the two Testaments.

Marcionites A group founded by Marcion in A.D. 144 when he was excommunicated from the church in Rome. The group was characterized by strict asceticism, distinctive practices of the sacraments, and an abbreviated Scripture.

Mariolatry Worship of Mary, the mother of Jesus.

Mariology Teachings regarding Mary, including (in Roman Catholicism) the immaculate conception and bodily assumption.

Maritain, Jacques (1882-1973) French philosopher who was the leading neo-Thomist of the twentieth century.

Mark of the beast A problematic expression found in Revelation 13:16-18, 14:11, 16:2, 19:20, and 20:4. Involving some type of brand or stamp, it seems to be identified with the number of the beast, 666 (Rev. 13:18). There has been much speculation as to its meaning and the identity of the beast.

Marks of the church Signs or qualities that indicate the presence of the true church.

Maronites A small Christian group in Lebanon. Although they are Roman Catholic, they have their own liturgy.

Marriage The uniting of two persons of the opposite sex in a union that is physical, emotional, and, in the Christian view, spiritual.

Marriage feast of the Lamb A metaphor depicting the consummation of the kingdom of God (Rev. 19:7-9).

Martyr Originally, one who gives witness to religious truth; in the later sense of the term, one who seals that testimony with his or her death.

Marx, Karl (1818-1883) German social philosopher whose work *Das Kapital* has become the virtual bible of communism. His setting Georg Hegel's dialectical view of history on a materialistic basis has come to be known as dialectical materialism.

Mary, Assumption of The Catholic dogma promulgated in 1950 by Pope Pius XII that the Virgin Mary did not die but was taken body and soul into heaven.

Mass A Roman Catholic term for the Eucharist or Lord's Supper. Since the fourth century, it has referred to the whole of the service in which Communion is observed.

Materialism The teaching that the ultimate reality is matter.

Materialism, Dialectical The philosophy underlying communism: Inherent forces within matter are working through a dialectical pattern to reach the classless society. Dialectical materialism is an adaptation of the philosophy of Georg Hegel.

Mathews, Shailer (1863-1941) Baptist educator and theologian who was a major proponent of theological liberalism. He was professor of theology and dean at the Divinity School of the University of Chicago.

Matins Part of the daily office: prayers said at midnight. The term is used in the Church of England for the service of Morning Prayer.

Matter In common language, concrete, physical, perceptible things. In philosophical and theological studies, matter is often contrasted with form.

Maundy Thursday The Thursday of Holy Week.

Maurice, John Frederick Denison (1805-1872) Anglican theologian who taught at King's College, London, but was dismissed for his denial of the doctrine of everlasting punishment. He disapproved of theological factions and was in some ways a forerunner of the modern ecumenical movement.

Mediating theology An effort, mostly in German in the middle of the nineteenth century, to find a middle ground between differing theologies.

Mediation The act of attempting to bring reconciliation between two parties.

Mediator One who goes between two parties in an attempt to reconcile them. In the case of Christianity, Jesus Christ is the Mediator between God and the human race.

Medieval scholasticism *See* SCHOLASTICISM.

Meditation, Silent or internal The act of pondering or reflecting on one's thoughts.

Meekness A humility that results in gentleness and moderation in relationships with others.

Meister Eckhart *See* ECKHART, MEISTER.

Melanchthon, Philipp (1497-1560) German Reformer who succeeded Luther as the major theologian of Lutheranism. His *Loci Communes* was the first systematic treatment of Lutheran theology.

Melchiorites Followers of Melchior Hoffmann, a sixteenth-century Anabaptist preacher.

Melchizedek Priest to whom Abraham paid tithes (Heb. 7:9-10). The name means "king of righteousness."

Memorialism The doctrine held by Ulrich Zwingli that the Lord's Supper is merely a commemoration of Christ's death.

Mennonites, the A group descended from Dutch, German, and Swiss Anabaptists. Among their emphases are believers' baptism, purity of life, and nonresistance or pacifism.

Menno Simons (1496-1561) Roman Catholic priest who left the Church of Rome because of its doctrines such as transubstantiation. He emphasized peace, nonresistance, prohibition of oaths, and separation of church and state.

Mental reservations Unexpressed limitations on that which one confesses.

Mercersburg theology A romantic Reformed theology in the middle of the nineteenth century. It is associated particularly with the names of John Williamson Nevin and Philip Schaff, who taught at the German Reformed seminary in Mercersburg, Pennsylvania.

Mercy Compassion, pardon, forgiveness.

Mercy of God *See* GOD, MERCY OF.

Mercy seat A slab of gold on top of the ark of the covenant. Symbolizing God's forgiveness of sins, the blood of atonement was sprinkled on the mercy seat.

Merit The deserving of some good thing.

Messiah Literally, "the anointed one," the leader appointed by God to carry out the special mission of redemption and liberation.

Messianic Pertaining to the work of the Messiah.

Messianic banquet *See* MARRIAGE FEAST OF THE LAMB.

Messianic consciousness A reference to the idea that Jesus was aware of his messianic mission.

Messianism Belief in a messiah.

Metanarrative An all-inclusive explanation or story that claims to be universal in its truth.

Metaphorical concept An idea that is not to be taken literally but figuratively.

Metaphysical gap A qualitative separation between types of beings, as between God and humanity or between humans and the rest of the creation.

Metaphysical union A reference to the idea that the human becomes absorbed into God, becoming essentially one with him.

Metaphysics The branch of philosophy

that deals with questions of the ultimate nature of reality.

Metempsychosis The theory that souls are reincarnated many times.

Methodism The branch or denomination of Christianity founded by John and Charles Wesley. Originating within but later separating from the Anglican church, Methodism emphasized a personal experience of salvation. It involves an episcopal polity.

Metropolitan A bishop who exercises authority over a province rather than a mere diocese.

Microevolution The idea that there may have been some limited development of one form from another through the process of evolution. It contrasts with macroevolution, which holds that the entire creation has developed from one initial form.

Middle knowledge The belief, going back to Molina, that God knows not only everything that will be, but also all the possibilities that could be but are not.

Midrash A Jewish rabbinic commentary on the Hebrew Scripture. There are halachic midrashim, which attempt to expound the deeper meaning of the law, and haggadic midrashim, which are homiletical, devotional interpretations of Scripture.

Midtribulationism The idea that the church will go through the first half of the great tribulation and then be raptured.

Mights One of three classes of angels described by pseudo-Dionysius the Areopagite, a fifth- or sixth-century writer who claimed to be the Dionysius converted by Paul in Athens (Acts 17:34).

Mill, John Stuart (1806-1873) Philosopher who propounded a utilitarian view of ethics: promoting the greatest good for the greatest number.

Millennialism Belief in a substantial period of divine rule on earth. In the most literal form of millennialism, this period is taken to be exactly one thousand years.

Millennialist One who believes in a millennium.

Millennial kingdom In premillennialism, the kingdom to be set up by Christ upon earth during the thousand years following his second coming; in postmillennialism, a reference to the idea that Christ's will shall be done on earth without his being personally present.

Millennium, the Period of a thousand years of Christ's reign on earth.

Miller, William (1782-1849) Baptist minister in New York whose teachings led to the establishment of what is today known as Seventh-day Adventism.

Mind The center of consciousness, thinking, and reason; it contrasts with the concept of body.

Mind, Bundle theory of The view advocated by David Hume that the mind is simply a bundle or collection of perceptions.

Mind, Substance theory of That aspect of the dualism of René Descartes that holds that the mind, like the body, is a distinct substance.

Minister One who serves by teaching and edifying. In common usage today, the term refers to an ordained clergyman; but it is not so restricted in Scripture.

Ministering spirits Angels (Heb. 1:14).

Ministry Service rendered to God or to other people.

Minor orders In Roman Catholic and Eastern Orthodox churches, the offices of acolyte, exorcist, reader (or lector), and doorkeeper (or porter).

Miracle An observable occurrence that, though it does not break the laws of nature, is remarkable in that the laws of nature, if fully understood, could not account for it.

Miracle narratives Scriptural accounts of the occurrence of miracles. They are found particularly in the Gospels.

Miracles, Gift of A spiritual gift that includes casting out spirits and healing bodily ailments (1 Cor. 12:10, 28-29).

Miracle stories *See* MIRACLE NARRATIVES.

Miracle-workers Those who claim to perform miracles. This often entails the claim of a special gift or office as well.

Miraculous conception Usually a reference to the virgin birth of Christ.

Miraculous gifts Spiritual gifts that are quite extraordinary, such as speaking in tongues, healing, and raising the dead.

Missiology The science of missions or of the communication of the Christian faith across cultures.

Mission of Christ The task or purpose for which Jesus came.

Missions The carrying of the message and work of Jesus Christ to others, especially to those of a different culture.

Mission schools Schools maintained on mission fields for the teaching of nationals and also for the teaching of the children of missionaries.

Missouri Synod Lutherans A conservative group of Lutherans in the United States.

Modalism The view that the three members of the Trinity are different modes of God's activity rather than distinct persons.

Modalistic monarchianism A movement that interpreted the Trinity as successive revelations of God—first as Father, then as Son, and finally as Holy Spirit. It began in the third century.

Moderator One who presides over the

business of a group or a particular church entity.

Modern ecumenical movement A movement in the twentieth century to unify believers. It began as a cooperative missionary endeavor to do the work of Christ. In some forms, it is intended to lead to the actual merger of denominations into one larger group.

Modernism Often synonymous with theological liberalism, the attempt to update ancient doctrines, frequently changing their substance in the process.

Modernism, Catholic A twentieth-century liberal movement within Roman Catholicism.

Modernist One who attempts to update or modernize the faith.

Modernist-fundamentalist controversy A twentieth-century controversy between conservative and liberal Christians; it was often carried on within a denomination.

Modern man One who accepts the beliefs and ways of thinking and acting of contemporary society.

Modern theology Theology of the nineteenth and twentieth centuries, beginning particularly with reactions to the thought of Immanuel Kant.

Modus ponens A form of logical reasoning in which, on the assumption that the antecedent implies the consequent, affirming the antecedent means that the consequent can also be affirmed;

in other words, if A implies B, then A being true, B is also true.

Modus tollens A form of logical reasoning in which, on the assumption that the antecedent implies the consequent, if the consequent is false, the antecedent may also be considered false; in other words, if A implies B, then B being false, A is also false.

Mohammed (ca. 570-632) Arab religious leader who, claiming to have received a revelation from God (which was written down as the Koran), became the founder of Islam, which regards him as the final and supreme prophet of God.

Molina, Luis (1535-1600) Spanish Jesuit who developed the theory of middle knowledge.

Moltmann, Jürgen (1926-) Contemporary Protestant theologian at the University of Tübingen who has propounded the theology of hope, which interprets the present, including the present nature of God, in the light of the future or that which will be. Moltmann makes eschatology not merely the last topic of theology but the perspective for the understanding of all theology.

Monarchianism An approach that stressed the unity of God, particularly a movement in the second and third centuries. It took two forms: dynamic monarchianism and modalistic monarchianism. *See* DYNAMIC MONARCHIANISM and MODALISTIC MONARCHIANISM.

Monarchianism, Dynamic A view that Jesus was not of the essence of God, but that God was at work in him.

Monarchianism, Modalistic A view that God was one person, not three, but that he revealed himself successively in three different roles.

Monarchical system of church government Any episcopal type of church government; like a monarchical civil government, it places authority in a particular office.

Monasticism Withdrawal from society into private groups that practice asceticism and other forms of spiritual discipline.

Monergism The view that conversion is accomplished totally by the working of God.

Monism A philosophy or theology that explains everything in terms of one principle; a view that reality is of only one type.

Monistic argument Any argument advanced against the idea that human nature is dualistic or composite.

Monogenism The idea that the entire human race has originated from one common pair.

Monophysitism The doctrine that Jesus had only one nature rather than two. It usually takes the form that the humanity of Jesus was absorbed into his deity.

Monotheism Belief in one God.

Montanism A movement deriving from the teachings of Montanus, especially the view that the Holy Spirit continues to speak through prophecy. Tertullian was a convert to Montanism, which flourished in Asia Minor in the second century and thereafter.

Moon, Sun Myung (1920-) Korean clergyman who is the head of the Unification Church. He published his views in *The Divine Principle*.

Moore, George Edward (G. E.) (1873-1958) English epistemologist and ethicist, and a leading exponent of analytic philosophy.

Moral Pertaining to principles of right and wrong behavior.

Moral actions Deeds that can be labeled ethically right (or wrong).

Moral agents Beings capable of engaging in moral action.

Moral argument for God A proof for the existence of God: God is needed as an explanation for moral values and the moral impulse.

Moral attributes of God Those qualities of God that pertain to his righteous treatment of his creatures. His moral attributes contrast with his sheer natural attributes, such as his knowledge, presence, and power.

Moral character The basic nature of persons with respect to matters of ethical right and wrong.

Moral choice Decisions that relate to matters having ethical significance, as contrasted with matters of mere etiquette or aesthetics.

Moral code A set of rules for moral behavior.

Moral competence Capability of understanding and making judgments in matters of morality.

Moral conduct One's behavior with respect to issues of right and wrong.

Moral conscientiousness The sense that in matters of right and wrong one has certain obligations.

Moral corruption The inability of persons, as a result of the Fall and subsequent sin, to choose rightly in moral matters.

Moral decision A determination having moral significance.

Moral disability *See* MORAL CORRUPTION.

Moral evil Evil within the universe that affects human beings and involves their actions toward each other. It contrasts with natural evil, which refers to features of the natural universe that cause difficulty but do not involve the exercise of human will.

Moral freedom The capability of making choices in matters of right and wrong.

Moral-influence theory of the atonement SEE ATONEMENT, MORAL-INFLUENCE THEORY OF

Moral norms Guides for ethical behavior.

Moral perfection The state of completely fulfilling the requirements of moral law.

Moral preparation In Roman Catholic theology and practice, the preparation of the person before participating in a sacrament. It involves removal of any previous indisposition that may work against the character of the sacrament.

Moral purity of God *See* GOD, MORAL PURITY OF.

Moral qualities Those attributes of God that pertain to his righteous relationship to human beings; they contrast with his natural qualities, his attributes of pure ability, such as his omniscience and omnipotence.

Moral Rearmament A later name for the Oxford Group, a movement stemming from the thought and work of Frank Buchman (1878-1961). It emphasized initially the importance of moral ideals and moral action.

Moral responsibility The condition of being able to distinguish issues of morality and to choose wisely.

Moral structures In the thought of John Yoder and others, those institutions of society that have moral implications; for example, tyrannical government, the market, the school, the courts, racism, and the nation.

Moral theology The Roman Catholic discipline corresponding to what Protestants usually call Christian ethics.

Moralist A student and teacher of morality.

Morality Conduct that is ethical.

Moravian Brethren A pietistic, evangelical, missionary-minded Christian movement beginning in Moravia. John Wesley was converted as a result of his contact with a group of Moravian Brethren.

Mormon, Book of The official authority of Mormonism. It consists of revelations that Joseph Smith claimed to have received. Among its doctrines are the idea that God the Father has a physical body and that humans are destined to evolve into deity.

Mormonism A religious group begun by Joseph Smith in 1830 in upstate New York. Following the death of Smith in 1844, the group divided into the Church of Jesus Christ of Latter-day Saints, which is headquartered in Salt Lake City, Utah, and the Reorganized Church of Jesus Christ of Latter-day Saints, which is based in Independence, Missouri.

Morning Prayer In the Anglican and Episcopal churches, a service that is part of the daily office. It is also known as matins.

Morphological categories Classifications on the basis of form.

Mortal body The body we have that is susceptible to death.

Mortal flesh *See* MORTAL BODY.

Mortalism, Pure *See* PURE MORTALISM.

Mortality Susceptibility to and the reality of dying.

Mortal sin *See* SIN, MORTAL.

Mosaic law The body of rules given through Moses.

Mosaic period The period in Israel's history from the Exodus until the entrance into the Promised Land.

Moses The leader of Israel during the Exodus through whom God revealed the Law. Moses was also the author of the Pentateuch.

Most High A name for God.

Most High, Power of the An expression used of the action of God, as in the announcement to Mary that she would bear the Messiah (Luke 1:35).

Most Holy Place The inner part of the tabernacle or temple. Only the high priest could enter it, and then only once a year on the Day of Atonement to offer sacrifice for cleansing. It is also known as the Holy of Holies.

Mother of God A title given to Mary at the Council of Ephesus in 431. The objection to this term by Nestorius, the patriarch of Constantinople, led to his being deposed. It later came to be used to exalt Mary and is found in Roman Catholic liturgy. The Bible does not use the term but refers to her as the mother of Jesus (e.g., John 2:1; Acts 1:14).

Mott, John Raleigh (1865-1955) American church leader who is regarded as a major force behind twentieth-century ecumenism. He served as general secretary of the International Committee of the Young Men's Christian Association (1915-1931).

Movable feasts Christian holidays the exact dates of which are determined by the phases of the moon. Thus they fall on different dates in different years. An example is Easter.

Münzer, Thomas (ca. 1489-1525) Fanatic Reformer who believed that God speaks directly to Christians, revealing his will through visions and dreams. Usually considered an early Anabaptist, he was a leader in the Peasants' Revolt.

Muratorian canon A manuscript fragment discovered by L. A. Muratori in 1740 that indicates what New Testament books late-second-century Rome considered canonical.

Murder The intentional, premeditated, and malicious taking of the life of a person not deserving nor wishing death.

Murray, Andrew (1828-1917) South African minister who was active in evangelism and in writing over 250 books and pamphlets. His theology was mystically inclined, and his emphasis upon a sec-

ond blessing and divine healing had an affinity with Pentecostalism.

Mutability, Holy *See* HOLY MUTABILITY.

Mysteries Truths not ordinarily known to humans. The New Testament teaches that the mysteries of God have been revealed to humans.

Mystery That which is unknown or not fully comprehended. Paul declares that God has revealed his mysteries so that they are no longer uncomprehended (e.g., Eph. 1:9; 3:3).

Mystery of iniquity A problematic phrase in 2 Thessalonians 2:7 (KJV; "the mystery of lawlessness," NASB, NKJV): The mystery of iniquity is already at work, but is being restrained by someone who will eventually be removed. A wide variety of interpretations and identifications have been given, including the explanation that the Holy Spirit is restraining the work of Satan.

Mystery religions Popular faiths in the Greco-Roman world. Persons who were initiated into these movements were given various truths that were to be kept secret.

Mystical relationship A reference to the view that the relationship between the believer and Christ is so deep and absorbing that the believer virtually loses his or her individuality.

Mystical union According to mystics, a union between a human and God that transcends the usual understanding of the relationship between the believer and God. Some mystics believe that this union is perpetual, others that it is intermittent.

Mysticism A form of religious practice that seeks a direct knowledge of God rather than a discursive or intellectual knowledge of him.

Myth Generally, a literary form or traditional story intended to convey a nonliteral meaning.

Nn

Narrative passages Those segments of the Bible that describe events of a historical nature.

Narrative theology Theology that regards doctrine as essentially of the nature of narrative, rather than rational propositions. Varying versions see the role of narrative as communicational, as the hermeneutical key to the Scriptures, or as possessing heuristic power. Some even believe that postbiblical and contemporary Christian biographies have revelatory value.

National Association of Evangelicals A fellowship of evangelical churches and denominations that was created in 1942 for cooperative action. Harold J. Ockenga was one of the leaders in the formation of this group. Its intention was positive action rather than negative protest, and consequently persons could belong even if they were members of the National Council of Churches (Federal Council of Churches).

National Council of the Churches of Christ in the United States of America A conciliar movement among denominations seeking to work cooperatively. Some within the movement are aiming at a merger of denominations into one unified church.

National Israel Israel thought of as a specific national group.

Nations, Judgment of the *See* JUDGMENT OF THE NATIONS.

Native religions The faiths practiced by the people indigenous to certain geographical areas.

Natural attributes of God Those attributes of God that pertain particularly to his relationship to the physical universe, such as his power, knowledge, and omnipresence.

Natural body The body that humans have prior to death and resurrection.

Natural causation Production of effects through ordinary rather than supernatural factors.

Natural contingency In the thought of Reinhold Niebuhr, a reference to the fact that human beings are finite and therefore insecure and dependent.

Natural ethic Principles of conduct that, instead of being received by special revelation, are developed simply by an observation of the world.

Natural evil Evil that is part of the creation independently of human will, such as disease, earthquakes, and floods.

Natural impulses The tendency or inclinations that we have simply by virtue of our sinful human nature.

Naturalism The belief that the system of nature is the whole of reality.

Natural law The basic principles found within nature, such as the law of gravity.

Natural man *See* MAN, NATURAL.

Natural processes Series of occurrences within the physical universe.

Natural realm The physical universe and the laws governing it.

Natural religion A belief system developed from observation of the physical world. Similar to natural theology, it is often associated with movements such as deism.

Natural revelation *See* REVELATION, NATURAL.

Natural righteousness The justness human beings have by their own effort.

Natural science The study of the physical universe—frequently contrasted with the social sciences.

Natural selection In the thought of Charles Darwin and other evolutionists, the process by which the stronger or fitter members of a group survive.

Natural theology Theology developed apart from the special revelation in Scripture; it attempts to demonstrate certain elements of theology from experience and reason alone.

Nature of God *See* GOD, NATURE OF.

Nature worship Worship of the created universe.

Nazarene One who is a resident of Nazareth; the term is applied especially to Jesus.

Neander, Johann August Wilhelm (1789-1850) German church historian generally regarded as the founder of modern church historiography.

Necessary being That which exists by virtue of having its own power of existence within; that which must exist.

Necessity That which must come to pass as a result of certain inherent laws of reality.

Negation, Method of An approach to investigating the attributes of God by excluding all the imperfections of human nature and ascribing to God their opposite perfections.

Negative theology Theology constructed by means of negation; in a more general sense, an orientation to theology that is primarily polemical and concerned with refutation of other views than with affirming its own.

Negligence, Sins of *See* SINS OF NEGLIGENCE.

Neill, Stephen Charles (1900-1984) British Anglican missionary, educator, scholar, and writer.

Neoevangelicalism *See* NEW EVANGELICALISM.

Neo-Kantians Philosophers and theologians who follow, in general, the approach of Immanuel Kant. They may well make some revisions of Kant's general approach.

Neonomianism A movement that arose in the early-eighteenth-century Church of Scotland during a controversy over the relationship between law and gospel in salvation. The Neonomians maintained that the gospel is a new law replacing the Old Testament law: The legal conditions of faith and repentance must be met before salvation can be offered.

Neoorthodoxy A system of theology associated particularly with Karl Barth, Emil Brunner, and Reinhold Niebuhr. While accepting biblical criticism and a certain amount of existential thought, the movement emphasized divine transcendence as well as human sinfulness and need. It represented a return to modified forms of orthodox doctrines as contrasted with the liberal abandonment of such doctrines.

Neo-Pentecostalism Later charismatic movement originating around the middle of the twentieth century. Unlike earlier Pentecostalism, it is found in major denominations rather than merely in isolated groups. The phenomena of the later movement often occur in more restrained form than in classical Pentecostalism.

Neophyte In the early church, a newly baptized convert who wore the white baptismal robe for eight days.

Neo-Platonism Later modified forms of the thought of Plato. Associated with thinkers such as Plotinus, it stressed that the fundamental character of reality is ideal or mental and often included the idea of creation as being an emanation from the nature of God.

Neopragmatism A philosophy associated with Richard Rorty. Rather than regarding truth as correspondence with reality or asking for justifying reasons for ethics, this view simply looks for what "works out."

Neo-Thomism Later modified forms of the thought of Thomas Aquinas.

Nestorianism A heretical view in effect dividing Christ into two persons, divine and human.

New Age religion A growing religion in the West that has roots in Eastern pantheistic philosophy. It sees sparks of the divine in all persons.

New birth Regeneration; God's giving new life to the believer.

New body The body that will be received in the resurrection.

New commandment An expression used of the divine injunction to love one another (John 13:34; 1 John 2:8).

New covenant The Christian dispensation and the economy introduced by Christ and the apostles. In some cases, the new covenant is a synonym for the gospel of Christ.

New creation A reference to the regeneration that takes place in the believer and also to the future remaking and restoring of the entire creation.

New earth That which together with the new heaven will be brought to pass in the future by the work of God (Rev. 21:1). *See* also NEW HEAVENS AND NEW EARTH.

New England Fellowship A fellowship of evangelicals organized in 1929 to implement Bible conferences, camps, and radio broadcasting. A nationwide session in April 1942, for which the leadership of this group had called, resulted in the present National Association of Evangelicals.

New England theology A theological tradition arising out of the work of Jonathan Edwards and continuing into the nineteenth century. The movement was characterized not so much by agreement on a common set of doctrines as by shared interest in issues such as the freedom of the human will and the morality of divine justice.

New evangelicalism A development in American evangelical Christianity following World War II; it emphasized the need for a greater intellectual involvement and for a social application of the gospel. Among the leaders of the early form of the movement were Harold J. Ockenga, Edward J. Carnell, Carl F. H.

Henry, Bernard Ramm, Vernon Grounds, and Billy Graham. In the later form sometimes referred to as neoevangelicalism, there were some modifications of classic doctrines, such as the inerrancy of Scripture.

New Hampshire Confession One of the foremost Baptist statements of faith. Published by a committee of the New Hampshire Baptist Convention in 1833, it contains eighteen short articles.

New Haven theology A late form of New England theology developed to meet the needs of the Second Great Awakening. It was associated particularly with the names of Timothy Dwight and Nathaniel Taylor. In its later forms the New Haven theology departed from the Calvinistic theology of Jonathan Edwards.

New heart An expression used by Ezekiel (18:31) in urging his hearers to repent of their sins: He encourages them to get a new heart and a new spirit. This is seen by some as an Old Testament reference to the doctrine of regeneration.

New heavens and new earth The redeemed and renewed universe of the future (Rom. 8:18-21; 2 Peter 3:13; Rev. 21:1-8).

New hermeneutic An interpretive approach that draws on existential philosophy to understand the Bible in terms of its effects upon a person rather than its objective meaning. The new hermeneutic is associated with names like Rudolf Bultmann, Ernst Fuchs, and Gerhard Ebeling.

New Israel The church.

New Jerusalem In Revelation 3:12 and 21:2, a reference to the ultimate state of the church.

New legalism Any approach that seeks to structure the Christian life in terms of certain invariable rules, the keeping of which is regarded as being virtuous.

New life The spiritual life given by Christ to the believer: The deadening effect of sin is negated, and new spiritual ability is instilled.

New Light schism A division within Presbyterianism and Congregationalism in the mid-eighteenth century. The Old Lights interpreted Calvinism rationally, holding that correct theological belief is more important than Christian living. The New Lights, on the other hand, stressed Puritan piety as essential to Calvinistic theology.

New man The regenerate person or believer.

Newman, John Henry (1801-1890) An English clergyman who in 1845 converted from Anglicanism to Roman Catholicism.

New morality A reference to twentieth-century modifications of traditional morality, particularly a greater permissiveness in the area of sexual ethics. The new morality is sometimes related to situation ethics.

New people of God, the The church.

New religious movements A number of religious groups arising in the late 1960s and early 1970s in North America and Europe. Some can best be described as cults; others derive from Eastern religions.

New School of theology A theological development in evangelical Christianity in the mid-nineteenth century. It grew out of the New Haven theology of Nathaniel Taylor and represented a stronger emphasis on human freedom and evangelistic decision. The New School adherents were expelled from the Presbyterian church in 1837 and reunited in 1869.

New search for the historical Jesus A renewal of the attempt to determine the nature of the historical personage Jesus. It was begun by Ernst Käsemann in 1954.

New spirit *See* NEW HEART.

New Testament The twenty-seven books that the church accepts as God's authoritative revelation about the life of Christ and the mission of the church.

New Testament canon An authoritative listing of the books included in the New Testament.

New Testament eschatology The teachings of the New Testament regarding the last things.

New world *See* NEW HEAVENS AND NEW EARTH.

Niagara conferences A series of late-nineteenth-century Bible conferences from which came certain statements of doctrines or lists of fundamentals that contributed significantly to the rise of the fundamentalist movement.

Nicea, Council of (325) An ecumenical council convened to deal with Arianism. The statement issued by the council declared that the Son is of one substance with the Father.

Nicea, Second Council of (787) Ecumenical council that authorized the veneration of images of various sorts, especially those of Christ, Mary, the angels, and the saints.

Nicene Creed A statement of beliefs issued by the Council of Nicea that insisted that the Son is of one substance with the Father. This was a clear rejection of Arianism.

Nicholas of Cusa (1401-1464) German philosopher and cardinal who at the Council of Basel advocated superiority of the council over the pope. He sought reunion of the Eastern and Western branches of the church.

Niebuhr, Helmut Richard (1894-1962) American theologian who taught at Eden Seminary, served as president of Elmhurst College, and then taught at Yale Divinity School from 1931 until his death. He was an advocate of an American version of neoorthodoxy. His most significant work was *The Meaning of Revelation* (1941). Brother of Reinhold Niebuhr.

Niebuhr, Reinhold (1892-1971) Best-known American advocate of neoorthodoxy. He served as a pastor for thirteen years in Detroit and then taught at Union Theological Seminary in New York City. His writings were largely in the area of theological ethics, his two most important books being *Moral Man and Immoral Society* and *The Nature and Destiny of Man*.

Nietzsche, Friedrich (1844-1900) German philosopher whose atheistic philosophy was one of the early forms of existentialism. His thought, especially regarding the superman, was drawn upon by Adolf Hitler and Nazism.

Nihilism A rejection of tradition, morality, and authority; to a large extent, it is philosophical skepticism with respect to both truth and morality.

Ninety-five Theses A list of ninety-five propositions that Martin Luther was prepared to debate. He nailed it to the door of the castle church in Wittenberg, Germany, on All Saints' Day, 1517. This event is often seen as the beginning of the Protestant Reformation.

Nirvana The goal of the Hindu. The cycle of reincarnation ceases, and the individual is absorbed into the Brahma.

Noah Old Testament patriarch who obeyed God by building an ark and was thus spared from destruction in the great flood.

Noetus of Smyrna (ca. 220-ca. 290) Third-century Christian philosopher whom Hippolytus identifies with monarchianism and patripassianism.

Nominalism The medieval doctrine that abstract concepts or universals do not have real existence but are simply names applied to qualities found within specific individual objects.

Nominalists Those who hold the view of nominalism.

Nonbiblical Pertaining to something not found within the Bible and perhaps even contradictory to it.

Non-Catholic Christianity Christianity that is not identified with the Roman Catholic Church; it includes Protestantism and the various Eastern Orthodox churches.

Non-Christian religions World faiths that are contradictory to the Christian religion; for example, Hinduism, Buddhism, Judaism, and Islam.

Non-Christians Those who are not believers in Jesus Christ.

Noncompatibilistic freedom A reference to the view that human freedom is not consistent with certainty regarding what is to happen, either through God rendering it certain or his foreknowing what will be done.

Noncompetitive endeavor A reference to the view of some liberals that because sin arises in part from individuals in competition with one another, non-competitive or cooperative endeavor will eliminate sin.

Nonconformity Unwillingness to comply with the established religion. Thus groups that are conformists in one state may be nonconformists in another.

Nondenominational church A church that does not identify itself with any particular confessional or organizational stance. It may sometimes identify itself as a community or Bible church.

Nonelect Those who have not been chosen by God for salvation.

Noneschatological view The view that something (e.g., a particular portion of Scripture or perhaps all of Christianity) is not eschatological in nature.

Nonliturgical Christian groups Groups that do not practice a fixed form of worship, sometimes in reaction against more liturgical groups. The Puritans in England are an example.

Nonmiraculous Jesus A reference to the belief that Jesus was purely human and his actions (including the apparent miracles) can be explained on natural grounds without appeal to the supernatural. This belief is often the result of applying to the Gospels a particular hermeneutic that removes the miraculous elements.

Nonperfectionist denominations Groups that do not teach that one can attain complete or perfect spirituality within this life.

Norm A measure or standard of belief or action.

Normative authority Authority that is binding upon us in terms of what we are to believe and do; it contrasts with historical authority, reliability in telling us what was normative for others or what happened at another period of time.

Northfield conferences A series of summer Bible conferences initiated by D. L. Moody in Northfield, Massachusetts, his boyhood home.

Novatianism A schismatic movement within the church from the middle of the third century until the sixth century. The movement practiced strict discipline and insisted that Christians who during the Decian persecutions (249-251) had offered sacrifices in the name of the emperor should not be accepted back into church fellowship.

Numerology, Biblical The study of the significance of various numbers in Scripture.

Numinous, The That which cannot be intellectually grasped or explained. The concept is found especially in Rudolf Otto's *Idea* of *the Holy* and the thought of mystics.

Oo

Obedience Doing that which is commanded. According to Scripture, obedience will inevitably follow from true faith.

Obedience of Christ Christ's willingness to carry out the will of the Father; for example, his submitting to crucifixion.

Oberlin theology A Wesleyan theology emphasizing perfectionism. It is especially identified with the thought of Charles Finney and the position of Oberlin College in the middle of the nineteenth century.

Objective guilt Guilt that is based on genuine wrongdoing; it contrasts with mere guilt feelings, which may not be appropriate or deserved.

Objective knowledge Knowledge of phenomena that exist independent of the knower.

Objective truth Facts about phenomena external to the person; in the thought of Søren Kierkegaard, facts that, while correctly describing external phenomena, do not really affect the knower.

Oblation Offering presented in worship. The term is particularly used of an inanimate offering in contrast to a sacrifice of a living thing.

Obscenity That which is filthy or lewd.

Occult That which is hidden or secret. The term often refers to practices such as spiritism and fortune-telling.

Ockham, William of SEE WILLIAM OF OCKHAM.

Ockhamists Those who follow the teaching of William of Ockham, particularly with respect to nominalism.

Offering, Burnt SEE BURNT OFFERING.

Offering of incense An offering made twice daily in the outer tent (the Holy Place) of the tabernacle.

Office, Daily (divine) Prescribed daily services of worship, especially in the Roman Catholic and Anglican churches and to a lesser extent in the Lutheran churches.

Officers, Church Officials who have authority to rule or teach in the local church or in fellowships of churches.

Offices of Christ The roles or functions of Christ, traditionally prophet, priest, and king.

Oil, Anointing with *See* ANOINTING.

Old Catholics A group of Roman Catholics who refuse to accept Vatican Council I's decree of papal infallibility.

Old Covenant *See* COVENANT OF WORKS.

Old dispensation The old covenant or God's relationship to humans prior to the coming of Christ.

Old life The life of the person prior to regeneration.

Old Lights *See* NEW LIGHT SCHISM.

Old man The person prior to new birth.

Old nature The sinful disposition of the person prior to regeneration. In a weakened form it continues in the believer, working against sanctification.

Old Princeton theology The theology of Princeton Theological Seminary in the nineteenth century, as enunciated by Charles Hodge, A. A. Hodge, Benjamin Warfield, and others. It was particularly noted for its staunch Calvinism and its strict view of biblical authority, inspiration, and inerrancy.

Old Roman Creed Most important predecessor of the Apostles' Creed, probably developed during the second half of the second century.

Old School theology Theology of traditional American Calvinists from the 1830s to the 1860s. Associated with names like Archibald Alexander Hodge and Charles Hodge at Princeton, the Old School attempted to maintain the strict Calvinistic position.

Old Testament The thirty-nine biblical books that were gathered by the Jews and were generally recognized at the time of Christ as being authoritative.

Old Testament believers Persons who were in a covenant relationship with God prior to the coming of Christ. Some date the end of the era of Old Testament believers to the time of Christ's resurrection; others date it to Pentecost.

Old Testament canon The list of books accepted by the church as God's special revelation prior to the coming of Christ.

Old Testament saints *See* OLD TESTAMENT BELIEVERS.

Oligarchical system of church government A presbyterian type of church polity: Authority is placed in the hands of certain representatives.

Oman, John Wood (1860-1939) A leading British theologian of a strongly liberal perspective. He pastored at Alnwick, Northumberland, and then taught at Westminster College, the Presbyterian theological school at Cambridge.

Omission, Sins of *See* SINS OF OMISSION.

Omnieschatological approach The approach of those who see eschatology throughout all of Scripture or see it as the key to Christianity and the biblical revelation.

Omnipotence, Divine *See* GOD, OMNIPOTENCE OF.

Omnipresence, Divine *See* GOD, OMNI-PRESENCE OF.

Omniscience, Divine *See* GOD, OMNI-SCIENCE OF.

Oneness of God *See* GOD, ONENESS OF.

Only begotten An expression emphasizing Christ's uniqueness as the Son of God (John 3:16). We humans are "children of God" in a qualitatively different sense.

Ontological argument An argument drawing on pure logical thought rather than sensory observation of the physical universe to prove the existence of God. A usual form is that God is the greatest of all conceivable beings. Such a being must exist because if he did not, one could still conceive of a greater being—namely, an identical being that also has the attribute of existence. Anselm and René Descartes are two of the most famous proponents of the ontological argument.

Ontological deity of Jesus A reference to the view that Jesus Christ actually possessed all of the qualities of deity; this view contrasts with the functional approach, which says simply that he did the work of God or acted on behalf of God.

Ontology The study of being.

Open theism Rejecting the classical view of God's immutability and omniscience, this theology holds that God grows, discovers things he did not know, and changes his mind. God has taken the risk of creating humans, whose actions he cannot necessarily foreknow.

Openness of God See OPEN THEISM.

Ophites A Gnostic sect that venerated the serpent, teaching that God was bad and the serpent good.

Opportunity, Universal *See* UNIVERSAL OPPORTUNITY.

Oppression Exploitative control of the powerless classes by the powerful. In liberal theology, it is the major dimension of sin.

Opus operatum See EX OPERE OPERATO.

Oracle of Delphi Greatest of the Greek prophetic shrines. Several methods of divination were employed, including strange language resembling the tongue-speaking phenomenon in Christianity.

Oral tradition That which is passed on by word of mouth rather than being written down. The Roman Catholic Church regards oral tradition as a second source of knowledge transmitted from the apostles, the first being Scripture.

Oral transmission The passing on of teachings and narratives by word of mouth rather than in written form. During the church period prior to the writing of the Gospels, information about the life of Christ was passed on orally.

Order of salvation The traditional sequence of discussions of the different aspects of salvation; for example, conversion, regeneration, justification, sanctification.

Orders, Holy The major offices of ministry in episcopal (Anglican, Roman Catholic, and Eastern Orthodox) churches; for example, bishop, priest, and deacon. Admission to these holy orders is by ordination.

Ordinance A practice established by Jesus Christ with the command that it is to be carried out. It is engaged in today as a memorial or as an act of obedience rather than as a sacrament. The term is used by nonsacramental traditions of Christianity to refer to certain practices, particularly baptism and the Lord's Supper.

Ordination The act of setting a person apart for ministerial office. Sacramentalists believe it confers certain powers of ministry. Others regard it as simply a public recognition of what God has already done.

Ordo salutis See ORDER OF SALVATION.

Organic unity An actual organizational connection, as in official church membership or the merger of churches into one corporate whole; it contrasts with spiritual unity, which is simply an agreement in matters of belief and practice.

Organized church The church existing in visible form with governmental structures and official membership lists.

Origen (ca. 185-254) A leading theologian in the early Greek church. His major writings were *Against Celsus* and *Fundamental Doctrines (De principiis)*. He believed that Christians are free to speculate on everything but the cardinal doctrines spelled out in Scripture. Among his speculations was a belief in reincarnation and the ultimate restoration of all beings, even the devil and his angels, to God. Three centuries after his death Origen was declared a heretic by the church.

Origenism Theology related to the teachings of Origen, particularly the belief in an eventual complete restoration of all things.

Original righteousness The uprightness or moral goodness of humans as first created by God. The human race lost this original righteousness as a result of Adam's fall.

Original sin The effect of the sin of our predecessors, and particularly of Adam, upon us. Affecting our behavior independent of and prior to any action of our own, original sin may include both corruption of human nature and guilt (or liability to punishment).

Origin of man The beginning of the human species. Whether it occurred by direct creation by God or evolutionary development from preexisting forms of life remains a question of debate between theologians and scientists.

Origin of the soul The question of whether each individual soul is directly created by God or is generated along with the body at the moment of conception.

Origin of the universe The beginning of the physical world. The means involved—whether a direct creation by God, an explosion of a compacted collection of matter, or whatever—is debated by theologians and scientists.

Orr, James (1844-1913) Scottish theologian and apologist for a moderate form of Calvinism. His most significant books include *The Resurrection of Jesus*, *God's Image in Man*, *The Problem* of *the Old Testament*, *Revelation and Inspiration*, *The Christian View* of *God and the World*, and *The Virgin Birth* of *Christ*.

Orthodox Literally "straight" or "proper," that which is in accord with correct doctrine or practice as established by an authority. The term may also mean simply "conventional," as opposed to "unconventional." Or it may refer to the Eastern branch of Christianity, which separated from the Latin Roman Catholic Church.

Orthodox Presbyterian Church A group that arose out of the Presbyterian Church in the United States of America in 1936. Separation followed the formation of Westminster Seminary and of an independent mission board by J. Gresham Machen and others.

Orthodox spirituality Religious observance as found within the Eastern Orthodox tradition, combining mysticism and an emphasis on contemplation with a deep liturgical interest in the sacraments and celebration of the church calendar.

Orthodox theology Theology that is in agreement with some officially established standard of belief.

Orthodox tradition The theological tradition of the Eastern Orthodox churches; also, the doctrines that have come to be regarded as the basic teachings of Scripture, such as the Trinity, the deity of Christ, the authority of Scripture, human sinfulness, and the need of regeneration.

Orthodox view The conventional, traditional, or correct position.

Orthodoxy The body of doctrines taught by Scripture, such as the deity of Christ, the Trinity, and the authority of Scripture; also, the segment of Christianity holding these doctrines. In addition, the term is used to refer to the Eastern branch of Christianity.

Osiander, Andreas (1498-1552) German theologian, Reformer, and follower of Martin Luther. His most significant work, *De Justificatione*, published in 1550, led to controversy. His understanding of justification was that it is not merely a forensic declaration of righteousness, but an actual impartation of righteousness through the indwelling of Christ in the believer. Thus Osiander tended to merge the traditional view of justification with that of regeneration.

Otherworldliness Relatively exclusive concern with personal spirituality or piety rather than with conditions in this world. It is sometimes associated with asceticism.

Otherworldly Pertaining to heaven and spiritual matters rather than to this world and its needs.

Otto, Rudolf (1869-1937) German theologian whose most significant book, *The Idea of the Holy*, emphasizes the numinous, the "ineffable Something" connected with the experience of the divine.

Ousia A word for being, referring especially to the undivided nature of God.

Outer darkness Exclusion from the presence of God. The term is used to describe hell in Matthew 8:12, 22:13, and 25:30.

Outward man A Pauline expression referring to that aspect of human nature that may be wasting away while the believer is being inwardly renewed (2 Cor. 4:16).

Overcoming A reference to the Christian idea that because Jesus has overcome the world (John 16:33), a believer is able to overcome the circumstances of life (Rom. 8:37).

Overseer A literal translation of the Greek word for "bishop"—one who is given responsibility to supervise the work of the church.

Owen, John (1616-1683) English Puritan theologian who strongly emphasized the congregational form of church government. He became a Nonconformist in the 1660s.

Oxford Group *See* MORAL REARMAMENT.

Oxford movement An important reform movement within the Church of England in the nineteenth century. In response to the rationalism, liberalism, and immorality of the day, it emphasized a return to the High Church tradition and to piety.

Ozman, Agnes Student at a Bible school in Topeka, Kansas, who claimed that on January 1, 1901, she received the Holy Spirit when Charles Parham laid his hands on her. She then prayed successively in several tongues unknown to her. This is sometimes regarded as the beginning of the modern Pentecostal movement.

Pp

Pacifism Usually, the position of those who refuse to participate in war; in general, a desire to avoid the use of force, particularly of a violent type.

Paedobaptism The practice of baptizing infants.

Paganism In general, religious and ethical systems other than Christianity.

Pain A sensation of unpleasantness that may be physical, emotional, or mental.

Pain of God theology A theological movement identified with the thought of Kazoh Kitamori, a professor at Tokyo Theological Seminary. In his book *Theology of the Pain of God* (1946), he emphasizes that the pain of God is the central meaning of the Christian gospel: God empathizes with and suffers on behalf of his people. This was an attempt to contextualize the Christian gospel in post-World War II Japan.

Palamas, Gregorius (ca. 1296-1359) Greek Orthodox theologian best known for his defense of hesychasm, which advanced a theology of direct experience of God.

Paleontology The study of fossil records as a means of attempting to determine the past.

Paley, William (1743-1805) Anglican theologian who taught at Christ's College, Cambridge. Quite liberal in theology, he believed that many of the 240 distinct propositions in the Thirty-nine Articles of the Church of England are inconsistent with each other. His most notable work was *A View of the Evidences of Christianity*. In that volume and in his *Natural Theology* he presents teleological arguments for the existence of God.

Palm Sunday The Sunday on which Christ's triumphal entry into Jerusalem is commemorated. It occurs the week before Easter.

Panentheism The belief that God is in, but is not to be equated with, everything that exists. By contrast, pantheism is the belief that God is all and all is God.

Panlogism The concept found especially in Hegelian philosophies that the ultimate reality is mental or rational in nature.

Pannenberg, Wolfhart (1928-) Theologian at the University of Munich whose rational, historically based theology represents a reversal of the Bultmannian approach.

Pannenberg circle A group of scholars in several theological disciplines who gathered to do cooperative theology and whose thought was associated particularly with Wolfhart Pannenberg.

Pantheism The belief that everything is divine.

Papacy The office of the bishop of Rome, the supreme pontiff of Roman Catholic Christianity.

Parable A simple story illustrating a spiritual truth. Jesus made extensive use of this teaching device.

Parables of Jesus Stories told by Jesus to illustrate and communicate spiritual truth.

Parachurch organizations Religious organizations created for particular tasks, such as evangelism or the reaching of young people. These organizations do not meet for regular Sunday worship services, administer the ordinances, or display other characteristics of the organized church. Their members frequently belong to various churches.

Paraclete A Greek term used to refer to the Holy Spirit (John 14:16, 26; 15:26; 16:7). It is usually translated "Counselor" or "Comforter."

Paradigm method A method of studying a particular concept by selecting one variety of it as a normative example.

Paradise Heaven or the presence of God.

Paradox An apparent contradiction in which two opposing theses are held in tension with one another.

Paradox, Theology of An existential or neoorthodox theology that sees the presence of apparent contradiction as a positive indication of truth. At this point occurs the crisis of faith.

Paralogism Reasoning contrary to rules of logic.

Pardon Release from the consequences of sin.

Parham, Charles (1873-1929) Head of a small Bible school in Topeka, Kansas, where charismatic phenomena broke out after he assigned the students to investigate the topic of the baptism of the Holy Spirit. This is often regarded as the beginning of the modern Pentecostal movement.

Parish A local congregation or the geographical area it comprises.

Parish view of the church The view that the church is to be identified with the parish or local congregation. This view is held by various groups, including Lutherans.

Parker Society Anglican society named for Matthew Parker, the first Protestant archbishop of Canterbury, that between 1840 and 1855 published the works of leading English Reformers of the sixteenth century. This was an attempt to return to the teachings of the Reformation, especially on justification by faith, and to counter the Tractarian movement, some members of which disparaged the English Reformation.

Parousia The second coming.

Partial rapture *See* RAPTURE, PARTIAL.

Particularism The idea that salvation is based on individual response to the grace of God; some, then, will be lost. The universalist position by contrast says that God will eventually restore all human beings to fellowship with him.

Particular redemption *See* ATONE-MENT, LIMITED.

Party spirit Divisiveness within Christian groups that results from strong identification with particular leaders. In Corinth, for example, some identified with Paul, others with Apollos, and still others with Cephas.

Pascal, Blaise (1623-1662) French mathematician, scientist, and religious thinker whose most significant ideas were recorded in the posthumous *Pensées* (thoughts on religion and some other subjects). He held that God is not known primarily through reason but is received intuitively by the heart. In his famous wager argument he asserted that prudence requires that we take the risk of faith in God.

Pascal's wager An argument made by Blaise Pascal in an attempt to jar the complacent or indifferent into thinking about the seriousness of the decision for or against Christ: We are betting either that there is a God or that there is not. If we incorrectly wager that there is a God, we have lost nothing; but if we correctly wager that there is a God, we have gained infinitely. On the other hand, if we correctly wager that there is no God, we have lost nothing; but if we incorrectly wager that there is no God, we have lost infinitely.

Paschal controversy Controversy regarding the fixing of the dates for Good Friday and Easter.

Passion Inner emotional experiences. In the thought of Søren Kierkegaard, inward passion rather than objective certainty is the correct measure of truth and faith.

Passion of Christ Christ's suffering, particularly the crucifixion.

Passover The initiatory event of the Exodus, when the angel of death took the firstborn of the families of Egypt but spared the firstborn of the people of Israel, who had marked their doorposts with blood. The event is still commemorated by Jews.

Passover lamb The lamb that was sacrificed at the Passover. In 1 Corinthians 5:7, Paul refers to Christ as our Passover lamb.

Passover meal A meal eaten by Jewish families in commemoration of the Passover.

Pastor A Christian minister in his capacity of teaching, spiritually nurturing, and caring for a local congregation.

Pastorals, Pastoral Epistles The letters of Paul relating to pastoral matters, specifically 1 and 2 Timothy and Titus.

Pastors and teachers One of the spiritual gifts (Eph. 4:11). The two terms are often thought of as referring to the same office.

Pathos Passionate emotion, particularly of sympathetic pity or compassion.

Patriarch The father of a family or chief of a tribe. The title is used of Abraham, Isaac, Jacob, and Jacob's sons, especially Joseph. It is also used in the Roman Catholic and Eastern Orthodox churches of bishops who have been exalted over other bishops. In particular, in the Eastern Orthodox churches a patriarch is a bishop in an especially significant city.

Patriarchal period In the book of Genesis, the period from Abraham through Joseph.

Patripassianism The idea that the Son was actually God the Father manifested in a different form and that, therefore, the Father suffered and died on the cross in the person of the Son.

Patristics The study of the lives and especially the teachings of the church fathers.

Paulicians An Eastern Christian sect that arose in the eighth century. They repudiated Mariolatry, intercession of the saints, the Roman hierarchy, and infant baptism. They were adoptionist in their Christology and valued very highly the writings of Paul.

Paulinism A theology based primarily on the writings of Paul rather than other New Testament authors.

Paul of Samosata Bishop of Antioch from 260 to 272 who was excommunicated by a synod held in 268. A dynamic monarchian, he believed that God worked through Jesus but that Jesus was not the Second Person of the Trinity.

Peace In the Bible, the idea of completeness, soundness, and wholeness. It may refer to health and prosperity and absence of strife, whether internal or external.

Peace offering A voluntary offering that an Israelite could make in addition to the sacrifices for atonement and consecration (Lev. 3; 7:11-38).

Pecock, Reginald (ca. 1395-1460) Bishop of Chichester and one of the early historical critics, arguing in 1450 that the "Donation of Constantine" was not authentic. He also tampered with the Apostles' Creed. Charged with heresy, he recanted and was confined to an abbey with a small pension for the rest of his life.

Pedobaptism The practice of baptizing infants.

Pelagianism The theology stemming from the thought of Pelagius, which emphasizes human ability and free will rather than depravity and sinfulness. In the view of most Pelagians, it is possible to live without sin. The effect of Adam's sin upon his descendants was simply that of a bad example.

Pelagius (ca. 360-420) British monk whose

views that human nature is essentially good and that unbaptized infants are not necessarily condemned brought him into conflict with the thought of Augustine.

Penal-substitution theory of the atonement *See* ATONEMENT, PENAL-SUB-STITUTION THEORY OF.

Penal sufferings Distress and pain experienced as punishment for sin.

Penance A discipline imposed by the church upon sinners who have confessed. It is a sacrament of the Eastern Orthodox and Roman Catholic churches. It involves performing certain acts as partial payment for the guilt of sins.

Penitence Often a synonym of repentance. Penitence may also be thought of as remorse over sin and thus be distinguished from repentance, which is the actual abandonment of the sin.

Penitential works Acts performed as indications of repentance.

Pentateuch The first five books of the Old Testament.

Pentecost From the Greek word for "fifty," a term designating the fiftieth day after the offering of the barley sheaf during the Passover celebration; specifically, the event occurring on the Pentecost following the resurrection of Christ in which the Holy Spirit came upon believers so that when they spoke, the multinational crowd heard the message in their own languages. This is generally accepted as the time of fulfillment of Jesus' promise that he would send the Holy Spirit. (The term also designates the season commemorating that event.)

Pentecostalism A movement that emphasizes both a special baptism of the Holy Spirit subsequent to regeneration and supernatural works of the Holy Spirit such as speaking in tongues and healing.

Pentecostal movement, Modern A movement beginning early in the twentieth century that regarded itself as a renewal of the first-century works of the Holy Spirit.

People of God The community of believers in God—Israel in the Old Testament and the church in the New. Vatican II included among the "people of God" non-Catholic Christians who are "linked" to the church and non-Christians who are "related" to the church.

Perdition Destruction, especially spiritual destruction.

Perfection Completeness or wholeness; in Wesleyan thought, the attainable ideal of not sinning. Other views emphasize the idea of completeness rather than flawlessness.

Perfectionism The view that it is possible to attain a state in which the believer no longer sins.

Perfectionist denominations Denominations of a Wesleyan bent that emphasize that spiritual perfection is to be sought and can be attained in the Christian life on earth.

Perfectionists Christians who emphasize holiness, including the concept that complete sinlessness can be attained within this life.

Perfect state The human condition of innocence and righteousness before the Fall.

Perichoresis Indwelling or mutual interpenetration. An ancient teaching that understands the Trinity as consisting of three persons, so closely bound together that the life of each flows through each of the others. Also used by some regarding the relationship between the two natures of Christ.

Perishable body The physical nature of humans that is subject to death and decay.

Permissive will of God God's allowing humans to commit acts that he himself would never choose.

Perpetual virginity The concept in Roman Catholicism that Mary not only was a virgin at the time of the conception and birth of Jesus, but remained so throughout her life. This means that she had no sexual relations and also that the process of birth did not nullify her physical virginity.

Perseverance, Doctrine of The teaching

that those who are genuine believers will endure in the faith to the end.

Persian mythology Stories found in Persian religion that include a powerful dualism in which the devil and demons are an independent force opposed to God.

Persistence of God *See* GOD, PERSISTENCE OF.

Person, God as The concept that God is not simply a force or an impersonal object, but has the characteristics of a person, such as emotion and will, and is capable of interacting with other persons.

Personal devotions *See* DEVOTIONS, PERSONAL.

Personal ethics The moral decisions and actions of individuals. Personal ethics contrasts with social ethics, which involves social entities and social practices.

Personal idealism A philosophy that stresses that the ultimate reality is persons or selves. This view is particularly associated with the thought of Borden Parker Bowne, Edgar Sheffield Brightman, and L. Harold DeWolf.

Personalism *See* PERSONAL IDEALISM.

Personality of God *See* GOD, PERSONALITY OF.

Personal salvation Salvation regarded in terms of the individual's relationship to

God rather than in terms of changing the structures of society.

Person of Christ The nature and identity of Christ, for example, as God and human. Study of his person is often distinguished from study of his work.

Pessimism A negative estimation, whether of human goodness and capability or of the possibility of the future turning out well.

Peter, Primacy of The idea generally accepted by both Protestants and Catholics that Peter was the first or the leader of the apostles. In Roman Catholicism this idea is the basis of the papacy (Peter was supposedly the first pope).

Peter Lombard (ca. 1100-1160) Medieval theologian who taught at the cathedral school in Paris and became bishop of Paris in 1159. Indebted to both Abelard and Bernard of Clairvaux, his theology involved both logical treatment and devotional commitment. His *Sententiae (Sentences)* was the major textbook in Roman Catholic institutions until the seventeenth century, when it was replaced by Thomas Aquinas's *Summa Theologica*.

Peter Martyr Vermigli (1499-1562) Major Reformer who, having fled from his native Italy in 1542, wrote and lectured in Switzerland, England, and France.

Pharisees Important Jewish religious group in Palestine from the late second century B.C. to the late first century A.D. whose legalism was often the target of Jesus' teachings. Their spiritual leaders were the scribes, and their focal point was the synagogue (their major rivals, the Sadducees, being more temple-oriented). In the early first century A.D., controversy broke out within the Pharisaic ranks between the followers of the conservative rabbi Shammai and the less rigorous Hillel.

Phenomena of Scripture Characteristics of Scripture (e.g., the rounding off of numbers and apparent disagreement between passages) that are potential problems in the formulation of a view of inerrancy.

Phenomenological analysis An examination of things as they appear to us in our experience.

Phenomenology A philosophy that in its contemporary form, stemming particularly from the thought of Edmund Husserl, seeks to bracket out the question of the existence of objects and to intuit their pure essences.

Philippists The followers of Philipp Melanchthon, who were regarded by the Gnesio-Lutherans or "genuine Lutherans" as too ready to compromise with Roman Catholicism.

Philo Judaeus (Alexandrinus) (ca. 20 B.C.-A.D. 42) Jewish philosopher who blended Old Testament thought with Greek Stoicism and Platonism. Much early Christian exposition of Scripture was influenced by his work.

Philosophical theology Theology that employs the resources of philosophy. This may involve either reflecting on the philosophical issues of theology, such as the existence of God and the problem of evil, or drawing more content from philosophy than from Scripture.

Philosophy Literally, "love of wisdom." Reflection on some of the major issues of life, including what is real, how truth is known, and what we are to do.

Philosophy, Analytical An attempt to shift the focus of philosophy away from its traditional issues (what is right, what is true, what is beautiful) to simply the meaning and function of language. The term is attached especially to a twentieth-century movement.

Philosophy of religion Philosophical scrutiny of and reflection on the nature and grounds of religion. As such, it is a branch of the broader discipline of philosophy.

Photian schism A ninth-century dispute between Eastern and Western Christianity that began when Photius, a professor of philosophy, was appointed patriarch of Constantinople. The dispute was both political and doctrinal, the latter relating to matters such as celibacy of the clergy, fasting, anointing with oil, and particularly the question of the double procession of the Holy Spirit.

Physical circumcision *See* CIRCUMCISION, PHYSICAL.

Physical creation That which God has brought into being that has a material or bodily character—that is, location, extension in space, tangibility, and so forth.

Physical death The termination of life in the human body, involving a breakdown of the psychosomatic unity of the person.

Physical evil *See* NATURAL EVIL.

Pictorial-day (literary-framework) theory An interpretation of the account of the six days of creation (Gen. 1) as a logical rather than chronological presentation. The sequence, then, need not be correlated with geology.

Pietism A variety of Christianity that emphasizes personal experience.

Pietism, German A movement beginning in the seventeenth century in reaction to Lutheran scholasticism. It emphasized personal faith and devotional life and sometimes tended toward anti-intellectualism. Philipp Spener and August Francke were major voices in the movement.

Pietistic approach to the doctrine of the church Defining, analyzing, and evaluating the church in terms of the spiritual experience and condition of individual members.

Pietists Christians who stress individual commitment to Christ, emphasizing the experiential dimension, personal study, holiness, seriousness, and dutifulness in religion.

Pit, Bottomless *See* BOTTOMLESS PIT.

Plain meaning The simplest or most obvious interpretation of a portion of Scripture.

Plato (427-347 B.C.) Greek philosopher active in Athens. A disciple of Socrates, he emphasized the reality of the ideal rather than the empirical. Plato has had a profound influence on Western philosophy and also on much Christian theology.

Platonism The philosophy stemming from the thought of Plato; it emphasizes the reality of ideals or of concepts as over against empirical entities.

Pleasure, God's good *See* GOD, GOOD PLEASURE OF.

Plenary inspiration *See* INSPIRATION, PLENARY.

Plenary sense *See* SENSUS PLENIOR.

Pleroma Greek word meaning "fullness" or "completeness."

Plerosis Greek word meaning "fullness."

Plotinus (ca. 205-270) Probably the most creative and influential neo-Platonic thinker. He emphasized that all things have emanated from God.

Plymouth Brethren A group that originated in Dublin, Ireland, but formed its first congregation in Plymouth, England, in 1831 as a reaction against the established Church of England. The services are simple, and there are no ordained clergymen. Open Brethren practice believers' baptism, while most Exclusive Brethren observe infant or household baptism. Through the teachings of John Nelson Darby, the Plymouth Brethren have had a great influence upon dispensationalism.

Pneumatomachians Literally, "Spirit-fighters," a fourth-century group that opposed the doctrine of the full deity of the Holy Spirit. They were also called Macedonians.

Pneumopsychosomatic Pertaining to the idea that the human is a unified physical, psychological, and spiritual whole and that each aspect of the person affects the others. Consequently, ministry must be to the whole person.

Polanus, Amandus (1561-1610) Theology professor at the University of Basel and a leading Reformed theologian of the period of Protestant orthodoxy.

Political Israel The political entity or nation of Israel.

Political science A discipline concerned with the study of governmental institutions and processes.

Polity The organization or governmental structure of a local church or fellowship of churches.

Polydaemonism Belief in a plurality of demons or demonical powers.

Polygamy The state of being married to more than one person at the same time.

Polytheism Belief in more than one God.

Pope The head of the Roman Catholic Church; also known as the supreme pontiff and the bishop of Rome.

Pornography Written or visual material that appeals to prurient interests contrary to the accepted standards of a particular community.

Positive thinking An approach to Christianity that stresses that optimistic thought will enable the person to fulfill particular ideals or to live a Christian life.

Positivism A philosophy founded by Auguste Comte that emphasizes the positive sciences and limits human knowledge to sense perceptions. It contrasts with earlier metaphysical approaches to reality.

Positivism, logical *See* LOGICAL POSITIVISM.

Postapostolic age The period of the church following the passing of the apostles from the scene.

Post-Christian era A reference to the concept that in the twentieth century, Christian beliefs and ideals have become obsolete, and we are therefore living in a period when Christianity's influence is greatly diminished.

Postconservative evangelicals Theologians and Christians who, while retaining the designation of evangelical, have modified the traditional evangelical theology in such doctrines as Scripture, the nature of God, and the extent of salvation. Leading theologians of this loose collection of thinkers include such persons as Clark Pinnock and Stanley Grenz.

Postconversion experience Christian experience occurring after conversion; in particular, the idea of a special work or baptism of the Holy Spirit subsequent to conversion and regeneration.

Postcritical Pertaining to a stage of life in which, having gone through a critical period, an individual or culture emerges with a more positive view without reverting to an uncritical view.

Postexilic Pertaining to the life of the Jewish people and nation following the exile.

Postlapsarianism The views of infra- and sublapsarianism.

Postliberalism A movement, associated with Yale theologians such as George Lindbeck and Hans Frei, that moves beyond the older liberal positions but without becoming conservative. *See also* NARRATIVE THEOLOGY and DOCTRINE, RULE THEORY OF.

Postmillennialism The eschatological approach that believes Christ will return following the thousand-year reign. This means he will reign without being physically present.

Postmodernism A late-twentieth-century movement in architecture, literary criticism, philosophy, and theology, as well as music and popular culture. It represents a reaction against the correspondence understanding of truth and universal explanatory schemes, as well as the Enlightenment view of objectivity, rationality, and progress. It tends toward pluralism and relativism.

Postmortem evangelism The doctrine that those who have not heard the gospel during their earthly lives will be given an opportunity to hear and choose after this life.

Postresurrection community Believers following the resurrection of Christ.

Postresurrection person The nature of the human being following bodily resurrection.

Poststructuralism An interpretational theory, following upon structuralism, that places more emphasis upon the role of the interpreter. It has strong affinities with postmodernism.

Posttribulationism The belief that the church will go through the tribulation, not being removed until the return of Christ at the end of that period. Those who hold this view ordinarily are premillennialists.

Poverty Great lack of the material necessities of life.

Power evangelism Evangelism that seeks to persuade by demonstration of contemporary miraculous signs and wonders, especially miracles of healing.

Power of being The capacity or ability to exist; in the theology of Paul Tillich, a synonym for ground of being.

Power of Christ Christ's capacity to enable the believer (see, e.g., 2 Cor. 12:9).

Power of God *See* GOD, POWER OF.

Power of sin Sin's control over unbelievers; it continues to some extent in the lives of believers.

Powers A problematic Pauline concept (Rom. 8:38-39; Eph. 6:12); in the thought of Hendrikus Berkhof and John Yoder, the very structures of society that form the framework within which persons function.

Pragmatics In the semantic theory of Charles Morris, the relationship between a sign and the knower or interpreter.

Pragmatism A movement that emphasizes that the meaning or the truth of any proposition is its practical effects. Beginning in the late nineteenth century and becoming influential in the first half of the twentieth century, particularly in the United States, the movement is associated with Charles S. Peirce, William James, and John Dewey.

Praise Homage and adoration, especially as directed to God.

Prayer Addressing God, whether in praise, petition, or confession.

Prayer of faith Generally, prayer that is uttered in and based on faith; in James 5:15, a prayer that will bring healing.

Prayers for the dead The practice of praying for those who are deceased. It is found in Roman Catholicism and some other varieties of Christianity.

Preaching Declaration of the truth of Scripture to an audience.

Preceptive will of God That which God commands to be done.

Precritical Pertaining to an approach that has not taken critical methodology into account.

Predestination The decision of God in choosing who will be saved and who will be lost. Single predestination is the teaching that God designates only those who will be saved; double predestination is the teaching that he chooses both classes. According to Arminianism, God foresees the faith of those who will believe and then elects them. According to Calvinism, the faith of the believer results from rather than causes God's choice.

Predictive prophecy Declaration of events that are to come to pass.

Preeminence Place of supreme standing. Unlike the Gnostics, who exalted angels, Paul emphasized the preeminence of Christ (Col. 1:15-20).

Preexistence A state of existence before this life. Classical Christianity uses the term for the preincarnate Second Person of the Trinity, who became incarnate as Jesus of Nazareth. Some forms of Eastern religion and Platonism use the term for an existence of human souls before this life.

Preexistence of souls A reference to the belief that the human soul existed before the conception and birth of the individual into this world.

Preexistent nature of Christ The preincarnate status of the Second Person of the Trinity.

Preincarnate humanity A reference to the belief that Jesus was human prior to his conception and birth as Jesus of Nazareth—he brought his human nature with him.

Prelacy From a medieval Latin term meaning "a high-ranking civil or religious official," the type of church government in which control is vested in officials such as archbishops (as in the Roman Catholic church) or metropolitans and patriarchs (as in the Eastern Orthodox church).

Premillennialism The belief that Christ will return and then set up his earthly reign for a period of one thousand years. Some premillennialists hold that this period need not be exactly one thousand calendar years.

Premillennialist One who holds to the view of premillennialism.

Preparation, Moral *See* MORAL PREP-ARATION.

Pre-Pentecost period The period prior to the coming of the Holy Spirit at Pentecost, including the events of both the Old Testament and the portion of the New Testament prior to Pentecost.

Presbyter An office involving teaching or ruling in the local church. In presbyterian forms of government, the presbyters of a given local church form its session, and presbyters from the churches in a given geographical area form its presbytery.

Presbyterianism The Christian movement that follows presbyterian polity and doctrine.

Presbytery In the presbyterian form of church government, the decision-making group for the organization of churches in a local area; it is made up of one lay elder from each local session and all the ministers in the area.

Presence, Bodily The doctrine that the body and blood of Christ are actually present in the bread and wine of the Lord's Supper.

Presence, Divine God's abiding everywhere, especially among his people and in heaven.

Presence of Christ Christ's abiding with his church, as he promised to his disciples (Matt. 28:20; John 14:23; 15:4-7). The nature of his presence in the Lord's Supper has long been a topic of controversy within Christian circles.

Presence of God *See* PRESENCE, DIVINE.

Present body The body that we as humans have in this life.

Present life The life we have on earth in our physical bodies.

Preservation That aspect of divine providence that pertains to God's maintaining in existence all that he has created.

Presuppositions Assumptions that are brought to the process of thought or reasoning; they are sometimes unexamined.

Preterist view An interpretation of eschatology and particularly the book of Revelation that holds that the events referred to had already taken place or were taking place at the time of writing.

Preterition From a Latin term meaning "to pass over"; God's passing over the nonelect, simply allowing them to go their chosen way. Preterition contrasts with the concept of reprobation, according to which God specifically determines that the nonelect shall be condemned.

Pretribulational rapture *See* RAPTURE, PRETRIBULATIONAL.

Pretribulationism The belief that Christ will rapture or remove the church from the world prior to the tribulation.

Preunderstanding A set of conceptions or dispositions that is brought to the process of theological understanding or living.

Prevenient grace *See* GRACE, PREVE-NIENT.

Pride Usually, excessive self-esteem, together with a looking down on others. On occasion the term may refer to a proper sense of self-esteem and satisfaction in one's well-being and accomplishments.

Priest, Christ as *See* CHRIST AS PRIEST.

Priesthood A system of interceding for humans and representing them before God, whether in terms of the Old Testament rites, the priesthood of Christ, or the priesthood of all believers. In sacerdotal religious systems, human priests represent the people.

Priesthood, Aaronic The priesthood conferred on Aaron and his successors by God.

Priesthood of all believers A reference to the idea that each person has direct access to God—there is no need of an intermediary; also, the idea that each believer is capable of acting as a priest for others.

Priestly role One of the three traditional offices of Christ: his act of atonement and his continuing intercession for his people.

Primary sense of Scripture The meaning that the author intended to convey to his original audience.

Primordial being In the thought of the Death of God theologians, and particularly of Thomas J. J. Altizer, a reference to the transcendent God prior to his progressively becoming incarnate in the world.

Primordial God *See* PRIMORDIAL BEING.

Primordial nature of God In Alfred North Whitehead's theology, the unchanging abstract essence of God.

Prince of the power of the air Satan (Eph. 2:2).

Princeton Theological Seminary Presbyterian seminary founded in 1812; until the early twentieth century it was noted as a center of staunch Calvinistic orthodoxy.

Princeton theology, Old *See* OLD PRINCETON THEOLOGY.

Principalities Spiritual forces referred to by Paul (Rom. 8:38; Eph. 6:12).

Principle of Hope (Das Prinzip Hoffnung) Work authored by the Marxist Ernst Bloch that stimulated Jürgen Moltmann to write his *Theology of Hope*.

Privatization of sin *See* SIN, PRIVATIZATION OF.

Probabiliorism In seventeenth-century casuistry, the rule that in cases of moral doubt a line of action shall be considered to fall under the law unless it is more probable that it does not.

Probabilism In Catholic casuistic theology, the view that any solidly probable line of action may be followed even though a contrary action may appear even more probable. This view led to moral laxity, for only slight probability was often accepted as sufficient justification for acting.

Probation The idea that our life on earth is a period of preparation for the life beyond.

Problem of evil *See* EVIL, PROBLEM OF.

Procession of the Spirit A reference to the question of whether the Spirit proceeds from the Father and the Son or only from the Father. The Eastern Orthodox church, objecting to a phrase in the Western version of the Nicene Creed that says the Holy Spirit proceeds from the Father and from the Son, separated from the Western church.

Process of regeneration A reference to the idea that God's transformation of the believer's life is not an instantaneous occurrence but takes place over a period of time.

Process philosophy A metaphysical system that emphasizes growth, progress, and evolution rather than fixed entities or substances. It stems especially from the thought of Alfred North Whitehead.

Process theology A twentieth-century theological movement that, stemming largely from the thought of Alfred North Whitehead, regards reality as primarily processive or evolving in nature. Moreover, God is so closely identified with the rest of reality that he too is thought to be growing and developing.

Proclamation Announcement or declaration of a message; especially, preaching of the Good News.

Professing Christians People who claim to be Christians.

Proglossolalia position The view that speaking in tongues is for Christians in the present day.

Progressive creationism *See* CREATIONISM, PROGRESSIVE.

Progressive education A popular twentieth-century educational theory developed largely by John Dewey on the basis of pragmatist and functionalist views: Education is to take place experientially and to stress the development of the student rather than traditional or classical subject matter and methodology.

Progressive revelation *See* REVELATION, PROGRESSIVE.

Promised Land, the The land of Palestine, which God had promised to his people Israel.

Proof text A text of Scripture offered in support of a particular view or teaching. Sometimes a proof text is rather artificially introduced, its connection to the point at issue being somewhat superficial, or its relationship to its context being disregarded.

Prophecy A speaking forth on behalf of God; in a narrower sense, the declaring of something that is to come to pass.

Prophecy, Gift of One of the gifts of the Spirit (1 Cor. 12:10; 14). Prophets are also referred to as a gift of the Spirit (Eph. 4:11).

Prophet One who speaks forth on behalf of God.

Prophet, Christ as One of the traditional offices of Christ: his teaching and revelatory ministry.

Prophets The occupants of the prophetic office in Israel; particularly, the writers of the prophetic books included in the Old Testament.

Propitiation A reference to the idea that Christ's atonement satisfies the wrath of God.

Propitiatory offerings Offerings to appease the wrath of God.

Propitiatory sacrifice A sacrifice offered to God to appease his wrath.

Propositional view of revelation *See* REVELATION, PROPOSITIONAL VIEW OF.

Proselytism The act of persuading those of another religious group to join one's own. It is sometimes contrasted with evangelization, which is then defined as persuading people who do not have a specific religious commitment.

Protestantism The branch of Christianity that in the sixteenth century separated from the Roman Catholic Church in protest against certain of its practices. In the broadest sense, Protestantism includes all Christian groups that are neither Roman Catholic nor Eastern Orthodox.

Protestant Reformation The break from the Roman Catholic Church especially in the sixteenth century. It began as an attempt to reform the Catholic Church but resulted in separation.

Protestant scholasticism Protestant theology, especially in the seventeenth century, which spelled out minute points of theology, as had Catholic scholasticism in an earlier period. It is also known as Protestant orthodoxy.

Protevangelium of James An apocryphal account of Jesus' birth. Claiming to have been written by James the brother of Jesus, it actually dates from the late second century.

Proverb A brief, wise saying. According to form criticism, the proverbs found in the wisdom literature of various religious cultures follow a comparatively fixed pattern.

Providence, Divine God's care for the creation, involving his preserving it in existence and guiding it to his intended ends.

Prudence Careful, judicious action, or the wisdom that lies behind such action.

Psalmist One who authors a psalm.

Pseudo-Isidorian Decretals A collection of letters supposedly authored by early popes and compiled by Isidore of Seville (ca. 560-636). They were generally regarded as genuine until Nicholas of Cusa (among others) demonstrated their spuriousness.

Psychological conditioning A reference to the idea that human behavior is influenced by psychological factors, and especially by psychological factors in one's background.

Psychological determinism The belief that human behavior is determined not by genetic or physical factors, but by psychological factors.

Psychology The study of the thoughts, emotions, and behavior of human beings.

Psychology, Behavioristic *See* BEHAVIORISM.

Psychology of religion Study that utilizes the categories of psychology to analyze religious experiences.

Psychophysical Pertaining to the relationship of the psychological and physical aspects of human nature.

Psychosomatic unity A reference to the idea that the human is neither pure body nor pure mind but a unity of the two.

Punishment The inflicting of suffering, pain, or loss as retribution for wrongdoing.

Punishment, Everlasting The unending suffering, pain, or loss that God will inflict on sinners.

Pure mortalism A form of the doctrine of annihilationism: Human life is so closely identified with the physical organism that the death of the body results in the cessation of life.

Purgative way In Christian mysticism, the first of the three stages of the mystical experience: One must be cleansed of sin and spiritual hindrances to receive the vision of God.

Purgatory In Catholic eschatology, a place to which persons go upon death who are neither sufficiently holy to go directly to heaven, nor sufficiently evil to be permanently assigned to hell. Through a process of purging experiences, they will be prepared for heaven.

Purification An act of cleansing.

Puritanism A movement aimed at purifying the Church of England, taking it beyond what had been done in the English Reformation. Originating in the sixteenth century, Puritanism involved an emphasis on simplicity of worship and life and on biblical and theological truth.

Puritan spirituality A form of religious orientation focusing on the Word of God, preaching, preparation of the heart to receive the Word, and obedience to God. This nonmystical approach developed in England and New England.

Purity, Church *See* CHURCH PURITY.

Purity of God *See* GOD, MORAL PURITY OF.

Purpose The aim or goal that governs life.

Pusey, Edward Bouverie (1800-1882) Leader of the Oxford or Tractarian movement of the Church of England.

Pythagorean thought The ideas of Pythagoras, who was born probably about 570 B.C. Among the major concepts are that the soul is immortal, philosophy is a means of becoming assimilated to the divine, and the universe is based on mathematical relationships. Much of the influence of Pythagorean thought came through its assimilation by Platonism.

Qq

"Q" The alleged source that the Gospel writers Matthew and Luke used to supplement the material in Mark. "Q" is an abbreviation for *Quelle*, a German word meaning "source."

Quadriga In medieval interpretation, the four senses of Scripture: literal, moral, allegorical, and anagogical.

Quakers *See* FRIENDS, SOCIETY OF.

Qualitative distinction A difference of kind rather than degree; according to the thought of Søren Kierkegaard, there is an infinite qualitative distinction between God and human beings.

Qualities, Absolute Those attributes of God that are independent of his relationship to created objects and persons.

Quantum mechanics An inclusive twentieth-century theory in physics, comprising many specific theories, according to which only statistical probability, not exact prediction, of certain behaviors of atomic and subatomic particles is possible. It has been objected to by some physicists, including Albert Einstein.

Quenstedt, Johannes Andreas (1617-1688) German Lutheran theologian of the Protestant scholastic or Protestant orthodox period.

Quickened with Christ A Pauline reference to the believer's being made spiritually alive or resurrected with Christ (e.g., Eph. 2:5).

Quietism Any approach that emphasizes contemplative passivity. In particular, a form of Roman Catholic mysticism in the seventeenth and eighteenth centuries.

Qumran The Essene community to which the production of the Dead Sea Scrolls is generally ascribed.

Rr

Rabbi A person qualified to teach the Jewish law.

Rabbinic Pertaining to the teachings and practice of the rabbis.

Rabbinic Judaism The type of Judaism taught by the rabbis.

Rabbinic theology Theology developed and passed on by the Jewish rabbis.

Racial prejudice Discrimination against those of a different ethnic background; it results from regarding them as inferior to one's own race.

Racial sin A reference to the fact that in Adam the entire human race sinned collectively.

Racovian Catechism Catechism drawn up in Racow, Poland, in 1605 by the followers of Faustus Socinus. It espoused an example theory of the atonement and was a forerunner of modern Unitarianism.

Radical Reformation The left wing of the Reformation or the Third Reformation; that is, those not included in the Lutheran and Reformed movements. It particularly involved the Anabaptists.

Radical theology Theology that takes an extreme position; especially, the Death of God theology in the mid-1960s.

Rahner, Karl (1904-1984) Liberal Roman Catholic theologian whose thought influenced Vatican Council II. He broadened the conception of the people of God to include some who have no formal connection with the church.

Raised with Christ A Pauline expression in Romans 6:1-11: The believer, having died and having been buried with Christ, will also be raised with him.

Ramm, Bernard (1916-1992) Baptist theologian and apologist whose writings contributed to the movement known as the New Evangelicalism.

Ransom theory of the atonement See ATONEMENT, RANSOM THEORY OF.

Rapture, the In premillennialism, Christ's removal of the church from the world. It is variously maintained that it will occur prior to, during, or following the great tribulation.

Rapture, Midtribulational view of the The idea that the church will go through half of the tribulation and then be raptured by Christ.

Rapture, Partial A reference to the idea that some persons will be raptured early and others later: The time depends on their readiness.

Rapture, Posttribulational view of the The doctrine that the church will go through the great tribulation and then will be caught up to meet Christ.

Rapture, Pretribulational view of the The idea that Christ will remove the church from the world prior to the great tribulation.

Rashdall, Hastings (1858-1924) English liberal theologian and personal idealist.

Rationalism Any emphasis on the role of reason. Epistemological rationalism is the theory that knowledge is gained through reasoning rather than through sense experience. Theological rationalism is basically the belief that reason has the capacity either to prove the truth of Christianity's claims or to interpret its contents. A more radical form of theological rationalism maintains that reason can discover spiritual truths and that only truths thus discovered should be accepted.

Rationalist One who emphasizes the role of reason.

Rauschenbusch, Walter (1861-1918) American Baptist pastor and educator sometimes referred to as the father of the social gospel. He taught at Rochester Theological Seminary.

Realism In medieval philosophy the idea that universals or general concepts have an existence separate from specific concrete entities. This view drew on the philosophy of Plato.

Realism, Scottish *See* SCOTTISH REALISM.

Realistic-headship view of the imputation of sin The belief of Augustine and others that all persons were seminally present in Adam, who was in effect the undistributed human race. When Adam sinned, therefore, all of us were actually present and participated in the act, though not individually and self-consciously.

Realized eschatology *See* ESCHATOLOGY, REALIZED.

Real presence of Christ The idea that the body and blood of Christ are actually physically present within the bread and wine of the sacrament of the Lord's Supper.

Reason The power of thinking, comprehending, and inferring.

Reatus culpae Liability to guilt or blame.

Reatus poenae Liability to punishment. The Protestant scholastics refused to distinguish *reatus culpae* from *reatus poenae.*

Rebaptism Baptism of a person who has already been baptized. It is often the administering of believers' baptism to a person who was baptized as an infant, or baptism by a different mode, particularly immersion.

Rebellion One of the biblical words for sin; it stresses unwillingness to submit to the power and authority of God.

Recapitulation The idea found especially in the thought of Irenaeus that Christ "recapitulated" humanity. This has been interpreted to mean either that Christ retraced the steps of Adam and humanity or that Christ comprehended or comprised in himself the whole of humanity.

Rechte Lehre Literally, "correct teaching" or "correct doctrine," a Lutheran emphasis in the period of Protestant scholasticism.

Recompense *See* REWARD.

Reconciliation The bringing together of two parties that are in dispute; particularly, Christ's bringing God and humanity together, the result of which is salvation.

Reconstituted body The body that believers will have in the resurrection; there will be some continuity with the body possessed in this life, but there will also be some significant differences.

Reconstruction A movement, associated with persons such as Gary North and Greg Bahnsen, that seeks to make biblical teachings the basis of public law and morality. Another name for this is theonomy.

Rector In Episcopalianism, the clergyman in charge of a parish; in Catholicism, the head priest of a church or other religious institution; also, the head of a school or university.

Reformed theology Theology that emphasizes the Calvinistic approach, especially with respect to the matter of salvation. It is often accompanied by a

presbyterian type of church government.

Reformed tradition The customary beliefs and practices of the Reformed churches as contrasted with Lutheran and other traditions. They derive especially from Switzerland, the Netherlands, and Scotland.

Regenerate Persons who have been born again.

Regeneration The work of the Holy Spirit in creating a new life in the sinful person who repents and comes to believe in Christ.

Regula fidei See RULE OF FAITH.

Reid, Thomas (1710-1796) Father of Scottish commonsense realism.

Reincarnation The doctrine that an individual soul may live successive lives incarnated in different persons or even different types of creatures.

Relational theology An approach to Christianity that stresses the relationship of persons to persons rather than doctrinal belief and direct relationship to God.

Realism, commonsense A philosophy associated especially with the thought of the Scottish philosopher Thomas Reid that holds that the objects we perceive are basically as we perceive them. Also referred to as Scottish commonsense philosophy.

Realism, Critical A belief in the existence

of the external world, but holding that we must take into account possible errors of perception.

Relative qualities Those attributes of God that are involved in his relationship to the creation.

Relativism Any view that holds that a concept, meaning, or truth is dependent upon a particular situation or object.

Relativism, Totalistic *See* TOTALISTIC RELATIVISM.

Relics Objects that are claimed to be from the early period of the church, particularly from the lives of Jesus, Mary, or the saints.

Religion Beliefs and practices related to a conviction that there is something or someone higher than the individual human being.

Religionless Christianity The logical endproduct of Dietrich Bonhoeffer's concept of the obsolescence of religion that needs God either to help solve its problems or to explain its mysteries. Religionless Christianity will enjoy God rather than use him.

Religious epistemology The study of how we gain religious knowledge.

Religious liberty Freedom to worship according to one's own convictions and conscience without coercion.

Remarkable gifts Those gifts of the Spirit that are unusual or spectacular in nature.

Remission of sins Release from the penalty for sins.

Remnant Jews who remained faithful to God.

Remonstrants Followers of James Arminius. In a document known as the Remonstrance (1610), they rejected the major Calvinistic dogma.

Renan, Joseph Ernest (1823-1892) French historian of religion who wrote *The Life of Jesus*, in which the origins of Christianity were argued to be legends.

Renewal Reawakening of life, whether in an individual or a group.

Renewal, Church Awakening or revitalization of the church.

Repeated reproduction In Frederic Bartlett's treatment of the spread of oral tradition, the concept of one person's telling over and over again what he or she has personally seen or heard. This contrasts with serial remembering, in which a story is passed on in a chain from one person to another.

Repentance Godly sorrow for one's sin and a resolve to turn from it.

Reprobate Those who are rejected or disapproved; in Scripture, those who have rejected God's offer of grace.

Reprobation God's choice of certain persons for damnation.

Responsibility The state of being capable and therefore answerable or accountable for one's actions.

Restorationism Belief in a return to a previous state of well-being. Either the final redemption of all creation or a universal salvation such as was maintained by Origen may be in view.

Restoration of Israel In the prophetic literature, a special future status for the nation of Israel. It is variously identified: the return from the Exile, the establishment of the modern state of Israel in 1948, and even displacement of the church as God's special people.

Restrainer, the In 2 Thessalonians 2:7, the person or group that holds back the power of lawlessness. The restrainer is variously identified as the Holy Spirit or the church.

Resurrection Usually, the future rising of all believers from the dead; sometimes unbelievers are also in view.

Resurrection, First A problematic reference in Revelation 20:5. Many amillennialists understand it as a spiritual resurrection or new birth; premillennialists understand it as a physical resurrection of believers alone. *See also* RESURRECTION, SECOND.

Resurrection, Second A reference to those who will not come to life until the end of the one thousand years. The concept is an inference drawn from the reference to "the first resurrection" in Revelation 20:5. Premillennialists understand the second resurrection as the bodily resurrection of unbelievers. Amillennialists usually consider it to be a physical resurrection involving all who have died, the first resurrection being a spiritual resurrection.

Resurrection body The body that believers will have upon being raised from the dead. It will have some continuity with the body of this present life, but will also be different in many ways.

Resurrection life Revitalization through the power of the resurrection and in light of the resurrection of Christ.

Resurrection of Christ The historical event and doctrine of Christ's coming back to life on the Sunday following his crucifixion.

Resurrection of judgment The resurrection of unbelievers (John 5:29).

Resurrection of life The resurrection of believers (John 5:29).

Resurrection of the dead Teaching found in both the Old and New Testament that at a future time all the dead will be brought back to life.

Resurrection of the just The resurrection of believers.

Resurrection of the righteous dead The resurrection of believers.

Resurrection of unbelievers Resurrection of those who, having never accepted Christ and been regenerated, died apart from him.

Retaliation The executing of vengeance for a wrong done.

Retribution Retaliation for a wrong done.

Retributive justice A reference to the idea that the justice of God aims not merely to correct sinners, but also to give them what their wrongdoing deserves.

Retributive punishment *See* RETRIBUTIVE JUSTICE.

Revelation The making known of what is unknown; the unveiling of what is veiled.

Revelation, Accommodated A reference to the idea that in making himself known, God adapts to the level of understanding of the recipient.

Revelation, Anthropic Revelation given in human form or in forms familiar to humans.

Revelation, Biblical The revelation that has been preserved in the Scriptures.

Revelation, General Revelation that is available to all persons at all times, particularly through the physical universe, history, and the makeup of human nature.

Revelation, Informational view of The view that God reveals himself by communicating factual information or truths rather than by making a personal encounter. This is sometimes also referred to as the propositional view of revelation.

Revelation, Natural Manifestation of God apart from his special revelation. Natural revelation pertains to those aspects of God's revelation accessible to all persons, such as his power in the physical universe.

Revelation, Nonpropositional view of The conception that God does not reveal truths but reveals himself.

Revelation, Progressive A reference to the doctrine that later revelation is built upon earlier revelation. Thus it contains truths that were not known before.

Revelation, Propositional view of The belief that God has communicated factual information about himself.

Revelation, Special God's manifestation of himself at particular times and places through particular events—for example, the Exodus and Isaiah's vision in chapter 6; also, the Scriptures.

Revenge *See* VENGEANCE.

Reverence for God Respect, worship, and honor of God for who and what he is.

Reversal, Law of *See* LAW OF REVERSAL.

Revival God's renewal of an individual's or a group's spiritual vitality and commitment.

Revivalism Emphasis on definite decisions to convert or to renew commitment.

Revival movements Trends at various times in history that have involved a resurgence or renewal of spiritual interest.

Reward Something given in recognition of past service or accomplishment; especially, what Christians will receive in the final judgment for faithful and righteous living.

Righteous indignation Just anger at a wrong that has been done.

Righteousness The state of being just or morally pure, whether in one's own strength or on the basis of imputed virtue.

Righteousness, Civil *See* CIVIL RIGHTEOUSNESS.

Righteousness, God's The quality or attribute of God by virtue of which he does that which is right or in accordance with his own nature, will, and law.

Righteousness, Human The virtue that humans have as their own accomplishment. In the sight of God it is never sufficient to qualify for salvation.

Righteousness, Original The human state of innocence prior to the fall.

Right hand of the Father Position of authority now occupied by Christ.

Ritschl, Albrecht (1822-1889) German Protestant theologian who, basing his

approach on the views of Immanuel Kant, constructed a form of liberalism that placed emphasis on value judgments rather than theoretical doctrines and upon the ethical and social responsibilities of believers.

Ritschlianism The system of thought attached to the name of Albrecht Ritschl; it emphasized value judgments rather than theoretical doctrines.

Ritual of purification A rite of cleansing administered after the birth of an infant (Lev. 12; Luke 2:22-39).

Robber Synod A council that met at Ephesus in 449 and reinstated Eutyches, declaring the idea that Christ had two natures after his incarnation to be heretical. Objection to this declaration led to the Council of Chalcedon in 451.

Robinson, Henry Wheeler (1872-1945) English Baptist pastor and Old Testament scholar who was principal of Regent's Park College from 1920 to 1942. During his principalship the college moved from London to Oxford.

Roman Catholic A communicant of the Roman Catholic Church; adjectivally, pertaining to the teaching or practice of Roman Catholicism.

Roman Catholicism The term in general use since the Reformation to identify the beliefs and practices of Christians who accept the pope as the head of the church and as its supreme earthly authority.

Roman Creed, Old *See* OLD ROMAN CREED.

Romanticism A literary and artistic movement that emphasized feeling as over against reason. It was particularly popular in the late eighteenth and early nineteenth century.

Royal priesthood A designation of Christians (1 Peter 2:9).

Rufinus (ca. 345-410) Palestinian presbyter who formulated a ransom theory of the atonement.

Rule of faith The sure doctrines of Christianity; the standard against which all beliefs and practices are to be measured. For the Reformers the rule of faith was Scripture alone; for Roman Catholics it is the whole body of official church teaching. The term was first used in the second century.

Ruling elders In churches following the presbyterian form of government, laypersons who serve on the consistory of the local church.

Rural dean Clergyman appointed by a bishop to head a group of parishes. The rural dean serves as an intermediary between the bishop and the clergy.

Ss

Sabaoth Literally, "of hosts," a word used in combination with *Yahweh* or sometimes *Yahweh* and *Elohim* to designate God as the "God of hosts" or "Lord of hosts." The compound name is not found in the Pentateuch, but is very common in the Psalms and the Prophets.

Sabbatarianism Strict observance (often by legal requirement) of one day of the week as a day of worship and rest.

Sabbath The day of rest and worship. Jews observe it on Saturday, most Christians on Sunday.

Sabbatical year In Judaism, every seventh year when landowners were not to sow in the field and the poor were allowed to gather what grew of itself (Exod. 23:10-11; Lev. 25:1-7).

Sabellianism A view deriving from the thought of Sabellius, which was essentially a modalistic monarchianism: God is one being, one person, who successively takes on three different forms or manifestations.

Sabellius A third-century theological teacher whose view of the Trinity was essentially modalistic.

Sacerdotalism The teaching that the act of ordination to certain religious offices conveys the ability to administer the sacraments and thus to dispense grace.

Sacral Pertaining to that which is set apart or separate from the mundane and secular.

Sacrament A religious rite regarded as a means or a sign of grace.

Sacramentalism The view that grace is conveyed through certain religious rites.

Sacramentalists Those people who believe that grace is conveyed through certain religious rites.

Sacramental sign In Roman Catholic theology, one of the essential elements of a sacrament. This visible sign consists of some form of matter (e.g., water in baptism) and a word of pronouncement.

Sacramental systems Religious rites by which grace is dispensed.

Sacrament of baptism A reference to the view that baptism is a means or sign of grace. *See also* BAPTISM.

Sacrament of marriage A reference to the Roman Catholic view that marriage is a sacrament. *See also* MARRIAGE.

Sacrificial animal An animal ritually slaughtered as an offering to God.

Sacrificial system Ritual procedure for

offering an animal, crops, or some other valuable object to God.

Sadducees Important Jewish religious group in Palestine from the late second century B.C. to the late first century A.D. who were opponents of Jesus. They rejected all Jewish observances not explicitly taught in the Pentateuch or Law. They also denied the doctrines of resurrection and rewards and punishments after death. Among their emphases was human freedom.

Saint In the New Testament, anyone who is a genuine believer in Christ; in Roman Catholicism, a believer now in heaven because of an exemplary life who can make intercession with God for both persons still alive and those in purgatory.

Sainthood The status of those who have been designated as saints by the Roman Catholic Church. After officially recognizing a list of miracles attributed to a particular person, the church may designate that individual a saint through a twofold process called beatification and canonization.

Saints, Invocation of In Roman Catholicism, calling upon the saints to intercede for someone.

Saints, Perseverance of the *See* PERSEVERANCE, DOCTRINE OF.

Saints, Veneration of Honoring of saints by both commemorating them and imitating their virtues. Verbal communion with them or reverencing them may also be involved.

Salvation The divine act of delivering a believer from the power and curse of sin and then restoring that individual to the fellowship with God for which humans were originally intended.

Salvation, Doctrine of Teachings concerning the whole of salvation and its various aspects, including conversion, regeneration, union with Christ, justification, adoption, sanctification, perseverance, and glorification.

Salvation Army An organization founded by William Booth in 1865 as an essentially evangelical, theologically conservative movement that aimed to minister to the practical needs of persons. It took the name Salvation Army in 1878.

Salvation by grace Salvation understood as a free gift undeserved by the recipient.

Salvation by works A reference to the belief that by performing certain virtuous deeds it is possible to qualify for divine favor and salvation.

Samosata, Paul of *See* PAUL OF SAMOSATA.

Sanctification The divine act of making the believer actually holy—that is, bringing the person's moral condition into conformity with the legal status established in justification.

Sanctifying grace In Roman Catholicism, the grace conveyed by the sacraments, combining what Protestants call justification and sanctification.

Sanday, William (1843-1920) Anglican New Testament scholar who was a pioneer in introducing biblical criticism from Germany into British scholarship.

Sardica, Council of (343-344) The council called by the emperors Constans and Constantius together with Pope Julius I in an attempt to settle the Arian controversy. It was held in Sardica (modern Sofia), which was midway between the East and the West. Athanasius, who had been previously exiled, was restored to his see, but the fundamental result of the council was a widening of the separation between East and West.

Sartre, Jean-Paul (1905-1980) French existentialist and atheist.

Sarx Greek word for "flesh."

Satan The devil, a high angelic creature who rebelled against God and therefore was cast out of heaven. He became the leader of the opposition to God and the heavenly forces.

Satan, Fall of Disobedience and rebellion of Satan prior to the creation of the human race.

Satanic forces Demons allied in support of Satan.

Satanism Worship of Satan.

Satisfaction Reparation or compensation for a wrong or a debt incurred.

Savior In the Old Testament, the anticipated Deliverer of the people of Israel. Jesus Christ by his atoning death became the Savior of the entire human race.

Saxon Confession An exposition (1551) of the Augsburg Confession. It was written by Philipp Melanchthon to present to the Council of Trent.

Sayers, Dorothy Leigh (1893-1957) Anglican writer and lay theologian who was an influential apologist for orthodox Christian faith.

Sayings of Jesus The actual utterances of Jesus.

Scapegoat The goat to which the sins of the Israelites were symbolically transferred on the Day of Atonement. It was then driven off into the wilderness.

Schaff, Philip (1819-1893) Swiss theologian and church historian. While teaching at the German Reformed seminary in Mercersburg, Pennsylvania, he was accused of heresy, but the attempt to convict him failed. He finished out his career at Union Theological Seminary in New York City. Among his most significant works are the seven-volume *History of the Christian Church*, the three-volume *Creeds of Christendom*, and the editing of the *Schaff-Herzog Encyclopedia of Religious Knowledge*.

Schism Formal division of a religious group.

Schism, Great The separation of the Eastern and Western churches in 1054.

Schleiermacher, Friedrich (1768-1834) Liberal Protestant theologian whose introduction of romanticism into theology led to the popularization of liberalism. He held that religion is not a matter of belief or practice but of feeling.

Schlick, Moritz (1882-1936) German philosopher who founded and led the group of logical positivists known as the Vienna Circle.

Scholasticism The theology and philosophy taught in the medieval schools from the eleventh to the fourteenth century. It took the form of textbook debates on various theses.

Scholasticism, Protestant The scholastic type of theology practiced by Protestantism and particularly by Lutheranism in the seventeenth century. It was concerned primarily with defining correct doctrine through a series of subtle arguments.

Scholastic theology Medieval theology that defined correct doctrine in great detail through a series of rational arguments and debates.

Schweitzer, Albert (1875-1965) German theologian, musician, and medical missionary. His most notable theological work was *The Quest of the Historical Jesus* (1906). He spent much of his life as a medical missionary at Lambaréné in Gabon (French Equatorial Africa).

Schwenckfeld, Kaspar (1489-1561) German mystic and lay theologian who was an early supporter of Luther, but broke with him over the nature and meaning of the Lord's Supper.

Scientia media Literally, "middle knowledge"; God's knowledge of what would happen on the basis of the free decisions of created beings. This concept of a third type of divine knowledge was introduced by Jesuits in the sixteenth century. It contrasts with (1) God's knowledge of what he can and cannot do and (2) his knowledge of what will happen on the basis of his own plan and will.

Scientific method The procedure used by positive sciences to gain and verify knowledge; it involves observation, prediction, and experimentation.

Scofield, Cyrus Ingerson (C. I.) (1843-1921) Congregational minister whose writings, especially *Rightly Dividing the Word of Truth* and *The Scofield Reference Bible*, did much to popularize fundamentalist and dispensational views.

Scofield Reference Bible A study Bible that has been very influential in American fundamentalism. It was originally produced by C. I. Scofield.

Scopes trial The 1925 trial of a biology teacher, John T. Scopes, in Dayton, Tennessee, over the issue of the legality of teaching evolution in Tennessee high schools. William Jennings Bryan, an antievolutionist, and Clarence

Darrow, the attorney for the defense, made the trial a debate over the relative values of the theory of evolution and the creationist interpretation of Scripture. In the newspaper reports of the trial, fundamentalists were given the image of cultural backwardness.

Scots Confession The first confession of faith of the Scottish Reformed Church. It was drawn up in 1560 by six Scottish Reformers.

Scottish realism A philosophical movement that attempted to respond to the epistemological skepticism of David Hume's empiricism with a common-sense realism. It was founded by Thomas Reid.

Scotus, Duns *See* DUNS SCOTUS, JOHN.

Scripture Literally, "writing"; the canonical books of the Old and New Testament.

Scripture, Authority of The right of the Scripture, as God's message to us, to prescribe faith and practice for Christian believers.

Scripture, Doctrine of Teachings concerning the nature and authority of Scripture.

Search for the historical Jesus *See* HISTORICAL JESUS, SEARCH FOR THE.

Second-Adam Christology Doctrinal study centered particularly on the picture of Christ as the second Adam, who reversed the effects of Adam's sin.

Second advent of Christ *See* SECOND COMING OF CHRIST.

Secondary separation Withdrawal from persons who have not detached themselves from the world.

Second chance A reference to the idea that at some time after death persons who have not accepted Christ in this life will have an opportunity to do so.

Second coming of Christ A reference to the belief that Christ will return to earth.

Second Council of Nicea *See* NICEA, SECOND COUNCIL OF.

Second death Eternal spiritual death (Rev. 2:11; 20:6, 14; and 21:8). It contrasts with physical death, which ends one's natural life.

Second Great Awakening *See* GREAT AWAKENINGS.

Second Person of the Trinity God the Son, Jesus Christ.

Second resurrection *See* RESURRECTION, SECOND.

Second Vatican Council *See* VATICAN COUNCIL II.

Sect Usually a group that has broken away from some larger religious group or holds distinctive and unusual views. There is often a particular leader whose unique teachings become the basis of belief for the group.

Sectarianism An excessively doctrinaire and exclusivistic commitment to one's own view. Those who disagree are condemned.

Secular clergy Those clergy in the Roman Catholic Church who are not committed to any particular religious community or order.

Secular humanism A philosophy that, while denying any religious or superhuman entities, is concerned for and committed to human beings.

Secularism Life and thought conducted without belief in or commitment to God or religion.

Secularization The process of moving from a religious orientation to one more centered on the world and natural things.

Secular theology Theology that emphasizes involvement in the world rather than withdrawing to a relationship with God. Dietrich Bonhoeffer was among the forerunners of this approach.

Security of the believer The view that Christians are kept by the power of God. The doctrine is also referred to as "perseverance of the saints."

Self-deceit Failure to admit the truth about oneself.

Self-determinism A reference to the belief that one is free to make one's own decisions independently of any external influence.

Self-esteem The favorable estimation that one has of oneself.

Self-examination Scrutiny of oneself in terms of one's virtues and motives.

Self-existence of God *See* GOD, SELF-EXISTENCE OF.

Selfishness Excessive concern for one's own welfare, comfort, and reputation.

Self-love Esteem and concern for oneself; in excessive form, egoism.

Self-revelation Disclosure of oneself to others.

Self-righteousness Appraisal of oneself as being morally upright and justified by one's own deeds.

Semantics The study of the meaning and function of signs, and especially of human language.

Semi-Arianism A position worked out by those who could accept neither the Arian position nor the orthodox position adopted at Nicea. They argued that Christ is *homoiousios* with the Father, which means that he is similar to the Father but not necessarily of the same substance or nature.

Semi-Pelagianism A doctrinal position developed during the fifth and early sixth centuries by persons who did not wish to adopt the views of either Pelagius or Augustine. The term *semi-*

Pelagianism, which was coined in the sixteenth century to describe this mediating position, is sometimes applied to Arminianism.

Semitic Pertaining to a group of people that in ancient times included Babylonians, Assyrians, Aramaeans, Canaanites, and Phoenicians, but in more recent times is represented particularly by Jews. The term is frequently used to refer to Hebrew ways of thinking.

Sensuousness theory of sin *See* SIN, SENSUOUSNESS THEORY OF.

Sensus deitatis or Sensus divinitatis A reference to the idea that humans have an innate knowledge or awareness of God.

Sensus plenior What the Bible has come to mean in the experience of Christian readers, generation by generation. This "fuller sense" is in addition to the author's conscious intent.

Sentences Medieval texts expounding theological truth in a disciplined and authoritative manner. The most famous are the *Sententiae* of Peter Lombard.

Separation The practice of removing oneself from the unholy or evil.

Separation, Ecclesiastical Withdrawal from church bodies that are thought of as impure, whether in doctrine or lifestyle.

Separation of church and state A reference to the doctrine that the church and state have distinct domains and should therefore be legally independent of each other.

Separatist One who ceases to associate with a particular religious group or practices a lifestyle of withdrawal.

Septuagesima The third Sunday before Lent.

Septuagint, the The earliest translation of the Old Testament from Hebrew into Greek, allegedly by seventy (or seventy-two) Jewish translators. It is sometimes abbreviated LXX—the Roman numeral for seventy.

Seraph, seraphim Heavenly beings often thought to be a class of angels (Isa. 6:2).

Serial remembering In Frederic Bartlett's classification of types of oral transmission, the passing on of a story in a chain from one person to another.

Sermon on the Mount Jesus' discourse in Matthew 5—7; it is frequently thought of as the highest of standards for Christian living.

Serpent The being that tempted Eve in the Garden of Eden. This is generally thought of as an appearance of Satan, the term being used of him elsewhere in Scripture (Rev. 20:2).

Servanthood The aspect of the Christian lifestyle that seeks to serve rather than to be served.

Servant of the Lord In general, a devoted follower of God; in Isaiah 40—53 the term *servant* appears twenty times, sometimes with reference to Israel, sometimes with reference to the Messiah.

Service, Gift of One of the gifts of the Spirit (Rom. 12:7; 1 Peter 4:11): a capacity to help others.

Session Literally, "a sitting," a reference to God's sitting on his throne, Christ's sitting at the right hand of the Father (Eph. 1:20-23; Phil. 2:9-11), or, in the presbyterian form of government, the governing body for the local church.

Seven deadly sins *See* SINS, SEVEN DEADLY.

Seventh-day Adventism A Christian denomination noted for its members' observance of the seventh day as the Sabbath and their belief that Christ's return is imminent. The group was first formally organized in New Hampshire in 1844.

Sexual ethics The moral issues and standards dealing with sexual relationships.

Shedd, William Greenough Thayer (1820-1894) Conservative American Calvinistic theologian who taught for thirty years at Union Theological Seminary in New York. His best-known work is his three-volume *Dogmatic Theology*.

Shekinah A nonbiblical word expressing God's nearness to his people, as, for example, in the cloud that covered the tabernacle as a visible manifestation of God's glory (Exod. 40:34).

Sheol An Old Testament term for the intermediate state of souls between life on earth and the final state.

Shroud of Turin *See* TURIN, SHROUD OF.

Shrove Tuesday The day before Ash Wednesday, which is the beginning of Lent.

Sign, Visible *See* VISIBLE SIGN.

Sign gifts Certain spectacular gifts of the Spirit, such as tongues and healing, that are regarded as special evidences of his work.

Signs A term frequently used of miracles, since at times they served as evidence of the supernatural authority of the person performing them.

Signs and wonders movement A Christian movement, generally thought to have been originated by John Wimber, that emphasizes miraculous healing. It is also referred to as the "third wave," following Pentecostalism and neo-Pentecostalism or the charismatic movement. See THIRD WAVE.

Simons, Menno *See* MENNO SIMONS.

Simplicity of God One of the attributes of God: his inviolable unity. As a pure spirit, he is not a composite and consequently cannot be divided.

Simpson, A. B. (1844-1919) American pastor and evangelist who founded the Christian and Missionary Alliance.

Sin Any act, attitude, or disposition that fails to completely fulfill or measure up to the standards of God's righteousness. It may involve an actual transgression of God's law or failure to live up to his norms.

Sin, Adam's The initial sin of Adam in the Garden of Eden. Constituting the Fall, it has had far-reaching consequences for the human race.

Sin, Animal-nature theory of The view that our sinful behavior is a result of our not having completely evolved from our animal nature.

Sin, Anxiety-of-finiteness theory of The view held by Reinhold Niebuhr that sin stems from our finiteness and consequent anxiety, which in turn results in endeavors to build our own security, often at the expense of others or independently of God.

Sin, Bondage to The enslaving or controlling effect of sin (Rom. 7).

Sin, Character of The underlying nature basic to all varieties of sin. The character of sin is distinguished from specific occurrences of sin.

Sin, Confession of *See* CONFESSION OF SIN.

Sin, Consequences of The temporal and eternal results of sin.

Sin, Conviction of *See* CONVICTION OF SIN.

Sin, Corporate effects of The consequences of wrongdoing on a group of people, whether one's family, the church, or, in the case of Adam, the entire human race.

Sin, Deliberate Wrongdoing in which one engages despite an awareness of the issues.

Sin, Deliverance from A reference to the concept that salvation involves not only a cancellation of the consequences of sin but freedom from its control as well.

Sin, Imputation of The charging or assessing of the consequences of sin, usually to another; particularly, the charging of Adam's sin to his descendants.

Sin, Individual Sin committed by one person; it contrasts with the sins of a society or of the race.

Sin, Individual effects of The results of sin on the person committing the sin or in some cases on the individual against whom the sin is committed. Group and societal structures are not involved.

Sin, Internal effects of Results of sin on the personality and character of the sinner.

Sin, Man of *See* MAN OF SIN.

Sin, Mortal Sin that causes spiritual death. In Roman Catholic theology, mortal sin extinguishes the life of God in the soul, while venial sin merely weakens that life. With mortal sin there is a deliberate and intentional determination to resist God in everything one does, but with venial sin there is a tension between the wrongful action and the person committing it.

Sin, Natural consequences of The effects that follow wrongdoing in a virtual cause-and-effect relationship.

Sin, Nature of *See* SIN, CHARACTER OF.

Sin, Original *See* ORIGINAL SIN.

Sin, Power of The habituating effect of sin.

Sin, Privatization of The tendency to regard sin as solely a matter of a broken individual relationship with God. The effects on other persons and society in general are disregarded.

Sin, Remission of *See* REMISSION OF SINS.

Sin, Selfishness theory of The idea that sin is essentially an excessive concern with oneself.

Sin, Sensuousness theory of The idea that sin is in essence the tendency of our physical nature to dominate our spiritual nature.

Sin, Slavery to *See* SIN, BONDAGE TO.

Sin, Universality of A reference to the fact that all persons are sinners and that sin is found in all cultures, races, and social classes.

Sin, Unpardonable Blasphemy against the Holy Spirit, a sin that Jesus declared "eternal," as contrasted with sins that can be forgiven (Matt. 12:31-32; Mark 3:28-29; Luke 12:10). Jesus made this statement after the Pharisees had attributed to Beelzebub the work that Jesus had done by the power of the Holy Spirit. The unpardonable sin is often thought of as a persistent denial of the work of God, resulting in a hardness of heart that prevents the individual from recognizing the truth and repenting of sin.

Sin, Venial In the Roman Catholic system, a sin that does not cause spiritual death. Venial sin is chosen, but not with the purpose of resisting God in everything that one does.

Sin, Wages of The consequences of wrongdoing: death (Rom. 6:23).

Sin and death, Law of The domination of sin (Rom. 8:2).

Sin as displacement of God A reference to the idea that the essence of sin is putting something else in God's place—that is, failing to let God be God.

Sin bearing A reference to the concept that Christ, like the scapegoat in the Old Testament, carries our sins away.

Sinlessness Freedom from sin.

Sinlessness of Christ A reference to the teaching that Christ never sinned. Some hold that he could not have sinned, while others hold that he could have sinned but did not actually do so.

The doctrine is based on several biblical references: 2 Corinthians 5:21; Hebrews 4:15; 7:26; and 1 John 3:5.

Sin offering An offering that each Israelite was required to make (1) for ritual cleansing, (2) for an unintentional sin against the law of God, and (3) at each of the Hebrew festivals. The sacrifice offered depended on the status of the person.

Sins, Seven deadly In Roman Catholicism, a list of seven particularly serious moral faults: pride, covetousness, lust, envy, gluttony, anger, and sloth. They are regarded as sinful tendencies rather than mortal sins.

Sins of ignorance Wrong acts done out of a lack of awareness of the issues. The Old Testament law provided relief from the penalty for sins committed without intent; for example, the Law established cities of refuge (Num. 35:6-34; Josh. 20).

Sins of negligence Sins resulting from inattention. According to Scripture, they generally carry less serious consequences, and yet the sinner is held responsible for them.

Sins of omission Sins of failure to do something or to carry out a responsibility. They contrast with actual violations of God's standards.

Sins of rebellion Sins involving unwillingness to submit to God's authority and direction.

Sins of the flesh Sins that involve wrongful use of the body; for example, fornication, licentiousness, and drunkenness. They contrast with attitudinal and social sins.

Sin unto death In 1 John 5:16, a reference to the unforgivable sin mentioned by Jesus. *See also* SIN, UNPARDONABLE.

Situational theology A theology worked out in response to particular circumstances or occurrences, such as the Pain of God theology worked out in Japan by Kazoh Kitamori following World War II.

Situation ethics A form of ethics that holds there are no absolute goods and no absolute duties except love. Any particular action, including even murder, may therefore be right in a given situation—that is, if it is the most loving course to follow in that situation. The chief exponent of situation ethics is Joseph Fletcher.

Sitz im Leben A German phrase meaning "setting in life"; that is, the particular life setting in which a teaching was given or formulated. In form and redaction criticism, *Sitz im Leben* may be the situation in which Jesus gave a teaching, the situation of the church as it preserved and expressed the teaching, or the situation to which the Gospel writer was addressing the final form of the teaching.

Six Articles One of a series of regulations established in the Church of England under Henry VIII. Promulgated in 1539, they gave a more Catholic turn to doctrine than had the Ten Articles of 1536.

Slavery The state of being forced to serve another. Although slavery is acknowledged in the Old and New Testaments and is not specifically attacked or condemned, the Bible does contain principles that eventually were seen to require the abolition of slavery.

Smalcald Articles Articles of faith written by Martin Luther for the Lutheran princes and theologians who met at the town of Smalcald in Germany in preparation for a council called by Pope Paul III. The articles are included in *The Book of Concord.*

Small Catechism A brief manual of instruction in the Christian faith written by Martin Luther in 1529 after discovering the widespread ignorance among clergy and laity in Saxony.

Smith, Hannah Whitall (1832-1911) American Quaker whose best-known book, *The Christian's Secret of a Happy Life,* emphasized inward rest and outward victory and had the effect of popularizing the doctrine that total sanctification is a second work of grace.

Smith, William Robertson (1846-1894) Scottish Old Testament scholar who taught at the Free Church College at Aberdeen but was dismissed in 1881 for views regarded as undermining

belief in the inspiration of Scripture. He later became editor-in-chief of the *Encyclopaedia Britannica* and professor of Arabic and head librarian at Cambridge University.

Social conditioning The idea that individuals' actions may be influenced and even totally determined by the effects of society on them.

Social ethics Questions of moral significance regarding conduct toward or the responsibilities of society.

Social gospel, the Within liberalism of the late nineteenth and early twentieth centuries, a tendency to replace the gospel of regeneration with an emphasis on transformation of society through alteration of its structures.

Social implications of the gospel Principles that the Christian message necessarily entails concerning individual and collective attitudes and action regarding the issues of society.

Socialism An economic and political system in which the means of production are owned collectively and the distribution of goods is controlled governmentally.

Socialism, Christian *See* CHRISTIAN SOCIALISM.

Society of Friends *See* FRIENDS, SOCIETY OF.

Socinianism A movement deriving from the thought of Faustus Socinus that emphasized morality; denied the deity of Christ, predestination, divine fore-knowledge, and original sin; and regarded the atonement of Christ as an example rather than as satisfaction paid to the Father.

Socinians Followers of Faustus Socinus.

Socinus, Faustus (1539-1604) Systematizer of a rationalistic type of Christianity that grew into modern Unitarianism.

Socinus, Laelius (1525-1562) Italian lawyer who was one of the early forerunners of modern Unitarianism. Uncle of Faustus Socinus.

Sociological determinism The belief that sociological factors determine human belief and conduct.

Sociopsychological effects of sin The consequences that sin has upon the mind, emotions, and social relationships.

Socrates (ca. 470-399 B.C.) Greek philosopher who is thought in many ways to have founded philosophy. Much of his thought is distilled from the dialogues of his student Plato.

Solafideism The teaching that salvation is by faith alone.

Solidarity of the human race A reference to the idea that all humans are descended from the same ancestors and therefore are affected by the actions of Adam, particularly the first sin in the Garden of Eden.

Solitary Christianity An attempt to practice the Christian life in isolation from other persons. There is an emphasis on the individual's personal relationship to God and a deemphasis of the collective aspects of Christianity.

Son of God Biblical expression indicating a unique relationship to God. It is used of Israel, of kings, and especially of Jesus with reference to his deity.

Son of man A somewhat enigmatic christological title that Jesus frequently used of himself. Against the background of Daniel 7:13-14, it seems to indicate someone who has the very prerogatives of God.

Son of perdition Someone whose life is controlled by the forces of destruction and who is therefore headed toward eternal ruin (2 Thess. 2:3). The term is applied to Judas in John 17:12.

Sonship The unique relationship to the Father that qualifies one for certain prerogatives.

Sophism The use of arguments that appear correct and impressive but are actually invalid.

Sophists A group of thinkers, especially in ancient Greece, who developed highly subjectivistic and specious arguments.

Soteriological Pertaining to salvation.

Soteriology The study of salvation.

Soul In Scripture, the life or self of the person or even the person himself; in theology, the immaterial aspect of the human being.

Soul, Creationist view of the origin of the The belief that God directly and specially creates each individual soul at the moment of conception or birth; in other words, the soul is not transmitted from the parents.

Soul, Traducianist view of the origin of the The belief that the soul together with the body is propagated by the parents.

Soul, Transmigration of the A reference to the belief that a soul may be reincarnated successively in different persons or even in different types of creatures.

Soul-extinction A reformulation of the concept of soul sleep as found in movements such as Seventh-day Adventism: There really is no soul to exist apart from the body; thus, after death one becomes nonexistent.

Soulish body In 1 Corinthians 15:44, the natural or physical body in distinction from the spiritual body of the resurrection.

Soul sleep A reference to the idea that between death and resurrection the person is in a state of unconsciousness, a deep and dreamless sleep.

Source criticism *See* CRITICISM, SOURCE.

Sovereignty of God God's rule and authority over all things.

Sovereign will A reference to the fact that God's choices and decisions are in no way constrained by factors outside himself; also, God's right to choose without being answerable to anyone or anything outside himself.

Special calling In Calvinistic thought, God's effectual working in the life of the elect to bring them to faith; it contrasts with his general calling, an invitation to all persons.

Special gifts The more spectacular or miraculous gifts of the Spirit; for example, healing, exorcism, raising the dead, and speaking in tongues.

Special revelation *See* REVELATION, SPECIAL.

Spectacles of faith A metaphor used by John Calvin to indicate that faith and special revelation give perspicuity in spiritual matters.

Speech-act theory A theory of language that emphasizes the manifold functions of speech, such as promising, commanding, etc., in addition to referring. Rather than merely raising the issue of the truth of an utterance, this approach inquires whether it is "happy" (i.e., effectual).

Spener, Philipp Jakob (1635-1705) German pastor who is generally regarded as the founder of Pietism.

Spinoza, Benedict de (1632-1677) Dutch Jewish philosopher who was a rationalist in epistemology and a pantheist in metaphysics.

Spiration Literally, "breathing," a term often used in reference to the idea found in 2 Timothy 3:16 that the Scriptures are God-breathed.

Spirit Literally, "breath" or "wind," the principle of life ascribed both to animals and to persons, whether human or divine.

Spirit, Outpouring of the Any special manifestation of the Holy Spirit, but especially that at Pentecost.

Spirit, Procession of the *See* PROCESSION OF THE SPIRIT.

Spirit, Sealed with the A reference to God's work of marking the believer with the Holy Spirit (Eph. 1:13).

Spirit-filled Pertaining to believers so controlled by the Holy Spirit that all of their life is spiritual in nature.

Spirit of God In the Old Testament, an expression frequently thought of as referring to the Holy Spirit and so identified by Peter in his quotation of Joel 2:29 (see Acts 2:18).

Spirit of sonship In Romans 8:15, the spirit that believers receive so that they are no longer fearful but call upon God as their Father.

Spirit of the world Earthly wisdom; in 1 Corinthians 2:12 it contrasts with the Spirit who is from God and who helps believers understand God's gifts.

Spirit of truth One of Jesus' designations of the Holy Spirit (John 14:17).

Spirit of wisdom The special blessing that Joshua received when Moses laid his hands upon him. It enabled Joshua to assist in Moses' work.

Spirits, Discernment of One of the gifts of the Spirit (1 Cor. 12:10): special ability to identify which spirits are of God.

Spirits in prison A problematic expression in 1 Peter 3:19: Christ preached to the spirits in prison. Some hold that this is a reference to the preaching in Noah's time. Others interpret the verse to mean that Jesus between his death and resurrection preached to those who were then in the intermediate state. Still others hold that we have here a reference to Jesus' preaching during his time of ministry on earth.

Spiritual ability A capacity to understand and respond to supernatural matters.

Spiritual blindness The inability of unbelievers to recognize divine truth (Rom. 1:21; 2 Cor. 4:4). A prime example is the Pharisees' hardness of heart toward Jesus' ministry.

Spiritual body The imperishable body that believers will possess in the resurrection (1 Cor. 15:42-49).

Spiritual children Individuals influenced by one's ministry; particularly, those who have come to know Christ through it.

Spiritual church *See* INVISIBLE CHURCH.

Spiritual circumcision A circumcision of the heart: dedication of oneself to the Lord. It contrasts with physical circumcision.

Spiritual coming A reference to the view that the second coming of Christ is nonbodily in nature and therefore may have already occurred at Pentecost.

Spiritual condition One's state with respect to otherworldly matters: Is one lost or saved? Spiritual or carnal? And so on.

Spiritual death Separation from God.

Spiritual development Advancement in one's level of spiritual maturity.

Spiritual discernment The ability to judge wisely in nonworldly matters.

Spiritual economy God's ordering of spiritual matters.

Spiritual fellowship A common interest in otherworldly matters, or a relationship or community that has no visible, concrete manifestation.

Spiritual force The power of someone or something unseen, whether divine or satanic.

Spiritual gifts *See* GIFTS, SPIRITUAL.

Spiritual growth Progressive maturing in spiritual matters.

Spiritual healing The curing of physical illnesses through nonphysical means, whether by Christ during his lifetime or by faith and prayer in the present time.

Spiritual health The condition of one's spiritual life.

Spiritual hosts of wickedness One form of the opposition against which the Christian wrestles (Eph. 6:12).

Spiritualism The belief and practice of those who seek to make contact with dead persons, particularly through mediums.

Spiritual Israel Believers in Christ— they have the faith, if not the blood, of Abraham.

Spirituality Deep commitment and likeness to God.

Spirituality of God The immaterial, nonphysical nature of God.

Spiritual kingdom The rule of Christ in the life of believers. This kingdom is not of this world and does not involve political or military power.

Spiritual life Sensitivity and responsiveness to otherworldly matters. Spiritual life goes beyond the merely physical or biological.

Spiritually dead The state of unbelievers. Because of sin's effect they are unresponsive to spiritual matters.

Spiritual meditation Reflection upon nonworldly matters.

Spiritual perfection Completion of the process of sanctification.

Spiritual presence A reference to the belief that Christ is not present physically and bodily in the elements of the Lord's Supper, but spiritually.

Spiritual qualities The characteristics that constitute spiritual maturity.

Spiritual realm The domain inhabited by spirits—God, the angels, and the demons. It contrasts with the physical realm.

Spiritual renewal Nonphysical reenergizing of a person or group.

Spiritual resurrection The new birth.

Spiritual sins Attitudes and dispositions that do not meet God's standard of righteousness. Spiritual sins contrast with wrongful physical acts.

Spiritual strength Capacity to engage effectively in the otherworldly dimensions of life, including spiritual ministry.

Spiritual truths Knowledge that cannot be grasped by the unaided human mind.

Spiritual union The nonphysical relationship Christians have with Christ or with one another.

Spiritual unity The nonvisible relationship all Christians have with one another. This contrasts with the visible unity of the organized church.

Spiritual warfare The Christian's struggle against otherworldly forces (Eph. 6:10-17).

Spotless Lamb of God Jesus the perfect sacrifice.

Sprinkling Scattering in drops or small particles. It is one mode of baptism.

Spurgeon, Charles Haddon (1834-1892) Influential Baptist preacher in England. Though never ordained, he had a powerful preaching ministry at a congregation in London for a period of thirty-eight years, much of that in a building called the Metropolitan Tabernacle, which seated six thousand persons. He also founded a college for the training of pastors. His theology was Calvinistic and his politics liberal.

State The governmental organization of a body of people permanently occupying a particular territory; in theology, political entities as distinguished from the church, a spiritual entity.

State of exaltation In classical Christology, the process of Christ's return to the glory that he had before coming to earth. It includes his resurrection, ascension, and session at the Father's right hand and will be climaxed by his second coming.

State of grace Unmerited condition of being in God's special favor.

State of humiliation Christ's self-limitation as he took on the conditions of human existence. Included in his humiliation are his incarnation, physical suffering, death, and, in the view of some, descent into Hades.

States of Jesus Christ The two major stages of Christ's life: his humiliation and exaltation.

Statutes Rules or laws enacted to govern behavior.

Staupitz, Johannes von (ca. 1465-1524) Roman Catholic scholar who encouraged Martin Luther to study for a doctorate and who later tried unsuccessfully to modify Luther's position.

Stealing Unauthorized taking of the property of another either by force or by stealth.

Stewardship Careful management of the resources of the kingdom of God that have been entrusted to a person or group.

Stigmata In mysticism, marks on the body that are reputed to be reproductions of Christ's wounds. They involve varying degrees of intensity, from faint red marks on the skin to actual bleeding wounds. The first well-known case is that of Francis of Assisi in 1224.

Stoddard, Solomon (1643-1729) Congregational preacher at Northampton, Massachusetts, who had a strong influence on Protestantism in New England. Grandfather of Jonathan Edwards.

Stoicism The philosophy of a school of Greek thought that took its name from the porch (*stoa*) in Athens where its founder taught. Stoicism is best known for its ethical system, which by emphasizing harmony with nature and freedom from emotion, enabled one to endure the fluctuating fortunes of life.

Strata of tradition The different layers that form critics believe they can identify in Scripture, particularly in the Gospels. These layers consist of the original material and earlier and later additions.

Strauss, David Friedrich (1808-1874) German theologian whose two-volume *Life of Jesus, Critically Examined* was one of the first radical accounts of Jesus. Strauss interpreted Christianity in the light of Hegelian philosophy.

Strong, Augustus Hopkins (1836-1921) American Baptist pastor, theologian, and educator who was president and professor of theology at Rochester Theological Seminary and first president of the Northern Baptist Convention (1905-1910). His *Systematic Theology* (1886) was a standard text for many years.

Structural(ist) exegesis An interpretive approach that holds that the biblical text has meaning independent of the composition process and the intention of the author. Stemming from the idea that there are certain recurring structures or patterns of thought, it attempts to find the interrelationships between the elements within the text (the superficial structure) and the anthropological realities to which these elements refer (the deep structure). Structuralism is often thought of as having been originated by a Swiss linguist, Ferdinand de Saussure. It makes a synchronic approach to the text rather than a diachronic approach and is a reaction to both the historical-critical method and the existential method of Rudolf Bultmann and the post-Bultmannians.

Subjective experience An event or occurrence so personal that it cannot be verified by others. In other words, there is no external object to which one can point for sensory verification.

Subjective knowledge An informational understanding that is not mere impassive observation but directly involves the person.

Subjective truth Facts considered in terms of their effect on the knower rather than in terms of their correspondence to the objects they describe.

Sublapsarianism The view that the divine decrees occurred (logically) in the following order: (1) to create human beings; (2) to permit the Fall; (3) to provide salvation sufficient for all; (4) to choose some to receive this salvation.

Subordinationism The doctrine that in essence and status the Son is inferior to the Father, or the Spirit is inferior to the Father and the Son. This is to be distinguished from functional subordinationism, which sees the role of the Son or the Spirit as temporarily subordinated to the Father during a period of ministry.

Substitution The act of taking the place of another.

Substitutionary death A reference to the idea that Jesus' death was in our place.

Suffering Physical, mental, or emotional pain or anguish.

Suffering Servant Isaianic reference to the Messiah and the anguish he would undergo on our behalf.

Suffering with Christ The Pauline concept of so identifying with Christ that we share in his pain and anguish or endure distress for his sake (Rom. 8:17; Phil. 3:10).

Suffragan bishop An assistant to a diocesan bishop. The term is also applied to a diocesan bishop when he joins with an archbishop or metropolitan in a synod.

Suicide The voluntary taking of one's own life, for reasons other than altruistic self-sacrifice.

Suicide, assisted (or physician-assisted) Terminology commonly attached to self-inflicted voluntary active euthanasia, committed with the advice or technical assistance of a physician.

Sunday The first day of the week; in the Christian Era it became the day of worship (the Lord's Day).

Sunday schools Schools conducted on Sundays (often in affiliation with a church) for the teaching of religious and biblical truth. The movement dates back to 1780 when Robert Raikes, a journalist in Gloucester, England, founded a school in the slums to teach children reading, writing, and scriptural truth.

Supererogation, Works of Works done of one's own free choice above and beyond the requirements of God's commands. The word *supererogation* means, literally, "paying more than is necessary."

Superhuman qualities Characteristics not possessed by human beings in their own strength (e.g., omniscience, omnipotence).

Superintendent An officer given responsibility for a particular area of activity—for example, the churches of a given region. Ordinarily the superintendent's authority is conferred by those over whom he has oversight.

Supernatural Pertaining to that which falls outside of or cannot be accounted for by the laws of the physical universe.

Supernatural endowment In the thought of Irenaeus and the medieval Catholic church, a supernatural gift added to basic human nature but lost in the Fall. This likeness to God, which consisted of his moral attributes, was distinguished from the image of God, his natural attributes of reason and will that humanity has retained.

Supernatural existential In the thought of Karl Rahner, the idea that each human has within himself the potential for knowing God and that this potential is already functioning. There is, there-fore, no such thing as being totally apart from grace.

Supernatural illumination A special enlightenment by the Holy Spirit that takes the recipient beyond normal human knowledge.

Supernaturalism Belief in powers beyond the observable universe.

Supernatural qualities Attributes not found in human beings or in nature apart from God's special working.

Supernatural realm That which lies outside the boundaries of the physical universe or of the natural system of causation.

Supernatural work Those acts of God that are beyond human capability.

Supersensuous sphere That which lies beyond the reach of human perception.

Superstition Literally, "a standing above," an unproved and irrational belief, often of a magical or religious nature.

Supplication A humble prayer to God.

Supralapsarianism The view that the decrees of God occurred (logically) in the following order: (1) to save some humans and condemn others; (2) to create both the elect and the reprobate; (3) to permit the fall of all humans; (4) to provide salvation only for the elect.

Surd evil In the thought of Edgar Sheffield Brightman, an evil that cannot be utilized for good, no matter what operations are performed on it.

Swedenborg, Emanuel (1688-1772) Swedish philosopher and religious thinker.

Swedenborgianism The views deriving from the thought of Emanuel Swedenborg, including (1) the neo-Platonic idea that the universe and humans were not created by but emanated from God, (2) a monopersonal Trinity, (3) an example theory of the atonement, and (4) belief in a second chance during the intermediate state.

Swete, Henry Barclay (1835-1917) Anglican scholar who taught at King's College (London) and Cambridge University and was noted for his conservative critical methods and writings on the Holy Spirit.

Syllogism A deductive argument in which a conclusion is drawn from a major and minor premise.

Symbol Something that stands for or represents something else. The two may have an inherent connection but are not literally equivalent.

Symbolic Pertaining to something that represents something else.

Symbolic logic A formal type of logic involving the use of symbols.

Symbolism The meaning that the use of one object or idea to represent another is intended to convey.

Sympathetic oneness A reference to the view that the believer's union with Christ is merely an external bond. It is like the agreement between people who are of one mind on certain important matters.

Synagogue Jewish place of worship. The first one was probably established during the Babylonian exile.

Synchronic approach The technique of studying something not by tracing its chronological development, but by comparing it with whatever may have existed simultaneously.

Syncretism The bringing together of differing beliefs; particularly, the assimilating of the views of one religion into those of another.

Syncretistic theology Contextualization of theology to the point where it becomes united with or incorporates elements of other religions such as Hinduism or Buddhism.

Synergism The idea that the human works together with God in certain aspects of salvation—for example, faith or regeneration.

Synod An official coming together of a group of Christians to discuss the business of the church. A group of churches is usually involved.

Synod of Dort *See* DORT, SYNOD OF.

Synod of Whitby *See* WHITBY, SYNOD OF.

Synoptic Gospels The three Gospels—

Matthew, Mark, and Luke—which, though each has distinctive emphases, approach the life of Christ from basically similar positions.

Synoptic problem The question of the relationship between the three Synoptic Gospels and their relative dependence on one another.

Syntactics That branch of semiotics (a general theory of signs) that deals with the relationship among the various signs or symbols in a given system.

Synthetic statement A cognitive proposition in which the predicate adds something to the content of the subject. It contrasts with an analytic statement, in which the predicate is contained, by definition, within the subject.

Systematic theology The discipline that attempts to arrange the doctrinal content of Scripture in a coherent fashion, express it in a contemporary form, and relate it to issues of practical Christian concern.

Tt

Tabernacle A large tentlike structure that served as the place of worship for Israel from the time of the wilderness sojourn until the building of Solomon's temple.

Tatian (ca. 110-172) Christian apologist and Gnostic whose major written contribution was the *Diatessaron*, a harmony of the Gospels.

Tauler, Johannes (ca. 1300-1361) Dominican preacher and mystic in what is now France, Switzerland, and Germany.

Tautology, tautological statement A compound proposition that is true regardless of the truth values of its component propositions.

Taylor, A. E. (1869-1945) British philosopher noted especially for his work on Plato and in ethics.

Taylor, Nathaniel William (1786-1858) Congregational preacher and theologian at Yale University who is generally thought of as the founder of the New Haven theology. He modified Calvinism, blending it with the emphases of revivalism.

Teachers, Pastors and One of the spiritual gifts (Eph. 4:11). The two terms are often thought of as referring to the same office.

Teaching, Gift of One of the spiritual gifts: the ability to impart knowledge (Rom. 12:7; 1 Cor. 12:28-29).

Teaching elders Elders who teach and preach; thus, clergy.

Teilhard de Chardin, Pierre (1881-1955) French Jesuit geologist who developed a view of cosmic evolution that in many ways is similar to process theology.

Teleological argument An argument for the existence of God: The order of the universe must be the work of a supreme Designer.

Teleology The study of apparent order or purpose in the universe.

Telos The end or purpose of something.

Temperance One of the seven cardinal virtues: moderation in everything. The term has come to have a specific application with respect to the drinking of alcoholic beverages. (The temperance movement actually suggested not only moderation but abstinence.)

Temple, the Structure erected at Jerusalem for the worship of God. Unlike the tabernacle, which was temporary and portable, the temple was a permanent house of worship; moreover, its dimensions were twice the size of those of the tabernacle. The first temple was constructed under the leadership of King Solomon.

Temple, William (1881-1944) Anglican scholar and churchman who served as archbishop of Canterbury. His most significant writings include *Christus Veritas*; *Nature, Man and God*; and *Christianity and Social Order*.

Temporal consequences of sin The results of sin that occur within this existence.

Temporal judgment Punishment that is administered through events within this life. It contrasts with the eternal judgment that is yet to come.

Temptation The act of inducing to sin, or the condition of being induced to sin.

Tempter One who induces to sin; particularly, Satan.

Ten Articles, the A doctrinal statement resulting from the religious revolution of King Henry VIII of England. Issued in 1536, the Ten Articles were his means of trying to satisfy a group of Reformers who were basically Lutheran in orientation.

Ten Commandments, the The most basic part of the law given by God to Israel at Mount Sinai. The Ten Commandments are recorded in Exodus 20 and Deuteronomy 5.

Tennant, Frederick Robert (1866-1957) Anglican theologian and philosopher of religion who taught at Cambridge University. His major work was done from an empirical epistemology.

Terminism The doctrine that God sets a time limit upon each individual's opportunity for conversion and salvation.

Territorialism The idea that a civil ruler has the right to establish an official religion in his domain.

Tertium quid A middle course or alternative to the horns of a dilemma.

Tertullian (ca. 155-220) Latin father who in his later years became a Montanist. His major contributions were his coining the term *Trinity* and suggesting that the Godhead is to be understood as one substance manifested in three persons. He also made significant contributions to the understanding of original sin and of the relationship between faith and reason.

Testament One of the two major divisions of Scripture: writings from the period prior to Christ and writings after his coming. The term originally meant "covenant."

Testimonium Spiritus Sancti internum See INTERNAL TESTIMONY OF THE HOLY SPIRIT.

Testimony Authenticating evidence or the act of witnessing.

Tetragrammaton The four letters in Hebrew for the name of Israel's God: YHWH.

Tetrapolitan Confession A confession worked out in 1530 during the Diet of Augsburg by Martin Bucer and Wolfgang Capito as an attempted compromise between the positions of

Luther and Zwingli. It paralleled the Augsburg Confession but gave a more mediating treatment to the Lord's Supper. It was not successful in uniting the two groups.

Textual criticism *See* CRITICISM, TEXTUAL.

Thank offering In the Old Testament sacrificial system, a type of peace offering given to God in gratitude for his favors.

Theism Belief in a personal God.

Theism, Absolute Edgar Sheffield Brightman's term for belief in an unlimited God. Brightman himself maintained that God is finite.

Theism, Dipolar In process theology, the idea that God has two poles or aspects: an unchanging abstract essence and a concrete actuality that relates to the world and undergoes change.

Theistic evolution *See* EVOLUTION, THEISTIC.

Theistic finitism Belief in a limited personal God. Among the exponents of this position, which is also known as finitistic theism, is Edgar Sheffield Brightman.

Theistic philosophy Philosophy that includes belief in a personal God.

Theocentric Pertaining to something that focuses on God as the highest value.

Theocracy A form of government that believes itself to be based on the law of God.

Theodicy An attempt to show that God is not responsible for evil.

Theodoret (ca. 393-458) Bishop of Cyrrhus in Syria who took a mediating position between the two parties in the Nestorian controversy. Deposed and exiled by the Robber Synod of Ephesus, he was restored by the Council of Chalcedon (451), which required him to participate in the condemnation of Nestorius.

Theodotus Byzantine leather merchant who introduced dynamic monarchianism to Rome about A.D. 190. In other areas of doctrine he was orthodox.

Theologia crucis *See* THEOLOGY OF THE CROSS.

Theologia gloiriae *See* THEOLOGY OF GLORY.

Theologian One who seeks to understand the doctrinal basis of a religion, ordinarily the religion that he or she espouses. A professional theologian is a person with advanced training in doctrinal studies who frequently also teaches and writes.

Theologians of balance In James Fowler's classification of liberation theologians, those who see wrong on both sides of today's social, political, and economic struggles: the oppressors and the oppressed.

Theological anthropology The study of human nature from the standpoint of theology and revelation.

Theological conservatism The position that there are certain basic abiding truths to be accepted and authorities to be obeyed.

Theological determinism Any system that holds that human behavior is caused (at least to some extent) by God; for example, the view that God has foreordained all things that come to pass.

Theological exegesis In the general sense, critical analysis of scriptural passages that is concerned with establishing doctrine; in a more specific sense, critical analysis that, assuming the unity of the canon, seeks to explain passages in light of the whole of Scripture.

Theological framework The doctrinal structure or Gestalt within which thought and life are conducted.

Theological methodology The techniques of constructing and evaluating a doctrinal system.

Theological seminaries Schools devoted to the study of theological subjects, particularly with the aim of preparing persons for professional ministerial service.

Theological tradition A particular set of teachings or framework of theology that has long been established and is still being adhered to.

Theology, Contextualization of The stating of religious doctrines in terms understandable and appropriate to a given culture.

Theology of feeling A theology, such as that of Friedrich Schleiermacher, that emphasizes emotion or feeling rather than belief or action.

Theology of glory Luther's term for the approach that claims to know God through his works—that is, through natural theology. The term would also apply to the triumphalism of some modern charismatics who see God at work in dramatic visions, miraculous healings, and glossolalia. The theology of glory is the antithesis of the theology of the cross.

Theology of hope An attempt to construct theology in terms of the future; it is particularly associated with Jürgen Moltmann.

Theology of liberation A theology that endeavors to end all forms of oppression—social, political, and economic. It emphasizes God's concern for the oppressed and seeks to work for their liberation.

Theology of paradox *See* PARADOX, THEOLOGY OF.

Theology of revivalism A theology that emphasizes human sinfulness and particularly the need of immediate and definite conversion. It often includes an emotional view of the nature of conversion.

Theology of the cross The doctrine formulated by Martin Luther that God is most revealed and encountered in the cross. The fullest knowledge of God is not to be found, then, in his glorious natural attributes (the theology of glory), but in the place where his glory is hidden by apparent weakness.

Theology proper Study of the doctrine of God.

Theonomism The belief that God is free to choose, and that whatever he wills is, therefore, good and right. In this approach, which relates particularly to the problem of evil, theology is prior to logic.

Theonomy *See* RECONSTRUCTION.

Theophany A visible appearance or manifestation of God, particularly in the Old Testament.

Theophoroi Literally, "God bearing" or "God borne," a term used of early Christians, signifying that they were indwelt by Christ or his Spirit.

Theosophy A mystical philosophy that involves a system of auto-salvation: Man is ever evolving toward divine nature through a series of reincarnations and through knowledge received either directly from the world of spirit or from the teachings of those who are closer to perfection.

Theotokos Literally, "God-bearing," an expression used of Mary, the mother of Jesus. Nestorius's refusal to accept the term was condemned by the Council of Ephesus in 431. *Theotokos* can be used either as an affirmation of the deity of Jesus Christ or as a form of Mariolatry.

Third-Eye Theology An Asian theology, associated with the thought of the Taiwanese theologian Choan-Seng Song, that emphasizes the intuitive role of the heart, which transcends reason and penetrates to the mystery of being. Song says that Asian Christians must learn to see Christ through Asian eyes.

Third Person of the Trinity God the Holy Spirit.

Third Reformation *See* RADICAL REFORMATION.

Third World theologies Contextualizations of Christian doctrine to Third World settings.

Third Wave A movement emphasizing miraculous gifts, following upon classical Pentecostalism and the charismatic movement, or neo-Pentecostalism. *See* SIGNS AND WONDERS.

Thirteen Articles A Latin manuscript drawn up by a conference between German Lutheran and English theologians in 1538. It was discovered among the papers of Archbishop Thomas Cranmer. Strongly dependent on the Augsburg Confession, the Thirteen Articles were never adopted by English civil or ecclesiastical authorities but may have been part of the basis of the Forty-Two Articles adopted in 1553.

Thirty-nine Articles The doctrinal standard of the Anglican church and of Episcopal churches worldwide. The document was first published in 1563 and adopted in 1571.

This age The era in which we are currently living. It contrasts with the age to come, which will be introduced by the return of Christ. Some aspects of the age to come, however, are already present in this age.

This-worldly Pertaining to the present world—that is, the secular.

Thomas à Kempis (ca. 1379-1471) German monk and spiritual writer best known for *The Imitation of Christ*, which emphasizes withdrawal from the attractions of the world.

Thomas Aquinas (1225-1274) Medieval Catholic theologian whose synthesis of Christian theology and Aristotelian philosophy became the classical system of Catholic theology for several centuries. He is especially noted for his fivefold proof of the existence of God.

Thomism The system of thought inspired by Thomas Aquinas's synthesis of Christian doctrine and Aristotle's philosophy. It includes an emphasis upon rational evidences for the existence of God.

Thomist One who follows the thinking of Thomas Aquinas.

Three-stage Christology *See* CHRISTOLOGY, THREE-STAGE.

Thrones Part of the first group of angels in the classification of Pseudo-Dionysius the Areopagite.

Tillich, Paul (1886-1965) An influential German-American theologian who sought to construct a theology using existential philosophy. Standing on the boundary line between East and West, liberalism and neoorthodoxy, and philosophy and theology, he developed what is called the method of correlation: Theological answers are correlated with the philosophical questions being asked by the culture. His view of God not as a being, not even as the Supreme Being, but as the ground or power of all being is basically panentheistic.

Time The period between the beginning of creation and the great consummation; it contrasts with eternity. In the New Testament, the word *chronos* generally refers to a period or sequence of time; *kairos*, on the other hand, refers to a definite point in time, and particularly, a significant event.

Timelessness *See* ATEMPORALITY.

Tindal, Matthew (ca. 1655-1733) English deist who caused a furor with his *Christianity as Old as the Creation; or, The Gospel, a Republication of the Religion of Nature*.

Tithe A tenth of one's income.

Tithing The practice of giving a tenth of one's income to the Lord.

TM *See* TRANSCENDENTAL MEDITATION.

Token of salvation, Baptism as A reference to the view that baptism is neither a means of grace nor an act of initiation corresponding to Old Testament circumcision, but an emblem or outward symbolic testimony of an inward change already effected.

Toland, John (1670-1722) English deist who rejected Christian mysteries and miracles lacking rational proofs. His best-known writing is *Christianity Not Mysterious*.

Tolerance Willingness to allow the existence of beliefs and practices different from one's own.

Tongues, Gift of One of the gifts of the Spirit; it involves speaking words that one has not previously known (Acts 2; 1 Cor. 12:10; 14). Some believe the modern-day phenomenon (which is also known as glossolalia) to be a matter of actual human languages, while others believe it to be a matter of unknown syllables.

Torah The Hebrew word for "law"; in the technical sense the term refers to the Pentateuch, the first five books in the Old Testament.

Torgau Articles Three documents composed by German Lutheran theologians in 1530, 1574, and 1576 respectively. The first of these was incorporated into the Augsburg Confession, as was the third into the Formula of Concord.

Toronto blessing Phenomena occurring at the then Toronto Airport Vineyard church, involving healing and unusual physical occurrences such as "holy laughter," twitching, and jerking.

Total abstinence Complete rejection of a particular practice or of the use of a particular substance, especially alcoholic beverages.

Total depravity A reference to the belief that humans begin life with all aspects of their nature corrupted by the effects of sin; thus, all their actions will lack totally pure motives. This does not mean, however, that they are absolutely devoid of any good impulses.

Total inability Human incapacity to do anything meritorious in the sight of God by one's own effort.

Totalistic relativism The position that all things are relative and that, consequently, there are no absolutes and no universally valid human knowledge.

Tractarianism The stage of the Oxford movement when the series of papers titled *Tracts for the Times* was being issued (1833-1841).

Tradition A set of beliefs or practices passed on from one generation to another.

Traditional theology Either conventional orthodox theology or theology that is routinely accepted without being examined.

Traducianism The belief that the human soul is received by transmission from one's parents.

Transcendence of God God's otherness or separateness from the creation and the human race.

Transcendentalism A nineteenth-century movement that emphasized intuitive knowledge, inspiration of the individual soul, and optimism regarding human nature. Among the prominent names associated with transcendentalism are Samuel Taylor Coleridge, Ralph Waldo Emerson, Margaret Fuller, and Theodore Parker.

Transcendental Meditation (TM) An Eastern meditative practice popularized in the West by Maharishi Mahesh Yogi. Though it claims to be simply a scientific technique giving happiness and restfulness, critics of the movement argue that it is Hindu religious practice.

Transcendent God A God who is separate and even somewhat remote from nature, history, and humanity.

Transdenominational Transcending denominational distinctions.

Transferral The passing of sin from sinners to Christ or of the righteousness of Christ to believers.

Transfiguration The mountaintop occurrence in which the appearance of Jesus was changed so that his face shone and his garments became glistening white (Matt. 17:2; Mark 9:2-3). The same

Greek word is used of the Christian in Romans 12:2 and 2 Corinthians 3:18, where it is generally rendered "transformation" rather than "transfiguration."

Transformation of life Regeneration.

Transformers Theologians who attempt to state religious concepts in contemporary form and, holding certain aspects of Christianity to be obsolete, are willing to eliminate certain doctrines or change their very essence.

Transforming grace God's undeserved work of regeneration.

Transgression A form of sin: overstepping the limits or boundaries established by God.

Transient forms Temporary or localized expressions that are not part of the essence of the message.

Transitive attributes *See* ATTRIBUTES OF GOD, TRANSITIVE OR RELATIVE.

Translation of persons The experience of Enoch and Elijah in being taken directly into the future state instead of dying.

Translations, Bible Renditions of the Bible from the original languages of Hebrew, Aramaic, and Greek into other languages.

Translators Theologians who attempt to state the Christian message in a contemporary form but without changing its essence in the process.

Translators, Biblical Persons who render the Bible into languages other than the original.

Transmigration of the soul *See* SOUL, TRANSMIGRATION OF THE.

Transubstantiation The Roman Catholic doctrine that the bread and the wine in the mass actually change into the substance of Christ's body and blood.

Treachery A variety of sin: betrayal of God.

Tree of the knowledge of good and evil The tree in the Garden of Eden of which Adam and Eve were forbidden to eat. When they nonetheless ate of it, they committed the first sin of the human race.

Trent, Council of (1545-1563) The official Roman Catholic response to the Lutheran Reformation. It sought to institute certain reforms in the church and to spell out its doctrines in relationship to those of the Reformers. Much of the definitive doctrine and practice of the church for many years to come was formulated at this council.

Trespass A term for sin: an overstepping of God-imposed limitations.

Trespass offering Payment of damages as restitution for a social, religious, or ritual wrong. Also referred to as a guilt offering, it entailed full restitution of the value of the goods involved and a penalty of one fifth (Lev. 5:14—6:7; 7:1-7).

Tribulation In Scripture generally, the suffering and anguish of God's people. The term is also used to refer to the great tribulation, an unparalleled period of trouble at the end of time. It will be initiated by the abomination of desolation and concluded by Christ's second coming. Some believe that the church will be removed from the world by a preliminary coming of Jesus at the beginning of the great tribulation.

Tribulational views Views on whether the church will go though the whole tribulation, just a part of it, or none of it, being removed beforehand. There also is some difference as to the duration of the tribulation, some people holding that it will be seven years, others that it will simply be an extended period of time.

Trichotomism The view that human nature is made up of three parts, usually identified as body, soul, and spirit.

Trinitarian functions Roles of God that are thought of as the working of all three persons of the Trinity conjointly.

Trinitarian properties Characteristics that are exhibited by all the members of the Trinity. These properties contrast with specific characteristics unique to the individual roles of the members of the Trinity, such as the humanity that is characteristic of Jesus but not of the Father or the Spirit.

Trinity A reference to the doctrine that

God is one and yet exists eternally in three persons.

Trinity, economic The Trinity as manifested in God's saving actions.

Trinity, immanent God's triune nature as he is in himself.

Trinity, First Person of the God the Father.

Trinity, logic of Attempting to analyze the meaning of the Trinity using logical categories.

Trinity, ontological The Trinity understood in terms of the actual nature of God.

Trinity, Second Person of the God the Son, Jesus Christ.

Trinity, Third Person of the God the Holy Spirit.

Tritheism Belief in three separate gods.

Triumphalism A view that emphasizes the victorious nature of the church or of the Christian life.

Triune God *See* TRINITY.

Troeltsch, Ernst (1865-1923) German theologian and social philosopher who served as a curate before teaching at Göttingen, Bonn, Heidelberg, and Berlin. A liberal, he followed a Hegelian interpretation of history as a movement of the spirit returning to God. In 1915 he switched from theology to philosophy. His best-known work is *The Social Teaching of the Christian Churches*.

Tropici Fourth-century group that interpreted the Scripture figuratively. Regarding the Spirit as an angel of the highest rank, they were opposed by Athanasius.

True church A church distinguished as genuine or as possessing the marks of the church. The definition of genuineness or the marks of the church varies from one denomination to another.

Trust Confidence in something or (especially) someone.

Truth That which accords with reality or is genuine.

Tübingen School A theological movement at the University of Tübingen that applied to the Bible antisupernaturalist assumptions and the historical-critical approach. The movement was headed by F. C. Baur but actually began with David Strauss's *Life of Jesus* (1835). Although it attracted a great deal of attention, this variety of liberalism did not have far-reaching advocacy.

TULIP Mnemonic abbreviation of the traditional five points of the Calvinistic view of salvation: *T*otal depravity, *U*nconditional predestination, *L*imited atonement, *I*rresistible grace, and *P*erseverance of the saints. The five points stem from the canons adopted by the Synod of Dort.

Turin, Shroud of A linen cloth containing what some believe to be an image of the crucified Christ. It is housed in Turin, Italy.

Turretin, Francis (1623-1687) Swiss Reformed theologian who represents Calvinistic scholasticism, spelling out minute points and extensive logical deductions. His best-known work is the three-volume *Institutio*.

Twelve disciples, the The original group of twelve called by Jesus: Simon Peter, his brother Andrew, James and his brother John (the sons of Zebedee), Philip, Bartholomew, Thomas, Matthew the tax collector, James the son of Alphaeus, Thaddaeus, Simon the Zealot, and Judas Iscariot. After the apostasy and death of Judas Iscariot, he was replaced by Matthias.

Twentieth Century Reformation Hour A radio program conducted by Carl McIntire.

Twofold nature of faith Faith considered as both acceptance of propositions or truths and trust in a person.

Twofold state of Jesus *See* STATES OF JESUS CHRIST.

Two-swords theory The doctrine that there are two earthly domains and powers—namely, the state and the church. It was originally stated by Pope Gelasius I in 494. The exact relationship between the state and the church has been the subject of a great amount of debate by theologians and canon lawyers.

Tyconius (active ca. 370-390) Donatist theologian whose postmillennial views influenced Augustine.

Type An actual historical event or person that in some ways symbolizes or anticipates a later occurrence; particularly, an Old Testament foreshadowing of a New Testament event.

Typological interpretation Understanding Old Testament events and persons as symbolic anticipation of New Testament occurrences.

Typology The study of Old Testament events and persons that symbolically anticipate the New Testament.

Tyrrell, George (1861-1909) Irish modernist theologian who left Anglicanism to enter the Jesuit order. His views critical of Roman Catholicism eventually resulted in his dismissal from the Jesuit order and his being deprived of the sacraments.

Uu

Ubiquity of God The omnipresence of God. The term is also used in Lutheran thought to explain how Christ's body can be present in the Eucharist while he is in heaven.

Ultradispensationalism An extreme form of dispensationalism that sees the beginning of the church occurring in Acts 28 when Paul at the end of his ministry declared that since Israel has rejected the kingdom of God, salvation is now given to the Gentiles. This position is often called "Bullingerism," after one of its leading advocates, Ethelbert William Bullinger (1837-1913). Another form of ultradispensationalism sees the church as beginning in Acts 13, when Paul was sent out on his first missionary journey. Ultradispensationalism is more inclined to identify certain passages as being only for particular ages than is the more moderate form of dispensationalism, which views Acts 2 (Pentecost) as the beginning of the church.

Ultramontanism A nineteenth-century Roman Catholic movement that encouraged centralization of power in the papacy as a means to spiritual renewal of the church.

Unbelief Lack of faith, particularly in the message of Christianity.

Unbeliever From the Christian perspective, a non-Christian or unregenerate person.

Uncertainty principle A key part of quantum mechanics, known as matrix mechanics, that states that some characteristics of atoms and their particles can be determined only with a degree of probability. Also known as the Heisenberg Principle, named for Werner Heisenberg.

Unchangeability of God God's constancy in all of his qualities, which means that he can be relied on to be the same in the future as he has been in the past. It does not mean, however, a fixity or lack of activity on God's part.

Unchurched Persons who have not been evangelized, or if they have been evangelized, have not been incorporated into the body of the church.

Uncircumcised The Gentiles.

Unclean Pertaining to a person or object that in some way is in violation of the ritual requirements of the law of Israel.

Uncleanness The condition of being in violation of the ritual law of Israel.

Unconditional choice *See* UNCONDITIONAL PREDESTINATION.

Unconditional covenant of God An agreement with humanity that God will fulfill simply because he has said so. It contrasts with a conditional covenant, fulfillment of which is dependent upon some action or response by humans.

Unconditional predestination A reference to the Calvinistic view that God's choice of certain persons to salvation is not dependent upon any foreseen virtue or faith on their part.

Unconditional selection *See* UNCONDITIONAL PREDESTINATION.

Unconscious faith Belief and commitment that exist apart from reasoning power and self-awareness. It has been suggested, for example, that baptized infants have unconscious faith.

Unconscious sin Wrongful acts committed without awareness of the evil involved.

Uncritical Pertaining to an approach that simply accepts a concept or truth claim on face value or without evidence.

Unction An anointing as a symbol of consecration.

Understanding A matter of comprehension or knowledge deeper than mere acquaintance.

Undistributed middle A logical fallacy that occurs when neither premise in a syllogism makes a universal statement about the term that does not appear in the conclusion; for example, since all A are X and B is also X, B must be an instance of A.

Unending fire Eternal punishment prepared for the devil, his angels, and evil humans (Matt. 25:41).

Unfaithfulness Failure to keep one's pledge or commitments. Unfaithfulness may refer to betrayal of or treachery against God. It may also be used in reference to human relationships, specifically, violation of the vows of exclusive commitment to one's marriage partner.

Unforgivable sin *See* SIN, UNPARDONABLE.

Unforgiven sin Wrongdoing that has not been pardoned, ordinarily because it has not been confessed and forgiveness sought.

Unfree Pertaining to an act that is caused or determined by external factors and therefore cannot be ascribed to the person.

Ungodliness The absence or opposite of a likeness to God in spiritual and moral matters.

Unification Church A twentieth-century cult that was founded in Korea by Sun Myung Moon that holds that because Jesus did not marry, his work of redemption was only spiritual. Consequently, there must yet be another messiah, the lord of the second advent, to bring about physical redemption. In *The Divine Principle* Moon implies that the lord of the second advent will be born in Korea and that all religions will unite under him. Some believe that Moon is that messiah; however, he has never made that claim officially. Followers of the movement, who are popularly called "Moonies," have received considerable publicity despite the fact that they number less than one million persons.

Uniformitarianism The conception in science and particularly in geology that the processes currently at work in the physical universe are the same as those in the past. Thus past events may be dated by extrapolation from present processes.

Unio mystica See MYSTICAL UNION.

Union of believers The bond connecting all Christians.

Union with Christ A basic dimension of the doctrine of salvation: By being identified with Christ in his atoning death as well as in his resurrection power, believers obtain his righteousness and vitality.

Union with God The restoration of a believer to the relationship with God that was originally intended. It has been brought about by the death of Christ.

Unitarianism Belief in God as one person alone.

Unitarians Generally, all those who hold that God is but one in person; specifically, members of an organized religious group with that belief.

Unitary view of human nature The idea that human nature is indivisible—it is not a composite of elements.

United Church of Canada A denomination formed in Canada by a union of the Presbyterians, Methodists, and Congregationalists in 1925.

United Church of Christ A denomination formed in the United States by a merger between the Congregational Church and the Evangelical and Reformed Church.

United Methodist Church A denomination formed in the United States by a union of the Evangelical United Brethren and the Methodist Episcopal Church.

Unitive way The highest and final stage in classical mysticism. It is built upon the purgative and illuminative ways.

Unity The oneness between the Father and the Son, between God and believers, and among believers.

Unity, Organic *See* ORGANIC UNITY.

Unity of believers The oneness between believers for which Jesus prayed in his high-priestly prayer (John 17:21). Some consider this to be simply a spiritual unity based upon the fact that all believe in the same God. Some maintain that it is to be a unity of actual active fellowship. Others interpret it as a unity of affiliation or a conciliar relationship. Still others envision actual organic union of all believers into one denomination.

Unity of God The doctrine that God is one in essence rather than three gods.

Unity of the human person, Conditional The idea that while the normal state of the human being is a material and non-material oneness, under certain conditions, such as death, that oneness breaks down.

Universal atonement The theory that Christ died for all persons.

Universal availability of salvation The teaching that God's redeeming grace is offered to everyone; all one need do is repent and believe.

Universal brotherhood The liberal view that all persons are children of God and, therefore, siblings of one another. Conservatives ordinarily hold that although all persons are by creation children of God, true brotherhood is present only among those who believe in Christ.

Universal church The idea that the church is composed of all believers everywhere.

Universal conversion The theory that all persons will turn from sin to Christ and thus be saved; that is, all will respond favorably to the gospel.

Universal death A reference to the fact that all persons die.

Universal depravity The doctrine that all persons are sinners (see, e.g., Rom. 3:23).

Universal explicit opportunity The view that every person will at some time be presented with a specific chance to believe. This position ordinarily includes the idea of a chance for belief after death for those who have not heard the message during their lifetime.

Universal grace *See* GRACE, COMMON.

Universal guilt The fact that all persons are liable to punishment for wrong-doing.

Universal history All the events of the past, present, and future. In the thought of Wolfhart Pannenberg and his circle, God works through and reveals himself in all of history rather than just the special redemptive acts recorded in Scripture.

Universalism The belief that in the end all humans will be restored to God.

Universalist One who believes in the salvation of all persons.

Universality of God's grace A reference to the idea that God's unmerited redemptive work has been provided for all persons.

Universal opportunity A reference to the view that all persons will have a chance sometime within life to respond savingly to Jesus Christ, whether they have consciously heard the gospel or not.

Universal pardon A reference to the teaching that God as a loving God will not condemn anyone but will forgive even those who have resisted him throughout life.

Universal priesthood *See* PRIESTHOOD OF ALL BELIEVERS.

Universal reconciliation A reference to the teaching that the death of Christ has restored all persons to God whether or not they have responded to him or are even aware of what has happened.

Universal response *See* UNIVERSAL CONVERSION.

Universal restoration A reference to the theory first set forth by Origen that at some point in the future all things will be returned to their original and intended state before God. This position often involves the idea that in the beginning of the life hereafter there will be a purgative period that will cause persons to respond to God.

Universal salvation A reference to the belief that all persons will be delivered from sin's effects.

Universal tendency A disposition found in all persons; primarily, the inclination toward sin.

Unleavened bread Bread that does not rise because it is baked without yeast; it is eaten in the Passover meal.

Unlimited atonement A reference to the doctrine that Christ's redemptive death was for all persons.

Unorthodox Pertaining to a departure from the official view. The term does not usually connote as serious a deviation as does "heterodox."

Unorthodoxy Any deviation from the standard or traditional position, particularly in the area of theology.

Unpardonable sin *See* SIN, UNPARDONABLE.

Unquenchable fire A metaphor for the unending nature of the punishment sinners will undergo. In Luke 3:17 John the Baptist declares that the coming Messiah will burn the chaff with unquenchable fire.

Unregenerate Those who have not been converted and thus born again.

Unrighteous Those who have not been justified and forgiven.

Unrighteousness Failure to conform to God's moral standard.

Unsaved Those who are still in their sins and therefore separated from God.

Unspiritual man In 1 Corinthians 2:14, the person who, not having the Holy Spirit, does not accept and cannot know the things that come from the Spirit, because they must be spiritually discerned.

Urgeschichte Either prehistory or events occurring in a realm beyond history.

Ursinus, Zacharias (1534-1583) One of the framers of the Heidelberg Catechism. He was dismissed from teaching positions at Breslau and Heidelberg for holding Calvinistic views of the Lord's Supper.

Ussher, James (1581-1656) Irish archbishop and scholar who is best known for dating the creation of the world at 4004 B.C., a conclusion that came to be included in many editions of the Bible.

Utilitarianism An ethical theory that evaluates acts by their consequences and particularly by the criterion of the greatest good for the greatest number.

Utopianism Belief in the possibility of a perfect society on earth.

Utrecht, Declaration of The official doctrinal basis of Old Catholic churches. Formulated by five Old Catholic bishops in 1889, it attempts to define Catholicism without commitment to the pope.

Vv

Valla, Laurentius (1407-1457) Italian Renaissance philologist and rhetorician among whose accomplishments was demonstration of the spuriousness of the Donation of Constantine.

Value Worth; also, a principle or standard that has or is judged to have worth.

Vatican Council I (1869-1870) Council convened in Rome by Pope Pius IX with the aim of defining clearly and authoritatively the church's doctrine, particularly in response to new challenges from theological liberalism and secular philosophical and political movements. The outbreak of the Franco-Prussian War and the occupation of Rome by Italian troops ended the council prematurely. The major result of the council was adoption of the doctrine of the infallibility of the pope.

Vatican Council II (1962-1965) Council convened in Rome by Pope John XXIII, which made far-reaching statements on the church, revelation, and salvation. In some senses, Vatican Council II was the resumption of Vatican Council I and its unfinished agenda.

Veneration of relics According of honor to certain objects believed to be associated with Christ or the saints.

Veneration of the saints *See* SAINTS, VENERATION OF.

Vengeance The executing of retribution on someone believed to have done wrong to another.

Venial sin *See* SIN, VENIAL.

Veracious authority The right to prescribe belief and/or action by virtue of possession of special knowledge.

Verbal inspiration A reference to the doctrine that the Holy Spirit so guided the writers of Scripture that even their choice of words conformed to God's intention.

Verificational analysis A form of analytic philosophy that emphasizes that a synthetic statement is meaningful only if there is a set of sense data that would verify or falsify it. Verificational analysis is basically equivalent to logical positivism.

Vermigli, Peter Martyr *See* PETER MARTYR VERMIGLI.

Vermittlungstheologie *See* MEDIATING THEOLOGY.

Vespers An evening service in the Catholic, Anglican, and Lutheran daily divine office. It is sometimes called evensong.

Via analogiae An attempt to gain knowledge of God by assuming that God has the positive qualities found in humans and that the proportion between these qualities in God and in humans is the same as the proportion between God's being and humans' being.

Via eminentiae An attempt to gain knowledge of God by taking positive qualities in human nature and extrapolating them to the infinite form.

Via illuminativa *See* ILLUMINATIVE WAY.

Via media A reference to the contention that the Anglican church represents a "middle way" between Roman Catholicism and Protestantism.

Via negativa A way of investigating the attributes of God: taking negative human qualities and ascribing to God their opposite perfection. If the human is finite, then God conversely is understood as infinite.

Via purgativa *See* PURGATIVE WAY.

Via unitiva *See* UNITIVE WAY.

Vicar Local parish minister in the Anglican church.

Vicarious death of Christ *See* CHRIST, VICARIOUS DEATH OF.

Vicarious faith A reference to the doctrine that it is possible to have faith on behalf of someone else; in particular, that it is possible for parents to have faith for their children.

Violence Use of force to inflict physical or mental harm on another.

Virgin, Assumption of the *See* MARY, ASSUMPTION OF.

Vineyard A network of churches of the signs-and-wonders or third-wave type.

Virgin(al) conception Expression used by Protestants and some others to distinguish their belief that Mary was a virgin at the point of Jesus' conception from the Catholic teaching that at birth Jesus simply passed through the wall of Mary's uterus instead of being delivered through the normal birth canal, so that her hymen was not ruptured. This Catholic teaching is part of the doctrine of the perpetual virginity of Mary.

Virgin birth A reference to the teaching that the conception of Jesus took place by a miraculous work of the Holy Spirit without Mary's having had any sexual relationship with a male. *See also* VIRGIN(AL) CONCEPTION.

Virginity, Perpetual *See* PERPETUAL VIRGINITY.

Virtual intention A reference to the Roman Catholic belief that if a priest intends to administer a sacrament, that sacrament is valid even if he is distracted in the act of administering it. That is to say, he need not be conscious of his intention at every moment during the sacrament.

Virtues Positive moral and spiritual qualities.

Visible church The official organized church on earth.

Visible foreground In Hendrikus Berkhof's thought, the physical part of reality; it contrasts with the invisible background, which is the unseen powers.

Visible sign In Catholic theology, one of the necessary elements in a sacrament: some form of matter (e.g., water in baptism) and a word of pronouncement.

Visio Dei See BEATIFIC VISION.

Vision of God *See* BEATIFIC VISION.

Visser't Hooft, Willem Adolf (1900-1985) Twentieth-century ecumenical leader who for a number of years was the head of the World Council of Churches.

Vital faith Faith as actual trust in a person. Synonymous with saving faith and the Latin word *fiducia*, the term *vital faith* was used by Edward Carnell in indicating that trust in a person must rest upon a general faith or a belief that something is true. Most orthodox theologians believe that trust in the person of Christ cannot be separated from belief in certain truths about him.

Vocation The Latin word for "calling," denoting God's invitation to salvation or to particular roles of service, whether individually or collectively.

Voluntarism A philosophical position that emphasizes the role of will as contrasted with that of reason or intellect.

Voodoo Forms of sorcery and black magic originating in Africa.

Vow A promise voluntarily made to God or to other persons.

Ww

Waldenses, Waldensians A medieval movement that followed the teachings of Peter Waldo: simplicity and purity of life and the evangelistic task.

Waldenström, Peter Paul (1838-1917) Swedish Pietist theologian whose influence can be seen in two American denominations of Swedish heritage: the Evangelical Covenant Church and the Evangelical Free Church. His most controversial teaching was a variety of the moral-influence theory of the atonement: The cross reconciles humanity to God rather than God to humanity.

Waldo, Peter A wealthy merchant of Lyons who between 1170 and 1180 had a deep personal spiritual experience. Followers of his teachings are known as Waldensians or Waldenses.

War Armed conflict between nations.

Warfield, Benjamin Breckinridge (B. B.) (1851-1921) Professor of theology at Princeton Seminary who was known for his staunch defense of orthodox Calvinism and particularly the view of the verbal inspiration and inerrancy of Scripture.

Water Buffalo Theology Emphasizing that the average Thai peasant is more concerned about his water buffalo than about abstract issues, Kosuke Koyama insisted that theology must address these practical matters.

Washing of feet *See* FOOT WASHING.

Watts, Isaac (1674-1748) Noted English hymn-writer.

Wave offering A communal offering described in Leviticus 7:28-34.

Way, The A designation of the Christian faith and community (Acts 9:2; 19:9, 23; 22:4; 24:14, 22). Paul classifies himself as an adherent (Acts 24:14).

Way International, The A cultic organization begun in the mid-1950s whose followers deny the deity of Christ and hold that speaking in tongues is the true worship of God.

Weiss, Johannes (1863-1914) German Protestant New Testament scholar whose book *Jesus' Proclamation of the Kingdom of God* held that the message of Jesus was consistently eschatological. Weiss's work, along with that of Albert Schweitzer, marked the end of the liberal accounts of Jesus.

Wesley, Charles (1707-1788) British evangelist and songwriter whose 7,270 hymns did much to spread the Christian message and Methodist faith that his more famous brother John preached.

Wesley, John (1703-1791) The founder of Methodism. Ordained in the Anglican church, he attended a Moravian Brethren meeting on Aldersgate Street in

London on May 24, 1738, and his heart was "strangely warmed." In Wesley's judgment, this was the beginning of a newness of life.

Wesleyanism Theology based on the teaching of John Wesley. Arminian in orientation, it emphasizes prevenient grace, by which God restores all persons to the point of being able to believe, and the possibility of total sanctification or perfection.

Wesleyan tradition Beliefs and practices that go back to John Wesley. It is Arminian in theology and emphasizes personal holiness.

Wescott, Brooke Foss (1825-1901) Outstanding British New Testament scholar who taught at Cambridge and then served as bishop of Durham. Conservative in theology and deeply involved in social issues, he is best known for an edition of the Greek New Testament text (which he produced in conjunction with Fenton John Anthony Hort) and commentaries on the Gospel of John, the Epistles of John, and the Epistle to the Hebrews.

Westminster Catechisms Two catechisms drawn up by the Westminster Assembly simultaneously with the *Westminster Confession of Faith*. Completed in 1647, the Shorter was intended for youth and the Larger for ministers.

Westminster Confession of Faith A statement of faith completed in 1646 by a group of clergymen assembled at the deanery of Westminster. Intended to bring the Anglican church closer to the Church of Scotland and other Reformed groups, it took the classical Calvinistic position. Though it governed the Church of England only briefly, the confession has long been used as a standard of belief by many Presbyterian and Reformed groups.

Westminster Theological Seminary Seminary espousing an orthodox Calvinistic Presbyterian theology. It was formed in Philadelphia in 1929 by a group including Robert Dick Wilson, Oswald T. Allis, and J. Gresham Machen, who had formerly been members of the faculty of Princeton Theological Seminary.

Whitby, Synod of A church assembly held in 664 to discuss various differences, particularly the date of Easter, between the Roman and Celtic groups of English Christianity. The Roman group prevailed, and the dissenters withdrew to Scotland, but no schism took place.

White, Ellen Gould (1827-1915) Seventh-day Adventist leader whose writings *Testimonies for the Church* and *Steps to Christ* had a strong influence on the movement.

Whitefield, George (1714-1770) Methodist evangelist who had great success in open-air preaching. Unlike the Wesleys, his theology was basically Calvinistic.

Whitehead, Alfred North (1861-1947) Mathematician and philosopher whose views have become the fountainhead of process philosophy and process theology.

Whitsunday Anglican term for Pentecost Sunday.

Wickedness Active opposition to God.

Will The capacity of choosing or that which is chosen.

Willful sin Wicked acts done consciously and with a definite determination to do wrong.

William of Ockham (ca. 1285-1349) Medieval English theologian greatly influenced by John Duns Scotus. He argued against the theology of Thomas Aquinas, insisting that reason cannot give us knowledge of God—such things can be obtained only by way of revelation and faith.

Will of God God's intention for humans.

Wisdom, Gift of One of the spiritual gifts (1 Cor. 12:8): special ability to discern or judge right and wrong.

Wisdom, John (1904-1993) British analytical philosopher closely associated with Ludwig Wittgenstein.

Wisdom literature The Old Testament books of Job, Proverbs, and Ecclesiastes, which offer counsel to humans.

Wisdom of God *See* GOD, WISDOM OF.

Witchcraft Sorcery involving magical rites, particularly with malevolent intent. The term may also refer to an irresistible influence or fascination.

Witness One who testifies or the act of testifying regarding that which is known or experienced, especially witness to the Christian gospel.

Witness of the Holy Spirit *See* INTERNAL TESTIMONY OF THE HOLY SPIRIT.

Wittenberg, Concord of An agreement that Lutheran and Zwinglian theologians reached in 1536 on the issue of the Lord's Supper.

Wittenberg, University of Institution where Martin Luther received his Bachelor's degree in biblical studies in 1509 and a doctorate in theology in 1512.

Wittgenstein, Ludwig (1889-1951) Austrian-born analytical philosopher who spent his teaching career at Cambridge University. His thought has had great influence in the areas of logical positivism and linguistic analysis.

Women in the church, Issue of The question of what role women should play in the church, including whether it is appropriate for them to serve as pastors and to be ordained.

Wonders A term for miracles that focuses on their ability to arouse astonishment.

Woolman, John (1720-1772) American

Quaker who advocated the abolition of slavery.

Word, the A term frequently used to refer to the Bible or Jesus Christ.

Word-flesh Christology *See* CHRISTOLOGY, WORD-FLESH.

Word-man Christology *See* CHRISTOLOGY, WORD-MAN.

Word of God The message that came from God. New Testament writers and Jesus refer to the Old Testament as the Word of God (see John 10:35). The Bible in its entirety is today spoken of as the Word of God.

Word of pronouncement In Roman Catholic theology, a formal statement that is essential to the efficacy of a sacrament.

Word of the Lord A term frequently used by the Old Testament prophets to identify their message as coming from God.

Work Activity aimed at accomplishing something. Scripture lays upon us the responsibility of doing the work of God.

Work of Christ The ministry of Christ, particularly his redemptive life and death.

Works The activity of God or humans.

Works, Covenant of *See* COVENANT OF WORKS.

Works, Good *See* GOOD WORKS.

Works righteousness A reference to the belief that humans can save themselves through their own meritorious deeds.

World, the In Scripture, the earth, the entire cosmos, or a spiritual force in opposition to God.

World Council of Churches Cooperative agency of churches and denominations that was founded in 1948. On the doctrinal basis of confessing "The Lord Jesus as God and Saviour according to the Scriptures," the members of the council "seek to fulfill together their common calling to the glory of the one God, Father, Son and Holy Spirit."

World evangelism The endeavor to convert the entire non-Christian world to faith in Jesus Christ.

Worldliness In one sense, a concern for life on this earth, including concern for social conditions; in another sense, an excessive identification with the world—conformity to it rather than transformation of it (see Rom. 12:2).

World Missionary Conference A missionary conference held at Edinburgh in 1910 in an endeavor to organize world missions in a cooperative way. It became the stimulus to modern ecumenism.

World missions The carrying of the message of salvation beyond one's own country to the entire world.

World religions Major faiths in addition to Christianity; for example, Buddhism, Hinduism, Islam, and Judaism.

World rulers A Pauline reference to the powers that control the present evil world (Eph. 6:12).

Worldview A broad conceptual synthesis that forms one's perspective on the whole of reality.

Worldwide Church of God A group that was founded by Herbert W. Armstrong and held to a syncretism of prophetic interpretations. The major means of propagating its teachings came to be the magazine *The Plain Truth*, the radio and television broadcast *The World Tomorrow*, and Ambassador College in Pasadena, California. In recent years, many members of the group have rejected Armstrong's teachings and have become thoroughly evangelical.

Worms, Diet of A meeting in 1521 at Worms in Germany at which Martin Luther was called upon to recant his teachings and refused to do so. The result of this meeting, which had been convened by Charles V, the Holy Roman Emperor, was that Luther was put under an imperial ban.

Worry Anxiety about specific events or possibilities.

Worship Offering of homage, honor, and praise to God.

Wrath of God God's opposition to and hatred of evil, together with his intention to punish it.

Wrede, William (1859-1906) German New Testament scholar who regarded Paul as the second founder of Christianity. In Wrede's view Paul's doctrines of the Incarnation, Atonement, and Resurrection changed the religion of Jesus.

Written code A set of standards that has been reduced to writing. It usually deals with morality or proper conduct.

Württemberg Confession A document produced by Protestant theologians in 1551 to present their position to the Council of Trent.

Wycliffe, John (ca. 1330-1384) English Reformer who has been called "The Morning Star of the Reformation." He spent much of his life at Oxford University. As a result of his criticism of the Catholic church, his followers at Oxford were placed under an ecclesiastical ban, and in 1428 his body was exhumed and burned and the ashes thrown into the Swift River. Wycliffe's major written contributions include a *summa theologica* and a translation of the Vulgate into English.

Yy

Yahweh Transliteration of the major Hebrew name for God.

Young Men's Christian Association A worldwide organization established by George Williams in London in 1844 with the intention of winning young men to saving faith in Christ. Today the YMCA is more of a social and educational organization.

Young Women's Christian Association A worldwide organization originally intended to evangelize young women but now geared more toward social and educational activities. The YWCA was founded in England in 1855 as two separate groups headed respectively by Emma Robarts and Lady Kinnaird. The two groups united in 1877.

Zz

Zeller, Eduard (1814-1908) German Protestant theologian and philosopher who became the leader of the so-called Tübingen School. He also taught at Bern, Marburg, Heidelberg, and Berlin. His major contributions were his *History of Greek Philosophy* and *Contents and Origin* of *the Acts* of *the Apostles, Critically Investigated*, which, using the critical methods of F. C. Baur and David Strauss, questioned the historicity of the book of Acts. Zeller rejected the orthodox view of God and the deity of Christ, adopting a pantheistic view instead.

Zinzendorf, Count Nikolaus Ludwig von (1700-1760) German founder of the Moravian church. While holding to the basic content of Lutheran theology, he emphasized the importance of personal, experiential knowledge of God. The Pietism of his group had a more joyous emphasis than did the Pietism of August Francke.

Zionism A movement attempting to restore the Jewish people to Israel.

Zionism, Christian A Christian movement that because of its premillennial eschatology has been supportive of Zionism's attempt to restore Jews to Israel.

Zoroastrianism A Persian religion dating back to about the sixth century B.C. Based upon the teachings of the prophet Zarathustra, it is a dualistic system that sees the world as a struggle between the lord of light and the spirit of evil.

Zurich Agreement A statement that affirmed the spiritual presence of Christ in the Lord's Supper. Formulated in 1549, it succeeded in preventing a split between the Calvinists and the Zwinglians.

Zwickau prophets Radicals who came to Wittenberg preaching a rejection of both infant baptism and the professional ministry, special revelation through visions and dreams, and the imminent return of Christ. They were expelled from Wittenberg in 1522.

Zwingli, Ulrich (1484-1531) Leader of the early Protestant Reformation in Switzerland. Around 1516 he came to view the Bible rather than the church as the source of doctrine. His major difference with Luther was over the latter's contention that Christ's body and blood are actually present in the Lord's Supper. Becoming more and more involved in political matters, Zwingli was killed at the battle of Kappel.